PLAY THE GAME:
THE PARENT'S GUIDE
TO VIDEO GAMES

JEANNIE NOVAK & LUIS LEVY

THOMSON
™
COURSE TECHNOLOGY
Professional ■ Technical ■ Reference

PLAY THE GAME:
THE PARENT'S GUIDE TO VIDEO GAMES

Publisher and General Manager, Thomson Course Technology PTR: Stacy L. Hiquet

Associate Director of Marketing: Sarah O'Donnell

Manager of Editorial Services: Heather Talbot

Marketing Manager: Jordan Casey

Senior Acquisitions Editor: Emi Smith

Marketing Assistant: Adena Flitt

Project Editor: Sandy Doell

PTR Editorial Services Coordinator: Erin Johnson

Interior Layout Tech: Judith Littlefield

Cover Designers: Jeannie Novak & Luis Levy

Cover Layout: Nikol Stein

Indexer: Larry Sweazy

Proofreader: Gene Redding

All trademarks are the property of their respective owners.

Important: Thomson Course Technology PTR cannot provide software support. Please contact the appropriate software manufacturer's technical support line or Web site for assistance.

Thomson Course Technology PTR and the authors have attempted throughout this book to distinguish proprietary trademarks from descriptive terms by following the capitalization style used by the manufacturer.

Information contained in this book has been obtained by Thomson Course Technology PTR from sources believed to be reliable. However, because of the possibility of human or mechanical error by our sources, Thomson Course Technology PTR, or others, the Publisher does not guarantee the accuracy, adequacy, or completeness of any information and is not responsible for any errors or omissions or the results obtained from use of such information. Readers should be particularly aware of the fact that the Internet is an ever-changing entity. Some facts may have changed since this book went to press.

Educational facilities, companies, and organizations interested in multiple copies or licensing of this book should contact the Publisher for quantity discount information. Training manuals, CD-ROMs, and portions of this book are also available individually or can be tailored for specific needs.

ISBN-10: 1-59863-341-4
ISBN-13: 978-1-59863-341-2
Library of Congress Catalog Card Number: 2006907930
Printed in the United States of America
08 09 10 11 12 TW 10 9 8 7 6 5 4 3 2 1

THOMSON
COURSE TECHNOLOGY
Professional ■ Technical ■ Reference

Thomson Course Technology PTR, a division of Thomson Learning Inc. 25 Thomson Place Boston, MA 02210

http://www.courseptr.com

Contents

Acknowledgments

The authors would like to thank the following people for their hard work and dedication to this project:

Emi Smith (Senior Acquisitions Editor, Course PTR/Charles River Media), for making this book happen.

Sandy Doell (Project Editor), for her professionalism, thorough copy editing, and insightful suggestions.

David Ladyman (Image Research & Permissions Specialist), for his superhuman efforts in clearing the many images in this book.

Ian Robert Vasquez, for his clever cover and in-book illustrations.

Per Olin, for his clean and organized diagrams.

Nikol Stein, for her aesthetically pleasing cover layout.

Jim Gish (Senior Acquisitions Editor, Thomson Learning), for helping to kick-start this project by introducing Jeannie Novak to Emi Smith.

A big thanks goes out to all the many people who contributed their thoughts and ideas to this book:

Aaron Marks

Bill Genereux (Kansas State University)

Billy Burger (Art Institute)

Brian Reynolds (Big Huge Games)

Catherine Clinch (Creative Screenwriting Magazine)

Chris Lenhart (NATO)

Cindi Lash

Colin Mack (THQ)

David Ladyman (IMGS)

Denice McLaughlin

Dennis J. Jirkovsky (Metropolitan Community College)

Destini Copp (South University)

Donna K. Kidwell (University of Texas at Austin)

Gordon Walton (BioWare)

Greg Costikyan (Manifesto Games)

Guy P. Vance

Jacques Montemoino (Gideon Games)

Janet Wilcox (UCLA Extension)

Jennifer Anderson

Jim Greenall

Jim McCampbell (Ringling School of Art & Design)

JoAnna Almasude (Art Institute Online)

John Francis Whelpley (Skibberrean Productions)

John Hight (Sony)

John Scott G ["The G-Man"] (Golosio Publishing)

Joseph Welsh

Kenneth C. Finney (Art Institute)

Martha Ladyman

Michael John (Method Games)

Patricia Dillon Sobczak (Chapman University)

Paul Orlando (Art Institute)

Rocksan Lessard

Rosanne Welch

Sandy Doell

Stacy Mengel

Steven Herrnstadt (Iowa State University)

Tommy Smith

Travis Ogurek

Thanks to the following people for their tremendous help with referrals and in securing permissions for images:

Ai Hasegawa & Hideki Yoshimoto (Namco)

Annie Belanger (Autodesk)

Big Stock Photo

Brian Hupp (Electronic Arts)

Brianna Messina & Denise Lopez (Blizzard)

Casey Maloney

Cathy Campos (Lionhead)

Chris Glover (Eidos)

Christina Cavallero (Sony Computer Entertainment)

Christine Seddon (Entertainment Software Rating Board)

Daniel James (Three Rings)

Daniel T. Wood (ResponDesign)

David Kwock & Gerilynn Okano (Blue Planet)

David Kwock (Tetris Holding, LLC)

David Swofford (NCsoft)

Dennis Shirk (Firaxis)

Eric Fritz (GarageGames)

Estela Lemus (Capcom)

Genevieve Waldman (Microsoft Corporation)

J. Finkelstein (Wikipedia Commons)

Jana Rubenstein, Makiko Nakamura & Yoshida Eijirou (Sega)

Jason Bramble

Jason Holtman (Valve)

Jim Miller

Kathryn Butters (Atari Interactive, Inc.)

Kelly Conway, Steve Weiss & Olivia Malmstrom (Sony Online Entertainment)

Kelvin Liu (Activision)

Kristen Keller (Atari, Inc.)

Lisa Hiroshige (Disney)

Lori Mezoff (US Army)

Maria Miller (TechExcel)

Mario Kroll (CDV Software)

Mark Rein (Epic Games)

Mark Soderwall (LucasArts)

Mark T. Morrison & Chari Ong (Midway)

Melissa Menton (The Game Factory)

Oni Lukos (Wikipedia Commons)

Pete Hines (Bethesda Softworks, LLC)

Piers Sutton (HopeLab)

Rama (Wikipedia Commons)

Robin Harper & Blue [Linden Lab]

Sophie Jakubowicz & Jocelyn Portacio (Ubisoft)

Stephen Millard

Sylvain Bizoirre (Old-Computers.com)

Ted Brockwood (Calico Media)

Terri Perkins (Funcom)

Tony Fryman (Cyan)

Valerie Massey (CCP Games)

Wendy Zaas & Cylor Spaulding (Rogers & Cowan)

About the Authors

Jeannie Novak is the founder of Indiespace—one of the first companies to promote and distribute interactive entertainment online—where she consults with creative professionals in the music, film, and television industries to help them migrate to the game industry. In addition to being lead author and series editor of the Game Development Essentials series, Jeannie is the co-author of three pioneering books on the interactive entertainment industry—including *Creating Internet Entertainment*. Jeannie is the Academic Program Director for the Game Art & Design and Media Arts & Animation programs at the Art Institute Online, where she is also producer and lead designer on a "course game" that is being built within the Second Life environment. She has also been a game instructor and course development expert at UCLA Extension, Art Center College of Design, Academy of Entertainment and Technology at Santa Monica College, DeVry University, Westwood College, and ITT Technical Institute—and she has consulted for the UC Berkeley Center for New Media. Jeannie has developed or participated in game workshops and panels in association with the British Academy of Television Arts & Sciences (BAFTA), Macworld, Digital Hollywood, and iHollywood Forum. She is a member of the International Game Developers Association (IGDA) and has served on selection committees for the Academy of Interactive Arts & Sciences (AIAS). Jeannie was chosen as one of the 100 most influential people in high technology by MicroTimes magazine—and she has been profiled by CNN, *Billboard Magazine*, Sundance Channel, *Daily Variety*, and the *Los Angeles Times*. She received an M.A. in Communication Management from the University of Southern California (USC), where she focused on games in online distance learning. She received a B.A. in Mass Communication from the University of California, Los Angeles (UCLA)—graduating summa cum laude and Phi Beta Kappa. When she isn't writing and teaching, Jeannie spends most of her time recording, performing, and composing music. More information on the author can be found at http://jeannie.com <http://jeannie.com> and http://indiespace.com <http://indiespace.com>.

Growing up in Sao Paulo, Brazil, **Luis Levy** was an extremely bright child, but he had trouble with his fine motor skills. His mother, a progressive psychologist, saw playing video games as the perfect remedy. She knew from early studies that games could help him fine-tune his movements in a fun and effective way. So on Luis's ninth birthday, he received a Sega Master System as a gift from his parents. The console's pioneering 3D graphics—with special LCD glasses—took Luis's imagination and dexterity to a whole new level. Games like *Phantasy Star* and *Space Harrier* also taught him his first words in English. As he grew up, Luis began creating batch programs in DOS for an old PC XT and even played *Prince of Persia* on the computer's rusty green screen monitor. He also took a major interest in all kinds of films, becoming a film buff and a member of a very exclusive film club at age 16. By that time, he had become the main "movie critic" for friends and family and also an expert in both hardware and software. Luis wrote intricate short stories and shot award-winning documentaries at Brazil's renowned private film school, FAAP, receiving a B.A. in Film and Television. He also made a daring trip to Brasilia, the country's capital, in a bus filled with homeless children and adults. The trip, shot in DV and Hi-8 analog video, became a prize winner itself. After working as a writer both in advertising agencies and Internet-new media corporations, Luis decided to move to America to pursue his true passions. Months after his arrival, Luis became an engineer at Activision, the world's second largest game publisher, where he tested and troubleshot AAA titles such as *Quake 4* and *Call of Duty 2*, in PC and both current and next-gen consoles. Luis also worked as an editor and writer at FJ Productions, an American-Brazilian production company that creates content in both Portuguese and English and produces the TV edition of *The Hollywood Reporter*. His most recent game project was *Call of Duty 3* at Treyarch, where he focused on the game's multiplayer capabilities.

Introduction

SAY HELLO TO YOUR NEW BEST FRIEND

The days of watching from a distance as your children play video games are over. In this book, you'll find out what your kids play—and why! You'll also discover the latest research on both violent and educational aspects of video games. Interviews with game developers, educators, psychologists, parents, and teens will provide you with a thorough understanding of the "state of play" associated with current video games. With topics such as game genres, platforms, styles, storylines, characters, ratings, players, and career opportunities, this guide will provide everything you need to know to truly communicate with your kids. You'll learn about how your kids are part of a new generation, known as "Millennials"—and how they are an entirely different breed from previous generations. You'll also discover the many career opportunities in the $50 billion game industry—and strategies for helping your "budding gamer" eventually become a game tester, engineer, designer, programmer, artist, or producer.

What kind of parent are you?

- **Curious.** You heard about the impact of games but don't know enough about them; you want to expand your knowledge through further education and research.
- **Gamer.** You play games yourself but have never thought about the impact they might have on your children. While you're already ahead of the curve, you wish you knew more about the "serious side" of gaming.
- **Concerned.** You worry your kids play games "way too much." You are looking for a guide that will help you understand games and create a bridge between you and your kids.
- **Puzzled.** Your kids play a lot of games and you don't have a problem with it. Still, you wish you fully understood their fascination with electronic games.
- **Progressive.** You are an early adopter. You always get the latest and greatest gadgets. Now you want to find out how to use games to further enhance your kids' lives.

No matter which of the above best describes you, this book will help to redefine or enhance your view of video games and how they relate to your kids. It has been said that technology makes parenting more difficult, often expanding the generation gap. Consider television and popular music in the 1950s, arcades and game consoles in the 1980s, and the commercial Internet beginning in the 1990s. These technologies posed new challenges for parents. Any technology can be disruptive, and games are no different; however, just like television and the Internet, games can also revolutionize the way we live our lives.

Our goal is to build and reinforce the connection between parents and kids through the same technology that might have been a cause for conflict in less progressive times. We believe that only through communication and sharing can this gap be bridged. There's much truth in the notion that playing games together creates bonds that last a lifetime; it's also unquestionable that, due to games, recent generations are very different than they were 20 years ago. With this book, we hope to show you that games are very powerful tools indeed and that learning how to use them constructively could be the turning point in many parent-child relationships.

What are you waiting for? It's time to press "start"!

Jeannie Novak & Luis Levy
Santa Monica, California

Questions and Feedback

We welcome your questions and feedback. If you have suggestions that you think others would benefit from, please let us know and we will try to include them in the next edition.

To send us your questions and/or feedback, you can contact the authors at:
Jeannie Novak & Luis Levy
P.O. Box 5458
Santa Monica, CA 90409
jeannie@jeannie.com / leglevy@gmail.com

Part I

The Basics

1 | Where It All Began

In This Chapter

- The Amusement of Arcades
- The Home Console Advantage
- Nomadic Gaming
- Your Friendly Home Computer
- Friends Everywhere

Believe it or not, the computer and video games your kids play today began as serious research. From the humble beginnings of a 1960s computer lab to the comfort of a modern living room, games have come a long way in redefining how and where kids play—whether alone, at a local hangout, with their families at home, or with friends all over the world!

BIRTH

In the 1960s, games were made possible because researchers dared to imagine a world in which human beings have fun and even learn with the aid of a machine. The nightmare technophobic scenarios of the time were ubiquitous—exhibited in science fiction movies depicting alien invasions, robots gone awry, or computers taking over the world (such as *2001* and *Colossus: The Forbin Project*). But these researchers envisioned the possibility of an *interface* (a bridge between eager human hands and a computer's harsh binary system of ones and zeroes) and the transformative power of games played, not on a soccer field but inside the confines of a living room—dominated by the television set. Even by '60s standards, which called for experimentation in almost all areas of human existence—social as well as technological—this was nothing short of revolutionary. In the early '60s, games were purely mechanical. Despite the invention of the transistor, computers at the time were still expensive *mainframes*—monsters of silicon filling whole floors of the largest corporations, universities, and government agencies. If computers were still this primitive, television itself was nothing more than a square box with very limited image quality. A cross between the two was unlikely at best.

The birth of video and computer games in the '60s was marked by four key moments:

1. *Tennis for Two*, built by Willy Higinbotham from lab equipment in 1958
2. Ralph Baer's console prototype, the Brown Box, which would later turn into the Magnavox Odyssey
3. *Spacewar!* (the first computer game) created by Steve Russell of the Massachusetts Institute of Technology (MIT)
4. Nolan Bushnell's *Computer Space* (the first arcade game), a version of *Spacewar!* that ran on less sophisticated hardware

At the Brookhaven National Laboratory (New York) in 1958, an electronic game was demonstrated by Willy Higinbotham. Dubbed *Tennis for Two,* it was a tennis simulation. Many claim that Higinbotham should be called the father of video games, but what he accomplished was really more of a "tech demo"—a demonstration of what could be done with the lab's advanced equipment. Still, with an analog computer and an oscilloscope as the display, it must have been an impressive demonstration.

Ralph Baer is usually credited as the true father of video games. Back in 1966, while manager of the equipment design division at U.S. defense contractor Sanders Associates, Baer asked himself what should be done with the channels that weren't being used to broadcast television programs. (In the '60s, many frequencies, or channels, were still vacant; in fact, you could count the number of networks on one hand.) The answer to this question was a paper entitled "Background Material—Conceptual, TV Gaming Display," written in September of the same year—where Baer describes game ideas, possible interfaces, and even genres such as racing games, all playable on a basic consumer-grade television monitors. This is unquestionably the first description of a game console (single-purpose game machines designed for home use).

Tennis for Two was the special attraction
at the Brookhaven National Laboratory.

Steve Russell, who is regarded as the first computer game designer and pro-grammer, built *Spacewar!* in 1962. The game ran on a DEC PDP-1—one of the first digital computers. *Spacewar!* spread like wildfire across college campuses in the United States, but Russell never made a penny from the game. An early hacker, Russell was solely interested in pushing the limits of the possible with the cutting-edge computers provided by MIT.

Spacewar!, created by MIT student Steve Russell, is considered
to be the first computer game. Spacewar!™ screenshot courtesy of Atari
Interactive, Inc. © 2007 Atari Interactive, Inc. All rights reserved.

The finishing touch to all these major developments was provided by Nolan Bushnell, a student at the University of Utah. One of his favorite computer games was *Spacewar!*, and Bushnell decided that he would find a way to have the game run on something cheaper than the $150,000 PDP-1. He created an adaptation of *Spacewar!* called *Computer Space*—and thanks to the production and funding assistance of arcade game manufacturer Nutting Associates, it became the first arcade game. Nolan Bushnell was so involved that he sculpted the cabinet himself, giving it space-age organic shapes straight from the set of *Barbarella*. The cabinet was available in several metalflake colors—including red, blue, green, and yellow. Although the unique game cabinets initially garnered some attention, *Computer Space* itself didn't catch on as an addictive game-playing experience. Unphased, Bushnell's next step was to create the first video game giant (Atari)—and with *Pong*, its first release, he successfully launched the commercial arcade game industry.

Computer Space, an adaptation of *Spacewar!* that was created by Nolan Bushnell, was the first commercial arcade game.

THE AMUSEMENT OF ARCADES

Lights blink through the smoke. The darkness is filled with endless laughter. Kids and teenagers rush from machine to machine, playing solo, against each other, or on the same team together against the toughest opponent—the arcade machine. A child entering an arcade for the first time feels a rush of excitement because these games are the fastest, most colorful, most involving ever seen! This describes an arcade "hangout" circa 1988, but arcades in the classic sense started in the early 20th century. Instead of video arcades, these hangouts contained nickelodeons—electromechanical coin-operated nickel machines—that allowed people to experience a pioneering way to watch moving pictures. Just as the nickelodeon arcade was the precursor to movie theaters (or maybe Blockbuster), the video arcade introduced electronic games to the world.

The image you may have of amusement arcades as "seedy little places" is nothing new. The arcade lifestyle did get a bad reputation among parents at the time, and sometimes deservedly so. But arcades also played an important part in creating a new way to experience entertainment. They represent the "humble beginnings" of what would become two of the most lucrative media in the world: movies and electronic games.

Arcades were popular hangouts for kids in the 1980s. Courtesy of Jim Miller

Until the 1930s, nickelodeon arcades were also heavily populated by slot machines (known then as *fruit machines*), which merrily took the money of those who dared tempt luck. (Slots eventually migrated to casinos and were replaced in the arcades by pinball machines, which are still found in the video arcades of today.) Finally, with the release of Nolan Bushnell's *Pong* in 1972, arcades converted themselves into centers of interactive entertainment, harboring all kinds of electronic games.

Pong, the first arcade game released by Nolan Bushnell after he founded Atari, was the true initiator of arcade gaming. Despite the overly simplistic first impression, this ping pong simulation was so addictive it could keep friends entertained for hours trying to best each other. *Computer Space* might have been the pioneer, but it was *Pong* that defined the medium.

> I was living in Frankfurt, Germany at the time, and I remember everyone talking about this new "video game" they had at the youth center. Like everyone else, I had to see what all the commotion was about; turns out it was *Pong*! After that day, I was there every afternoon for the next year watching and playing—just wanting to be part of it all!
>
> —Aaron Marks (composer/sound designer/parent)

> My first video game memory? Sitting on our ugly, scratchy, green living room carpet and playing *Pong* with my father, who was a gadget kind of guy. He brought home an Atari console, complete with a silly rifle for skeet that never worked. I was never an athlete (and he was an excellent one), nor was I the son I suspect he secretly craved—so I cherished this time spent laughing and competing with him.
>
> —Cindi Lash (longtime news reporter & game critic,
> formerly with the *Pittsburgh Post-Gazette*)

Space Invaders, released in 1978, was the first massive hit—soon engulfing the United States after a warm start in Japan. Never before had a game been so popular with the general public; its popularity might have been due to the massive sci-fi craze brought on by *Star Wars*—not to mention some very frantic action. *Galaxian*, another game that involved shooting alien vessels, would be the first arcade game in color.

Pac-Man is known as the first arcade game *blockbuster*. Released in 1980, it took everyone by surprise by proving that games didn't need to be violent to be fun. It was such a paradigm shift that the player market expanded from solely 12- to 18-year-old boys to girls and even adults (who flocked to machines installed in supermarkets, convenience stores, and even cocktail tables in restaurant bars). The usual cliché—that arcade games only involved a combination of teenage boys, quarters, and evil square-ish space aliens—was forever swallowed by that yellow disc-shaped creature who evaded ghosts and munched on power pills. The game was so popular that even a Saturday morning cartoon series featuring Pac-Man, his wife, Mrs. Pepper Pac-Man, and their son, Baby-Pac, was produced and managed to be on the air for two full seasons.

> The fact that *Pac-Man* was a visual magnet for focused attention, that it ate (or destroyed) something in its path, was disturbingly enticing.
>
> —John Francis Whelpley (writer-producer, Skibberrean Productions, Inc.)

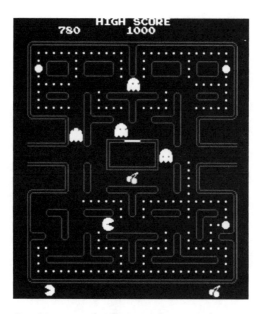

Pac-Man was the first arcade game that appealed to both boys and girls. PAC-MAN®
© 1980 NAMCO BANDAI Games Inc. Courtesy of NAMCO
BANDAI Games America Inc.

Pac-Man Enters the TV Maze

In 1982, a *Pac-Man*–themed cartoon premiered on U.S. television. It would be the first time a game character was seen on television. *Pac-Man* was a certifiable craze in the early 1980s; even a song, "Pac-Man Fever," was composed for the game. The video game industry expanded further when the game hit it big with market segments that didn't usually play video games—women/girls and adults. The cartoon was produced by Hanna-Barbera and followed the arcade game closely. The ghosts now had a leader, Mezmeron—and Pac-Man landed a job as official protector of the Power Pellet Forest, instead of only eating pellets in case of need! Although the show never came close to the original arcade game's success, it was still a remarkable crossover between games and traditional entertainment (television).

Space Invaders, Pac-Man, and *Galaxian* represent the seed of what is known as the arcade's Golden Age, a period of time that started in 1978 and lasted until the mid-'90s. Each of these three games was successful in its own way, inspiring worthy sequels, imitators, and newcomers. The games also set the standard for arcade gameplay—simple, addictive, and increasingly difficult—the markings of a satisfying arcade experience.

Old-School 3D

In the late 1970s, arcade games began to use vector graphics—comprised of geometric constructs such as polygons—to create the illusion of three dimensions. The popular *Star Wars* arcade game was vector based, as were *Asteroids* and *Lunar Lander*. All vector-based games contained detailed 2D shapes, and some of them even managed to achieve primitive 3D graphics. (The attack run on the Death Star in *Star Wars* comes to mind!) Vector graphics died out in favor of basic 2D, yet modern-day games ironically use textured and shaded polygons to create updated 3D graphics. Vector games were indeed ahead of their time!

My dad had a soda vending business. He bought the business from a guy who also had an arcade business. We used to go to Los Angeles and spend a whole day at C.A. Robinson, where the arcade guy used to buy the machines. We would play all the new games for free before they were out on the streets. We would then go home and tell him what games we liked the best. The first time we went, *Asteroids* was there. It was a blast!

—Jim Greenall (animatronics designer/fabricator/puppeteer)

By 1988, action games such as *Golden Axe* and *Double Dragon* took the next step by showing everyone the true meaning of playing games *together*. *Double Dragon* supported two players, Jimmy Lee and Johnny Lee (the Dragon Brothers). *Golden Axe* allowed for three players at the same time—one for each character—and they all fought *cooperatively* on the same team (except when everybody rushed to grab some of the magic pots carried by the dwarfs)! This rash of multiplayer games was already pointing to the future of electronic games: networked play.

For over a decade, arcade games pushed the envelope with graphics and sound. This trend lasted until the mid-'90s, when consoles became more sophisticated and eventually made arcades obsolete. By then, arcades began to focus on games such as *Dance Dance Revolution*, which required proprietary hardware and attracted an *exhibitionist* scene—with players competing for the best dance moves, cheered on by *groupie* onlookers!

Virtua Racing was a groundbreaking 3D arcade racing game. © Sega.

Chuck E. Cheese: Arcade's Friendly Face

Nolan Bushnell, founder of Atari, loved the arcades. However, he also knew that arcades had a bad reputation with some parents. It was said that arcades were too dark and *underground* to be safe for kids. Parents feared violent games, drug dealers, and dangerous peer pressure—and they made every effort to prevent younger kids from enjoying the latest arcade games. Out of all the protests and bans, Bushnell saw a great opportunity. Why not start a chain of restaurants where playing games would be *safe*? His answer: Chuck E. Cheese's Pizza Time Theatre. Tokens allowed kids to play while their food was being prepared—giving a rest to the parents—and robot animals would come to the rescue during the meals themselves. Most fond memories of visits to Chuck E. Cheese are not based on the food or service, but on the entertainment and atmosphere!

I've spent some miserable hours at Chuck E. Cheese just trying to keep track of one little blonde head in a sea of little bobbing heads. I prefer the arcades in malls now and will play a lot of those games myself.

—Sandy Doell (author, editor, mother, grandmother, and gamer)

As a kid, I spent a lot of time playing video games in arcades, in bowling alleys, and at home. It was a chance to be with friends, and that is why I did it. I let my friends put the majority of quarters in as I watched. I enjoyed seeing the progress of the early games—and, as technology advanced, they didn't seem as special any more. I never did like the newer home and computer games that would go on and on. I liked the quicker games where you and your friends would play a game and then try to better a score. Not too long ago, I was playing a new *Star Wars* game at my dad's house on his Xbox and got bored. I kept waiting for something new to happen or for it to end. I finally quit. I then played a tennis game with him and had a blast. It was fun to learn new tricks and play to the end of the match and then play again.

—Jim Greenall (animatronics designer/fabricator/puppeteer)

THE HOME CONSOLE ADVANTAGE

Playing games at home was a completely different experience than doing so at a video arcade. First, players no longer had to feed a machine with quarters. Second, mom and dad were right there—supervising and sometimes even participating! Third, and most importantly, it was now affordable for players to collect games. Instead of having to purchase an arcade machine for every game they wanted to play (an option only available to the wealthy), players would buy just one fairly inexpensive system known as a *console*, which hooked up to a television monitor. Games (also inexpensive) were sold separately, but there was a whole library of them available. Like stamps and books, games proved to be highly collectible items.

Since playing games at home was the perfect *protected* environment, the social atmosphere of gaming changed—with groups of kids hanging out at a friend's house, playing games for hours on end. This new form of social interaction, akin to playing board games such as *Monopoly* and *Life,* would define most traits associated with social console gaming until the advent of Xbox Live and other online services (discussed later in this chapter). Consoles very soon turned into objects of desire. The latest model was met with a lot of hype, and owners could expect an update in status among friends. A new console also meant new games, which were essential to a healthy gaming market. Let's take a look at the machines that brought games home.

FIRST GENERATION: THE ODYSSEY BEGINS

The Magnavox Odyssey was the realization of Ralph Baer's plans back in 1966—and it was extremely simple by all standards. The system had only a few built-in games, overlays that subbed for graphics, and very clumsy controllers. Still, it sold over 100,000 units and is considered a milestone for game consoles. Being "King of the Arcades" wasn't enough for Nolan Bushnell, who probably realized that arcades were a limited medium at best: How many grocery stores, gas stations, movie theaters, and restaurants would carry the same game? (And that's if you don't consider the many lower quality *Pong* copycats that were flooding the market.) Bushnell knew that his games needed to be inside people's homes—where the whole family could play together. This was the inspiration for Bushnell's first attempt at a home console system—a machine that could only play *Pong*.

SECOND GENERATION: THE ATARI VCS/2600

Bushnell's next move was to develop hardware that was to become the first commercially successful home console system: the Atari VCS/2600—the first console of many of the so-called "old school" gamers. The very idea of playing a game that escapes the whole "*Pong* frame of mind"—sticks and dots posing as objects—was only made real by this powerful new system. With an Atari in the home, sometimes the entire family would play *Combat, Pitfall, Adventure,* and *River Raid* together. Earlier consoles such as the *Pong,* Fairchild Channel F, and Odyssey systems, while impressive in their own way, didn't have the comfortable Atari joystick or the vision to license a Hollywood movie and turn it into a console game. (Licensed arcade games based on *Tron* and *Star Wars* had been launched previously.) While the game adaptation in question was *ET: The Extra Terrestrial* (regarded as one of the worst games of all time), the very idea of making a game based on a film paved the way for the mesh between Hollywood and the game industry—which would become a powerful driving force in later years. Games on the Atari had color, detail, and actual sounds (as opposed to the bleeps and blips of *Pong* and its contemporaries). Also, Atari unknowingly started the game development business—now that new games could be brought to market easily. Soon enough, the first independent publisher, Activision, started churning out game after game to a starving market —and a multimillion dollar industry was born.

> My first experience playing an electronic game was *Superman* on the Atari 2600 and the feeling of achievement when I first got all the bad guys jailed in less than two minutes [was great].
>
> —Donna K. Kidwell (commercialization consultant, University of Texas at Austin)

Atari VCS/2600 courtesy of Atari Interactive, Inc. © 2007 Atari
Interactive, Inc. All rights reserved.

Pitfall, for the Atari game console, was the first electronic game I had ever played. I grew up in an indigent demographic, and just by knowing someone with an Atari (which was very expensive at the time, considering home electronic game consoles were relatively new and regarded by many adults as a fad and a waste of money), I was able to experience the wonder of electronic gaming. The user interface was stiff and very unaccommodating, but as an introductory experience into electronic gaming, it dazzled and mesmerized me. It served as a new way to play games yet offered a new benefit aside from the usual recreation that came from playing the physically interactive games that children play when outdoors. This new device challenged my problem-solving capabilities [and] decision-making aptitude, as well as my hand-eye coordination. It had been the first activity that I had ever experienced that equally tested (what I now know as) my right and left brain faculties. Although electronic games were not socially and physically demanding, the Atari was addictive and mentally engaging all at once.

—Jacques Montemoino (student/game developer; Gideon Games, LLC)

Easter Egg *Adventure*

Easter eggs are hidden features left inside commercial games. They're all over the place; even the 1997 version of Microsoft Excel contains a hidden flight simulator! But before 1979, no one had ever thought of doing such a thing. An employee of Atari at the time, Warren Robinett, was the main programmer behind *Adventure*, one of the best-selling Atari games to date. Since Atari

→

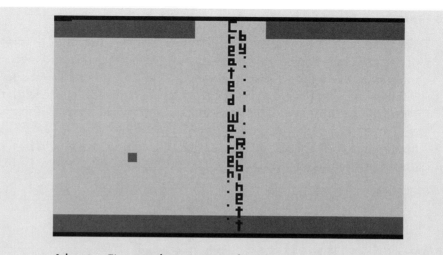

Adventure™ screenshot courtesy of Atari Interactive, Inc. © 2007 Atari
Interactive, Inc. All rights reserved.

didn't give credit to developers—no name on the box and no royalty payments
whatsoever—Robinett (in protest) decided to hide his name inside his own
game. It was a complicated process; an almost invisible *magic dot* had to be
found and then taken to a certain wall. Then, in a room behind that wall, his
name would be displayed in very colorful, low-resolution text. A precocious 12-
year-old in Utah eventually found it and sent a letter to Atari. From then on,
video and computer games would always have these endearing hidden secrets.

Need Memory?

One factor that differentiates first- and second-generation consoles is the use of
cartridges. All systems released before 1976 were programmable but had no
memory, so multiple games were variations on the main program and not
separate programs. If you bought a later *Pong* console, such as *Super Pong*, you
could play four games that were really just four different ways of playing . . . you
guessed it . . . *Pong*. With cartridges, games could now be stored in a cartridge's
ROM (read-only memory), so a game like *Pitfall* could use 4 Kilobytes for
graphics and sound. This allowed for much needed variety because new games
could be bought in stores—and they were new games indeed! The Fairchild
Channel F was the first console to use cartridges, but this new way of storing
games would only be perfected by the Atari VCS/2600.

THIRD GENERATION: *MARIO* TO THE RESCUE

The infamous video game crash that began in 1983–84 and lasted throughout much of the '80s almost ruined the industry. Low-quality releases and a general lack of innovation overloaded the market with games that no one wanted to play. This resulted in a number of bankruptcies, and people started to lose faith in the game industry. Many believed it was just another passing fad. Parents also started to see computers as a better investment; they allowed kids to play games *and* do their homework on one machine! (We discuss the computer segment of the game industry later in this chapter.)

Mario, one of the most recognized
video game characters—and Nintendo's
mascot. Courtesy of Nintendo

The release of the Nintendo Entertainment System (NES) in the United States in 1985 would bring new life to the video game industry. First, the 8-bit NES was much more technically advanced than anything in the second generation—including most personal computers. Second, Nintendo had absolute control over who could make a game for the NES and who could not. This meant that every single game released had to have the Nintendo Seal of Quality—negating the market to opportunists and independent developers in general and thus allowing Nintendo to carve a safe, family-friendly niche for itself. The *blockiness* from earlier consoles

The Nintendo Entertainment System (NES) brought the game industry back to life. Courtesy of Nintendo

would finally give way to the distinctive, cartoonish look of third- and fourth-generation consoles. NES games such as *The Legend of Zelda, Super Mario Bros. 3,* and *Mega Man* were very sophisticated—requiring a lot more time and depth of play to be appreciated. In fact, the NES represented a move away from arcade or "pick-up-and-play" games. In turn, arcade gameplay would be embraced by the now cult Sega Master System (SMS). By 1987, the market was fully reawakened. The NES had saved the industry from self-destruction, and Nintendo was more than ready to reap the benefits. By 1988, Sega had captured most of the European market—and Nintendo dominated everywhere else. The SMS sold poorly in the United States, failing to differentiate itself from the NES. Sega knew it had to turn the market upside down . . . or else.

FOURTH GENERATION: *SONIC* BOOM

No stranger to the arcade industry, SEGA (derived from SErvice GAmes) originally imported jukeboxes and pinball machines to U.S. military bases in Japan in the early '60s. The company knew that arcade technology was the key to taking the market from Nintendo's hands. SEGA executives figured out that they already had 16-bit CPU hardware in the arcades, and so adapting it to fit a console wouldn't be that difficult. Nintendo was so comfortable in its lead that it had made itself vulnerable to SEGA's move.

SEGA's Sonic The Hedgehog—a surprise
challenge to Mario.

The Sega Genesis helped SEGA erode Nintendo's lead.

The release of the Sega Genesis marked the first act of what became known as the *16-bit Console Wars*. The 16-bit Genesis could access much more memory than the 8-bit NES, leaving the latter in the dust. Also, Genesis games had stereo music and very fast pacing, thanks to the system's speedy processor. NES games seemed lifeless by comparison. Released in the United States in 1989, the Genesis catered to an older, edgier audience in its teens and 20s. Genesis games would bring graphic violence to console games for the first time, with titles such as *Altered Beast, Road Rash,* and a much talked about home version of *Mortal Kombat.*

In 1991 SEGA unleashed *Sonic The Hedgehog,* boosting sales of the system to the stratosphere and threatening Mario's throne. For an audience used to the relatively plodding gait of Mario, Sonic The Hedgehog was exhilarating. In line with Sega's focus on the teens and 20s player market, Sonic The Hedgehog had the swiftness and freedom of a typical teenager—being able to rush through levels like no other game character had done before.

For roughly three years, SEGA was a force to be reckoned with. The company had everything: the hardware, the games, the cash, the following. What happens next is the stuff of legend and is usually regarded as the second act of the 16-bit Console Wars.

Nintendo took a hit from SEGA, but it had enough resources and smarts to survive a single lost battle. The company took its time to fine-tune the follow-up to the NES—a 16-bit powerhouse that would be known as the Super Nintendo Entertainment System (SNES).

The Super Nintendo Entertainment System (SNES) was the winner of the 16-bit Console Wars. Courtesy of Nintendo

Nintendo built the SNES to address the Genesis' weaknesses: When designing the Genesis, Sega had slipped on the sound, which (although in stereo) made most games sound harsh. Nintendo hired Sony to design the SNES sound chip, which resulted in a much cleaner hi-fi quality to both music and sound effects. The Genesis was also limited in the amount of color it could display onscreen at the same time—61 out of 512 available colors. The SNES could show 512 . . . out of 32,000! The only remaining advantage of Sega's system was the faster processor—more than triple the SNES' performance. SNES games had a pastel, soft look, while the Genesis went for a monochromatic style that made games look dark and edgy. Genesis games also focused more on speed and sports, while the SNES showcased deeper and more complex story-based games. Eventually, Sega released two ill-fated add-ons (Sega CD and Sega 32X), and the SNES overtook the Genesis in sales by 1994—never to lose the lead again in the 16-bit market.

Avoiding FMV Fever

The early '90s suffered from an affliction known as "FMV fever." *FMV* (full motion video), or in-game live action footage, is common today with PlayStation 2 and Xbox games, but back when cartridges couldn't store a 30-second TV commercial, it was the next big thing. Since Sega thought that FMV was the best way to showcase the newly released Sega CD, the company decided to push these kinds of games instead of using CD-ROMs as extra storage. A great example is *Sewer Shark*, Sega's launch title for the Sega CD. The game put the player in a sewer-roaming hovercraft with which he could hunt mutated animals and other post-apocalyptic menaces while struggling to avoid deadly dead-ends, all with a mixture of video and computer graphics. However, FMV games soon proved to be an expensive way to develop what turned out to be fairly uninteresting games that focused more on eye candy than compelling action. Players lost interest . . . fast. The dive was so pronounced that it destroyed not only the Sega CD but other similar systems such as the Phillips CD-i and Trip Hawkins' 3DO.

FIFTH GENERATION: NINTENDO'S DEMISE & SONY'S RISE

Around the time the Sega CD was released in 1992, Nintendo was hard at work developing its own CD-ROM add-on. Its partner, Sony, had developed a similar disc drive for the Sega CD and had built a custom sound chip for the SNES. Sony was close to a final prototype (PlayStation) when—fearing that an old 1988 contract gave Sony too much power—Nintendo decided to jump ship. This move was ultimately disastrous for Nintendo, which lost its technological edge and would only go back to discs with the release of the GameCube in 2001; it was also disadvantageous for Sony, which suffered a dishonorable defeat at the hands of a former ally, not to mention millions lost in research and development!

The Sony PlayStation was born out of this dramatic scenario. What started as a console add-on was soon reshaped into the first 32-bit, 3D-centric console. Sony got the best custom parts available and built a polygon-mashing monster with the leftovers from Nintendo's broken deal—samurai style!

The PlayStation prototype led to the breakup of a partnership between Sony and Nintendo. Sony Computer Entertainment America

The Sony PlayStation took the game industry by storm. Sony Computer Entertainment America

Released in 1994, the PlayStation was the very first console that could rival an arcade machine in speed and graphics quality. *Ridge Racer*, Namco's 3D racing game, made a big splash, and along with *Tekken*, it turned the PlayStation and its successors into the most successful console family in history. A few popular games that launched on the first PlayStation were *Gran Turismo* (attracting serious racing fans), *Metal Gear Solid* (showing that stealth and cunning could be more effective than shooting), and *Tomb Raider* (featuring one of the first female heroines who had brains as well as beauty). In time, the PlayStation's weaknesses (long disc access time, jittery polygons, and limited memory) would be evident, but for many years, nothing could beat the console that broke Nintendo's back.

Sony didn't have the 32-bit market all to itself. Sega launched the Sega Saturn four months before the PlayStation, and Nintendo gave it a shot in 1996 with the Nintendo 64 (N64). Unfortunately, none of these systems ever really had a chance.

The Saturn was an impressive piece of engineering. Sega of Japan designed it to be the "ultimate" 2D console. It was so powerful that it could actually run arcade-perfect ports of very demanding 2D games such as *Marvel vs. Capcom* and *Street Fighter 2*. The problem with the Saturn wasn't its power, but its *concept*.

Back in 1994, 3D games were all the rage. Nobody cared about FMV anymore, since it left such a bad taste in everyone's mouths—developers and players alike. Nonetheless, the Saturn was a super 2D machine but only a mediocre 3D machine, which further drove players to the PlayStation. The Saturn was also extremely difficult to develop for because it had two main processors instead of a single one like traditional consoles. It died a quick death in the United States, but Japanese gamers would embrace it until 2000.

The Nintendo 64 started life as Project Reality, Ultra 64, and finally, Nintendo 64 (N64). Nintendo's objective was to surpass Sony in graphics while attracting gamers with the promise of zero load times. While the N64 was a great system, it had an enormous flaw: It still used cartridges rather than CD-ROMs. At $70 each, cartridges were significantly more expensive than $40 CD-ROMs, and they had limited storage space in comparison (12 megabytes maximum for one cartridge versus 650 megabytes for one CD-ROM). Game developers did not like working with the N64 system because they had to cram their games into a tight little space—while the PlayStation's CD-ROMs had plenty of room to spare. The relatively higher price of cartridges also translated into scant sales of the system's titles. Nintendo had miscalculated—banking on customers preferring zero load times to higher expense.

The N64 had just been released, and I was playing Super Mario 64. My daughter was three years old at the time and was sitting in the middle of the coffee table watching me play the game. As I was negotiating *Bob-omb Battelfield,* she got up and went to the kitchen. I heard pots and pans rattling. In a few moments she returned, wearing a large soup pot on her head for protection. She resumed her former post in the middle of the table and kept watching. She didn't smile or wink . . . she was legitimately concerned for her safety and figured the makeshift helmet would do the trick. At that moment, I understood just how immersive a game could be, regardless of the level of sophistication of the graphics.

—Jim McCampbell (department head, computer animation;
Ringling School of Art & Design)

The Waiting Game

"Loading" is a message displayed onscreen every time the console has to load images, audio, or video from a CD- or DVD-ROM. Both the Saturn and PlayStation had long loading times. Players face loading times before starting an action sequence (such as combat) or accessing a large, detailed game environment. Using cartridges and not discs, there was instant load in every N64 title.

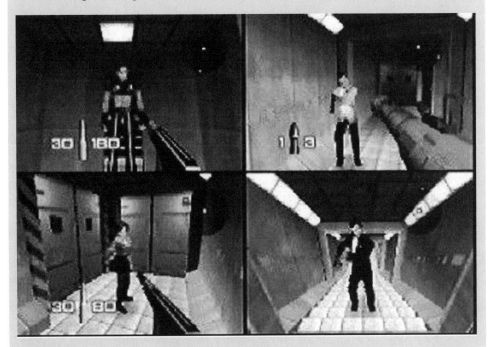

Goldeneye 007 had a revolutionary multiplayer mode. Courtesy of Nintendo

With the N64, Nintendo continued to focus on family-friendly titles. While this is an honorable objective, it caused Nintendo to lose a great deal of market share. The players were getting older, but Nintendo still wanted to focus on a younger market niche. The N64 did not sell well, and the best it could offer was classic Nintendo franchises, such as *Mario* and *Zelda*, or masterpieces like *Goldeneye 007* (the very first console game that allowed up to four players to battle simultaneously in the personas of famous Bond characters) and *Donkey Kong 64* (which featured a huge sprawling world full of unlockable items and secrets).

Nintendo's "Kiddie" Games

Nintendo's focus on kids happened almost by accident—a response to a brief change in climate that hit the U.S. game industry at a specific moment in time. Back in 1983, right before the notorious Video Game Crash, hundreds of adult-themed games (many of them low quality) were released for the Atari VCS/2600. These games had inadvertently muddied the water in parents' views—helping to push the game industry further down the chasm. By 1984, when Nintendo decided to release game titles for the U.S. market, games had developed a horrible reputation in the United States, losing status and sales by the minute. In order to counter this trend, Nintendo created the "Nintendo Seal of Quality"—a sticker that assured parents "this game will not contain any sexual references or excessive violence." The marketing operation worked so well for Nintendo that the company then decided to have all future consoles steer toward a younger audience—since "safer" games were a surefire hit with families and more conservative parents. Although Nintendo would eventually release violent games, such as *Mortal Kombat 2* for the SNES and *Resident Evil 4* for the GameCube, sexual content is still a "no-no" at Nintendo to this day.

SEGA'S DREAM

The last chapter in console history is a sad one. This is the story of the Sega Dreamcast, released in 1998 but gone only two years later. Following the failure of both 32X (an add-on that was intended to upgrade the Sega Genesis to a 32-bit machine) and Saturn, Sega suddenly saw itself without a viable game system. The Sony PlayStation had taken the market by storm, much to Sega and Nintendo's surprise—and Sega knew it might have one last chance to save the company's traditional hardware business. Like the famous phrase from *Field of Dreams* ("If you build it, they will come"), Sega felt that if it made a console that corrected all of

The Sega Dreamcast was caught between generations.

Saturn's mistakes, buyers and developers alike would flock to it and give Sega a much-needed cash influx. It was a daunting task, but Sega really had no other choice in a Sony-dominated market.

The Sega Dreamcast was far ahead of anything the competition had released at the time. It also used a special GD-ROM disc system that had 1.5 times the storage of a CD-ROM, giving the developers all the room they could possibly need. Due to its straightforward design, Sega Dreamcast was very easy to develop for and had un-precedented performance—unlike the Saturn. On top of all that, the console was the very first to come equipped with a built-in 56k modem. SegaNet, Sega's online service, would not start operations until 2000, but the fact that the Dreamcast could actually offer online games was unrivaled. Games such as *Soul Calibur* (the best-looking 3D fighting game seen thus far) and *Sonic Adventure* (which successfully converted the *Sonic The Hedgehog* franchise to a vivid 3D environment) were spell-binding. The jump in graphics power was immense. The public woke up to the next generation of console gaming, and Sega was right there.

Soul Calibur raised the bar for fighting games during the Sega Dreamcast era.
SOULCALIBUR® © 1998 1998 NAMCO BANDAI Games Inc. Courtesy of NAMCO BANDAI Games America Inc.

For the first year, the Sega Dreamcast sold out. Quality releases and great publicity brought Sega back to life, a reality that most of the industry deemed impossible. The Sega Dreamcast was the system of choice for all early adopters. But the good times came to an end. The fall of the Sega Dreamcast began with hype over the powerful follow-up to the PlayStation—the PlayStation 2 (PS2). Players reacted to the impending release of a supposedly more powerful system by losing faith in Sega, and Sony loyalists opted to wait for the release of the PS2 instead of upgrading to a Sega Dreamcast. The situation worsened when pre-orders for the PS2 gained momentum several months before the system's 1999 release. The overflow of customers for the still unproven console scared some developers into canceling Sega Dreamcast titles in favor of the new Sony machine. In 2001, cash-strapped Sega admitted defeat and cancelled the Sega Dreamcast altogether. It would be the company's last console system.

Consoles brought games into our living rooms—impacting the social landscape in a powerful way. This was the first time that parents really got a chance to supervise their kids—limiting and choosing what their kids played. Also, the convenience of console cartridges allowed kids to exchange games with friends—building new relationships based on common interests and helping them play more games than they could actually afford. Multiplayer console games provided the opportunity for both siblings and parents to play together—breaking down the walls between gender and generations. In Chapter 2, we'll continue our discussion of consoles—focusing on those systems that are in current use today.

Nomadic Gaming

One thing that consoles didn't manage to do was to follow their owners wherever they went. That's because consoles are always bound to a power outlet and also to the TV through audio and video cables. Consoles are simply *destined* to stay home!

Kids wouldn't settle for only playing coin-op games in arcades, yet they didn't always want to be forced to stay home either. Playing a game "on the go" made waiting bearable, whether at a school bus stop, during recess, or in the orthodontist's office. Books also did the trick, but sometimes nothing could be more engrossing than a challenging game.

Portables were invented in the mid-1970s to tag along with players everywhere. At first, technological limits forced them to be even simpler than the consoles of the time. Like mini arcade games, many of them could only play one game, which could be remedied by collecting every handheld available. Mattel Electronics, for example, put out a series of action and sports games, such as football, baseball, and basketball, that used light emitting diode (LED) displays. Soon enough, successive jumps in technology brought handhelds very close to what was available for home use. Let's touch on some of the classic portable systems that made a difference.

My first experience playing an electronic game was with a football game my father bought me. It was one of the only things I could actually compete with him at, so I really enjoyed it!

—Chris Lenhart (network technician, NATO)

I have fond memories of trying to run the score (in *Mattel Basketball*) up to 100–0—and noticing how it would "cheat" to make my play less effective as I got further ahead. That was when I first thought about how games were made and what needed to be done to make single-player games seem fun.

—Colin Mack (project manager, THQ Inc.)

NINTENDO GAME & WATCH

In 1980, Nintendo tried something new by releasing a portable game console disguised as a digital clock. Annoying alarm ringing aside, this early liquid crystal display (LCD) portable system still holds a place in many hearts. Like the Mattel LED portables, there were no cartridges; only one game could be played on each unit. The screen had no colors, and no true animation was possible because it didn't have a dot matrix display (made up of an array of dots). Nonetheless, the games were fun to play, up to Nintendo's high standards, and long-lasting due to an excellent battery life. Some classic games played on the system included *Octopus*, *Popeye*, *Mario's Cement Factory*, and *Safe Buster*. Interestingly, the Game & Watch clamshell design and dual-screen layout would show up decades later in the Nintendo DS (discussed in Chapter 2).

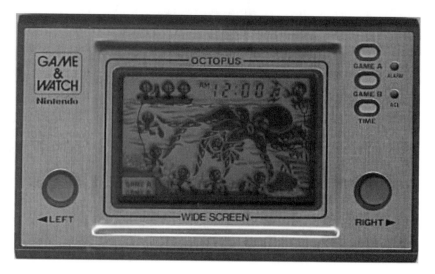

Courtesy of Nintendo

NINTENDO GAME BOY

Many call the Nintendo Game Boy the most successful game system ever. The reason for this is simple: For years, the Game Boy had no competition. From its release in 1989 to the introduction of its successor (the Game Boy Advance), the original Game Boy became an institution in portable gaming. Others have tried to seize the market, but nobody could touch it. The Game Boy had a blurry grayscale dot matrix display and stunning stereo sound (one of the least-remembered features but surely one that made a difference). Games for the portable reached the thousands, and sales have always been impressive; the Game Boy has been Nintendo's "secret weapon" for quite some time.

Courtesy of Nintendo

Since the Game Boy was launched, versions of almost all of Nintendo's franchises have been created for the system, and one game in particular, *Super Mario Land,* became the "system seller." Is some ways, the game was much better than the original *Super Mario Brothers* due to the variety of actions. Coupled with *Tetris,* which was bundled with the console, *Super Mario Land* helped the Game Boy practically sell itself from day one. In 1998, Nintendo released the Game Boy Color, an update to the then very old-fashioned grayscale screen. A stopgap measure, it would secure the market until the release of the more sophisticated Game Boy Advance in 2001.

SEGA GAME GEAR

In 1991, Sega's answer to the Game Boy was the Game Gear. Based on Sega Master System technology, the 8-bit Game Gear was one of the first portables to use a back-lit color display. Leagues ahead of the Game Boy, the Game Gear's screen was very popular among players. On the other hand, it had a battery life of only five hours. Since six new AA batteries were needed to resume play, players soon realized that a Game Gear could be an expensive addition to anyone's collection, surely more than kids could afford. This meant more sales for the Game Boy because it only ate four AAs for 10 or more hours of play, and it already had an established image with players. While a worthy adversary, the lack of variety in games and the short battery life slowly pushed the Game Gear into obscurity.

SEGA NOMAD

The aptly named Sega Nomad (released in 1995) is now considered a cult system—elevating anyone who owns one into some kind of gaming Olympus. Since it was essentially a downsized version of the Sega Genesis console, the Nomad was an extremely powerful portable system. A 16-bit portable was available before in the NEC Turbo Express, but the Nomad allowed Sega fans to take all their Genesis games anywhere. (The complete Genesis library of over 800 titles could be used on the Nomad without having to purchase new cartridges.) Other interesting features included the beautiful high-res LCD screen, a joystick input, and one video output. This allowed two-player games (one player with a Genesis controller) to be displayed on a TV screen. But then reality hit. Like the Game Gear before it, the Nomad's battery life was poor—rarely lasting more than three hours. This and a high price of $199.99 at launch meant that this exceptional handheld was destined to never be more than a blip on the radar, failing to bring Sega any significant percentage of the market.

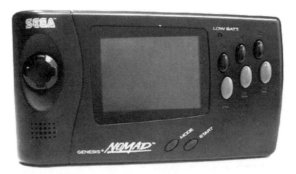

GAME BOY ADVANCE

Based on Super Nintendo Entertainment System (SNES) hardware, the Game Boy Advance (GBA) was very powerful and had none of the Nomad's shortcomings. It was actually a direct descendant of Nintendo's 16-bit system with added late-1990s functionality. Games on the Game Boy Advance were often better looking than anything seen on the SNES because the system had a built-in SuperFX 2 chip that allowed 3D graphics. SuperFX 2 chips were seen in some of the most advanced SNES games—*Star Fox* and *Yoshi's Island*. Like the SNES, it displayed over 32,000 different colors (512 at the same time), and it was capable of pseudo-3D games like *Iridion 3D*. All Game Boy and Game Boy Color games could be played on the GBA, and newer games, made especially for it, looked truly beautiful.

Courtesy of Nintendo

There have been two variants released since the SNES debuted in 2001. One, the Game Boy Advance SP, moved from the widescreen layout to a playful square-ish clamshell design that resembled a mini laptop. (Nintendo also added a much-needed backlight to the system.) The second model was the Game Boy Micro, a stylish portable for older, fashion-conscious gamers. The chromed look gave the Game Boy Micro an upscale, sophisticated aura never seen before in portables.

Despite its core audience consisting of kids and teenagers, the GBA is still a hit with the late 20s/early 30s crowd. This is due in part to its colorful 2D games, which are reminiscent of the great 16-bit systems. And although the GBA is not considered a "current generation" system, many new games are still being developed for it. The GBA has "classic system" written all over it. (Nintendo's current portable system is the DS, discussed in Chapter 2.)

YOUR FRIENDLY HOME COMPUTER

Back in the mid-1980s, when the industry was going through the video game crash, many parents bought their kids personal computers (PCs) instead of consoles. This was a more practical decision, since computers could be used for multiple purposes (accounting, letter writing, desktop publishing) and weren't solely focused on games. Computers brought true "solo" play to games. Since it was very rare to have two joysticks or two keyboards, it was natural to have primarily single-player games. Computers also allowed kids to have their first contact with the online universe through the first modem units (*boxes* that helped computers connect to each other through a phone line—similar to the modems of today, but not nearly as fast). Last but not least, computers were programmable; kids who grew up with a computer in the home would sometimes learn how to program their *own* games. In fact, many game developers of today got their start this way; their parents had inadvertently given them an incentive to go far beyond just *playing* games!

APPLE'S TAME GAME MACHINE

It all started with the Apple II, the very first affordable personal computer. Until its release, the only other option was the Altair—an odd machine that lacked both a keyboard and a screen. The Apple II was truly the first computer that could be called "personal." It was non-threatening, user friendly, aesthetically pleasing, and it looked comfortable sitting next to the other home appliances. The Apple II sparked the personal computer revolution. Sales were brisk, and with the advent of the Visicalc spreadsheet application, the Apple II also became a hot item at the office. It was a major system until the early '90s, spreading through libraries, schools, and colleges. Since many Apple IIs were bought by parents, game developers realized the machine was positioned perfectly in the marketplace. This sparked the production of all sorts of Apple-compatible computer games; many of these were more sophisticated than console offerings, because a dedicated computer usually had more memory and storage—it also had a keyboard that facilitated "thinking games" (as opposed to "twitch" arcade games), such as Brøderbund's *The Ancient Art of War*.

The Apple II introduced computers to a new market.
Courtesy of Rama (Wikipedia Commons)

THE COMMODORE TAKES OVER

One of the most popular personal computers of all time was the Commodore 64—released in 1982. The C64 would outdo all other computers until the IBM PC got more horsepower under the hood (see next section). A major gaming system, the C64 soon began to devour console sales; the system was only marginally more expensive than a console while being a multipurpose system—a much better bang for the buck. (The multipurpose advantage of PCs would later be one of the reasons for the video game crash of 1983–84.) High-quality versions (known as *ports*) of arcade games, such as *Donkey Kong* and *Ms. Pac-Man*, were published for the C64. But this was just the beginning; the C64—with its 160k of storage, superior graphics, and sound—launched the trend of developing games containing large and detailed virtual worlds. *The Bard's Tale*—a pioneering 3D role-playing game that invited players to explore dungeons in search of gold and experience points—was a direct evolution of the text-based adventures from the late '70s such as *Colossal Cave* and *Zork*, which would be played by typing two-word commands such as "go west" and "drink potion" (discussed further in Chapter 2). The C64 sound chip also had a cult following because the music designed and played on it had a very distinct sound, alternatively featuring full-length songs, instrumental solos, and several simultaneous instruments.

Commodore Computers

Edutainment's Rise and Fall

With the advent of CD-ROMs, some in the industry believed that the new storage medium would provide enough resources to teach kids while avoiding the risk of "boredom" associated with some traditional teaching methods. This is the origin of the term "edutainment"—a tentative mix of education and entertainment. Part of a classic 1990s utopian ideal, edutainment games tried to be fun and instructive at the same time—but with the content leaning more heavily toward education than entertainment, this limited the effectiveness of the

→

results. Some home systems and computers were designed from the start to run edutainment software (Phillips CD-i and Commodore CDTV), while others were able to do it if necessary (Sega CD and Panasonic 3DO). After failing the final exam two times in a row (no fun plus barebones learning), it's not surprising that edutainment games fared badly both in sales and overall product quality. The "crash" was prominent: Edutainment software went from premium to budget overnight. But there's a resurgence of games being developed for the educational market (now referred to as "serious" or simply "educational" rather than the buzzword descriptor "edutainment"). We will discuss these games in more detail in Chapter 2 and Chapter 5.

IBM PC AND CLONES WANT TO PLAY, TOO!

The latest and most lasting system for computer games was the IBM PC (known simply as the PC), the very first model of Intel-based personal computers. Released in 1981, the PC was originally a business computer that was purchased only for corporate offices, but it soon made its way into homes due to the popularity of the PC standard. Since the PC started life as a business machine, it wasn't initially the best game system. The sound quality was extremely low, and the graphics looked shabby compared to the C64 and the Amiga 1000. The PC would only become a proper game machine in 1991 with the advent of faster processors, add-on sound cards such as the SoundBlaster 16, and the introduction of the CD-ROM. Newer versions of MS-DOS (Microsoft's old text-based operating system) gave game developers more flexibility, and with the added functionality of new technological advances, PC games started to get very sophisticated. For example, the groundbreaking 3D PC action game, *Doom* (in which a space marine must battle demons), was released in 1993, but it wouldn't get to home console systems until 1995. With the release of *Doom*, PCs would always be much more capable than consoles, leading in every area.

My first memory of computer gaming is from high school in 1973, playing *Star Trek* with a gang of six guys at school on the sole school computer with no monitor—where we typed in our moves and got a paper printout showing the current position of our *Enterprise* and the Bird of Prey we were fighting. No game has matched up to that one!

—Martha Ladyman (mom, substitute teacher, contract writer; Office Manager, IMGS, Inc.)

Courtesy of Sylvain Bizoirre (Old-Computers.com)

FRIENDS EVERYWHERE

Playing games with a friend is nothing new. *Spacewar!,* the first computer game, began as a two-player game, and all first- and second-generation consoles depended on a second player because the systems were not powerful enough to support computer-controlled opponents. Through the '70s and '80s, computers struggled to support two players in front of a single machine, but this was just too awkward for players (other than the "parent with child on lap" combination). Computers then began to make significant advances in what would be known as networked multiplayer games, leaving consoles in the dust. After multiplayer games in which players would share a screen in the same space, networked play would be the next incarnation of multiplayer gaming. These games would be played online or over a local network against multiple opponents.

"Networked" Doesn't Mean "Online"!

Networked and online games are similar, but there's a crucial distinction between the two: *Networked* is what we call a game played over a local area network (LAN). At a "LAN party," for example, players lug their desktops or laptops to one location and connect to a single network. Corporate networks were also popular for this type of gaming; it was convenient to play *Doom* during lunch hour or after work at the office because the network and computers were already in place. *Online* implies that a computer is used only to connect to the Internet—ruling out any kind of local network.

LAN parties kicked off the phenomenon of networked games.

EverQuest (discussed later in this chapter) is a perfect example of an online game because it is played on a much wider network, the Internet. Players are not in the same physical space, and there's the possibility of having a much larger number of people playing. Thus, online games are played much differently than networked games. Many online games are also never-ending persistent worlds that are available 24 hours per day. (These games, known as massively multiplayer online games, will be discussed in more detail in Chapter 2.) Note that classic "online services" such as CompuServe were not connected to the Internet but ran on proprietary networks with members-only access.

Arcades slowly began to carry two-player action games (often fighting games), and there was even a fairly popular four-player game, *Gauntlet*. Consoles were initially limited to two-player games, but this changed with the introduction of four-player adaptors in the early '90s. Newer game consoles such as the Nintendo 64 contained four built-in controller ports later in the '90s; *Goldeneye 007* received a lot of good press for its fun-filled four player battles.

Games began to move from LAN parties (see sidebar) to *virtual* events in 1996. Full-scale online games began with *Quake* in 1996. In the ensuing years, playing games online became a whole industry segment, with services such as Blizzard's battle.net, Valve's Steam, and Microsoft's Xbox Live leading the pack. Text-based networked games known as multi-user dungeons (MUDs) got their start in the university system during the '60s, and they continued to expand through the decades; once we were able to use web browsers to access the Internet in the early '90s, MUDs transformed into graphical multiplayer games such as *Ultima Online* and *EverQuest*, which were housed on networked servers that could host upward of 1,000 players at a time. To give you an idea of how massive this market is, consider *World of Warcraft* (discussed in Chapter 2), the most popular online game in the world; it has over 7 million subscribers and exerts a virtual monopoly over PC gaming.

Today games usually have two *modes*: single-player and multiplayer. Single-player only games are getting rarer by the minute, while some games opt to rule out single-player altogether—such as id Software's forthcoming *Quake Wars*.

Playing games with thousands of people is very different than playing at a friend's house. Many times, the "best" player in a group of friends suffers humiliating defeats when playing online! This happens because the competition provided by a large number of human opponents is much tougher than computer-controlled enemies, a simple fact that is usually forgotten by the reigning "champion."

Online games can be played through computers or through consoles (such as the Xbox Live service). Since online games attract such a wide variety of players, they are much more challenging for parents regarding ratings and themes. For one thing, there is no true way to forbid swearing and other objectionable behavior in online games. At most, a feedback system will attempt to self-regulate the game, but this is usually not enough to keep the game family friendly. Console online games played through Xbox Live are usually populated by male teenagers and young adults—and testosterone-fueled trash talk is the rule. In contrast, PC online games attract a mixed age group consisting of a 60/40 split between males and females, resulting in a balanced environment more conducive to a healthy dialogue. The anonymity factor in online games can ironically unleash all sorts of antisocial behavior—shown in anything from virtual heckling to unfair competition. Even inferiority complexes emerge in the form of players who choose big mean Orcs rather than elves as their characters so that they can vanquish all the other players in the game!

EDUCATION NETWORK: PLATO

Online games started in the early '60s with PLATO (Programmed Logic for Automatic Teaching Operations), a computer-based education program at the University of Illinois that Rick Blomme transformed into the first multiplayer gaming network. Through PLATO, lucky college students could play networked versions of *Spacewar!*, *Empire*, and *Airflight* (a flight simulator). By the '70s, PLATO introduced *Avatar*, a text-based game that was known as a *dungeon* (a genre in its own right that reflected the excitement and danger of exploring huge labyrinths). In 1978, these adventures were renamed multi-user dungeons (MUDs), after mutating into persistent dungeons that could be populated by more than one player. MUDs used ARPAnet (the precursor to the Internet) to connect different computers/players and were all text based.

ONLINE SERVICES: COMPUSERVE, QUANTUMLINK, AND GENIE

Beginning in the 1980s, first CompuServe and then QuantumLink (which would later become AOL) would give players the very first graphics-based dungeons through a network. They were both very expensive—sometimes charging $25–$65 per hour of play. GEnie (GE Network for Information Exchange) introduced a truly pioneering game, *Air Warrior*—a World War II flight simulator that for the first time allowed online play though the use of a graphical interface, a feat for the time.

LAN PARTIES: *DOOM, QUAKE,* AND *HALF-LIFE: COUNTER-STRIKE*

In 1993, with the release of *Doom*, the game world would never be the same. This is the game that coined the playing style known as "death match"—an all-out battle for life in a virtual environment. *Doom* allowed for eight-player death matches that soon invaded offices and schools worldwide. The company responsible, id Software, perfected the idea behind *Doom* with *Quake*—the first fully 3D shooter (discussed in Chapter 2) and also the first to have online lobbies where players could pick a "server" or host their own games. Created by John Carmack, lead programmer and one of the founders of id, *Quake* garnered a cult following and the sales to back it up, generating three sequels. All of them had online play; in fact, *Quake III* was so focused on the multiplayer feature that it didn't have a single-player campaign at all.

The widely popular *Doom* created the game style known as "death match."
DOOM used by permission from id Software Inc.

Quake III Arena was a landmark multiplayer networked game. QUAKE III
ARENA used by permission from id Software Inc.

My most memorable moment? Playing *Quake* on the office LAN with my older daughters and co-workers.

—Greg Costikyan (chief executive officer, Manifesto Games)

The big name in online shooters, however, turned out to be *Counter-Strike.* In 1999, games were still getting used to the new 3D accelerator cards known as GPUs (graphics processing units). One of the first games to make full use of these cards was *Half-Life.* The game looked and played beautifully—stunning everyone with the textured, high-res look of maps and characters. Many consider *Half-Life* the greatest shooter ever made. (Many of these shooters are now commonly referred to as first-person shooters, or FPSs, discussed in Chapter 2.)

Counter-Strike was a *mod* for *Half-Life*—created by players who "modified" *Half-Life* by using world-building tools that are shipped with the game. Modding (described in Chapters 2 and 7) has been a great way for kids to learn how to develop games. In *Half-Life: Counter-Strike,* one team of players is comprised of terrorists, and the other is comprised of counterterrorist operatives; both teams fight epic battles to free hostages and defuse bombs, as opposed to the simple (by comparison) death matches of *Quake* and *Doom.* This type of game was truly revolutionary; the only other game mode that required team skills was CTF (*Capture the Flag*), which was much less rigid than a hardcore *Counter-Strike* game.

Counter-Strike was released in 1999, well into the broadband revolution; it was a perfect time for online games. The high-speed Internet connections were essential for games such as *Counter-Strike* because speed defined how fast a player could react in the game world; the lack of speed came to be known as *lag.* Since *Counter-Strike* was based on real-world terrorist events and was a mod, players soon started designing new weapons and maps for the game—keeping it interesting for much longer—which increased what is known as *replay value.* Today, *Counter-Strike* is played in championships all over the world for honor, fun—and even money!

BRAVE NEW WORLDS: *ULTIMA ONLINE, LINEAGE,* AND *EVERQUEST*

Three games set the standard for games that came to be known as massively multiplayer online games (MMOGs, discussed in Chapter 2). These games are all descendants of MUDs, spicing up the story and dungeon exploration with vast and detailed worlds aided by aesthetic 3D graphics. *Ultima Online (UO),* launched in 1997, was the pioneer. A networked follower of *Diablo, UO* was the first online multiplayer game that combined advanced graphics and interactivity to create a very addicting persisting medieval world. *UO* is also one of the first games to let go of the "pay by the hour" format, charging a monthly subscription instead. In 2003, it eventually reached 350,000 subscribers. (A sequel is planned for 2007.)

I remember running quests on *Ultima Online* with my oldest son sitting with me. He would help me think of things to do with the other players on the quest. To this day, he can remember most of the details about any of the quests he helped me on.

—Jennifer Anderson (tech support rep/Student)

Lineage followed the same online multiplayer model and was a huge success in South Korea (the leader in online multiplayer games due to its strong broadband base). The world of *Lineage* featured fantasy/sci-fi monsters and treasures. It was a "slam dunk" in subscriber numbers (a few million in South Korea alone). It also boasted one of the first *virtual economies*, an in-game monetary system that allowed players to sell and buy virtual goods. Soon, this economy expanded into the real world—and people started paying real money for in-game, rare items such as a magical sword or shield. *Lineage* grew to 4.5 millions users in its heyday.

EverQuest introduced massively multiplayer online games to the U.S. market. Used with permission of Sony Online Entertainment.

EverQuest, released in 2001, was the first game to draw large-scale attention to the online multiplayer experience in the United States. As addictive as *UO* and *Lineage*, it was soon nicknamed "EverCrack" because it turned once normal individuals into zombies (metaphorically speaking, of course). By 2003, countless research papers were showing that games could actually steal the audience and buying power from more traditional media such as film and television. Instead of selling virtual items and characters within the game, players built up powerful characters and sold them on auction sites such as eBay. One former University of Southern California student cleared $10,000 per month by selling his very powerful virtual characters to *newbies* (inexperienced players, also known as *noobs*)! *EverQuest* has validated the technical and economic significance of virtual universes—a "how-to" that will eventually be used for newer long distance, computer-based educational systems.

Gasp!

If you made it here, the enormous scope of the gaming industry is hopefully quite clear to you. In order to help you understand how your kids play games (and *why*), we went back in time to where it all began. This ride through history—with stops in the research lab, local hangout, living room, home office, and cyberspace—saw the birth of a new industry that has had a cultural impact not unlike that of traditional media such as film. Knowing the history of games also means understanding where games are now and what will become of them in the near future. Your new historical perspective will allow you to understand most of today's dilemmas regarding games and kids—and it puts you in good standing with players around the world. In the next chapter, we will go beyond history and take an in-depth look at the vocabulary associated with games, which will help you and your kids speak the same language.

2 Games 101

In This Chapter

- The Facts: Stats That Will Surprise You!
- The Fundamentals: Terms That Every Parent Should Know
- Platforms
- Ratings
- Genres
- Market
- Story: *What Do We Play?*
- Gameplay: *How Do We Play?*
- It All Begins on First Base

In order to truly understand the appeal of games, it's important for parents to become familiar with the vocabulary associated with them. Games are often referred to as "interactive entertainment"—*interactive* because they involve active participation on the part of the audience (players), and *entertainment* because their basic storytelling mechanisms are derived from traditional entertainment industry segments such as cinema, comic books, and even television series. Like film, games have *genres* and *ratings*. However, as you learned in Chapter 1, "Where It All Began," games are also quite unlike traditional entertainment—because they can be experienced on several different systems (arcades, consoles, computers, handhelds); also, players can control their game experiences through accessories such as joysticks, gamepads, and driving wheels. This chapter focuses on basic game elements (such as genres, goals, platforms, ratings, gameplay, and story)—and some surprising and little-known game industry facts.

THE FACTS: STATS THAT WILL SURPRISE YOU!

We're about to share some game industry facts that might catch you by surprise. You are most likely unaware of them because the media often characterize games as a negative force in society. However, as the following facts will reveal, games are increasingly being used as positive and transformative tools:

Q. How many American households have video games?
A. **Almost 70%.** (You didn't think they were so common, did you?)

Q. How old is the average player?
A. **33 years old.** (Teenagers actually represent only 31% of the player population.)

Q. What's the percentage of games rated M (Mature; 17 and older)?
A. **15%.** (Violent games are not the rule, but the exception.)

Q. What's the percentage of female players?
A. **38%.** (Female players are very real and on the rise!)

Q. Do people over the age of 50 play games?
A. **Yes. 25% of gamers are over 50 years old.** (This is the top age group that plays puzzle and computer games.)

Q. How many hours per week does the average gamer play games?
A. **Males, 7.6 hours; females, 7.4 hours.** (This is probably much less than you expected—and very similar across genders.)

Q. Do players spend the same energy on sports?
A. **Yes. A whopping 79% of gamers play at least 20 hours of sports per month.** (Gamers may love their pizza, but they also crave exercise.)

Q. What about culture? Do players go to museums and concerts? Do they read books?
A. **Yes—62% attend cultural events, while 92% read daily newspapers and books.** (Impressive, huh?)

All of the above facts are backed by research collected by the Entertainment Software Association (http://www.theesa.com). What some still call a new medium is already a major part of most people's lives. Furthermore, players could be considered relatively normal people who may stand out due not to antisocial behavior but to superior manual dexterity, intelligence, curiosity, problem-solving skills, and autonomy.

THE FUNDAMENTALS: TERMS THAT EVERY PARENT SHOULD KNOW

The following terms have been used in the electronic game industry since its inception. Some of them might seem antiquated, but they are all part of the foundation on which modern games are based. Let's take a deeper look at the basic vocabulary:

LIVES

Back in the arcade era, every game had a simple, unspoken rule: "Do well and live; do badly and die." Each quarter that was deposited into the arcade machine gave the player one try against the game. When games migrated to the home, quarters did not apply anymore; a different way of counting the player's "credits" was required. After many late hours (and lots of coffee), someone must have figured out that, if player died in-game, they lost a life. And thus game lives were born. *Lives* represented the old-fashioned way to limit the number of tries available to the player. Difficult games might have had only a single life, while others allowed players to select a number that best fits their level of expertise. However, while most games gave players extra lives (known as "one-ups"), zero lives usually meant "game over."

Only two lives are left in this image from *Alex Kidd in the Enchanted Castle.* © Sega. All rights reserved.

CONTINUES

Although no more lives usually signaled the end of a game, there were some games that allowed players to get "reborn" through additional lives known as *continues*. So if you died battling the green monster inside the cave—and you had run out of lives—*maybe* a continue would be available. Continues either were earned or could sometimes be available by default.

In *Golden Axe II*, players could use a "continue" to have a brand new set of lives.

LEVELS

The word *levels* has been said to have originated from the role-playing games of the 1970s, when players would start at Level 1 in the dungeon and progress to a higher level (such as Level 9). When arcade games first began (also in the '70s), a word was needed to describe the many different stages that a player progressed through. It was a natural fit; levels began to make a lot of sense, and the term was adopted without much effort. Current games have levels, too, but they are much more complex, sometimes sprawling areas with terrain, structures, climate, characters, and themes. Levels are the *worlds* in which the game is played.

DIFFICULTY

Unlike the level structure discussed previously, difficulty levels describe the intensity of the game's challenges. Electronic games have always included a variety of built-in difficulty levels to address a wide range of players. Certain games are notoriously difficult, while others try not to challenge players too much to avoid frustration in favor of more relaxed play. Most current games have variations of the three classic difficulty levels: easy, medium, and hard; others add a more advanced level (sometimes "crazy" or "maniac") to challenge the most hardcore players.

CONTROLLERS

From the very beginning, players were always the ones in control of the game experience. This player control was first achieved with computer keyboards and later with aptly named *controllers*—wired input mechanisms that, through a directional pad and buttons, allowed players to jump, dodge, draw swords, select dialogue choices, and add items to their inventory among other game actions. Today, many types of controllers are available. We'll discuss these later in this chapter.

The controller for the PlayStation 2 is considered to be comfortable for most hand sizes. Sony Computer Entertainment America

BOSSES

Bosses are nothing more than tougher-than-average "evil entities" that usually appear at the end of every level. The purpose of a boss is to give the player that extra challenge necessary to clear a level, contributing to player confidence . . . or frustration (depending on how tough the boss is to beat). Back when a level was just a more difficult version of the same level that preceded it, bosses didn't exist. There simply was no need for them. Then, as games became more complex, the first signs of a three-act dramatic structure (beginning with *Ms. Pac-Man*) started seeping into games, resulting in the need for a climax at the end of each level. A much harder, scarier "final boss" in the game's last level is a given in almost every game.

Bowser is a boss in the unique *Paper Mario*.
Courtesy of Nintendo

FRAME RATE

Not all games run at the same speed. The "Holy Grail" of gaming is 60 frames per second (FPS, which is double the *frame rate* of U.S. television. Other games have to settle for 30 FPS due to high graphic demands or poor programming, which is less than ideal, but surely acceptable. Games that run under 30 FPS can be considered poor and will certainly annoy players.

PLATFORMS

In Chapter 1, we discussed the different eras involved in game development. Each era was marked by a primary game system (arcade, console, handheld, computer). These systems are known in the game industry as *platforms*. A game developed for one platform will usually not work on another; for example, an Xbox game won't work on a PlayStation 2, and vice-versa. Let's take a look at some modern-day platforms.

CONSOLES

Dedicated game machines, *consoles*, have quickly become the preferred platform of choice in the United States for games. For one thing, consoles are much simpler to operate—needing only to be connected to a TV and sound system in order to play. Console games are also "plug and play," since they run straight from DVD or Blu-Ray discs; unlike PCs, there's no need to install anything on the hard drive. Finally, consoles have eclipsed PCs as game platforms because consoles remain current for roughly five years, while a PC may become "old" in six months. This allows consoles to give players optimal game conditions, such as high frame rate and consistent picture quality during the console's lifetime, without the risk of being too slow for a demanding game. *Current-gen* (or current generation) consoles are those currently in use, including the Sony PlayStation 2, Nintendo GameCube, and Microsoft Xbox. *Next-gen* (or next generation) platforms are those that remain unreleased or that have been in the market for only a year or so. Through the decades, many consoles that are now no longer in primary use were once referred to as "next-gen"—including the Sega Genesis, Sony PlayStation, and even the now current-gen PlayStation 2. Next-gen consoles for 2007 include the Microsoft Xbox 360, the Nintendo Wii, and the Sony PlayStation 3.

Sony Playstation 2

> **Year of release:** 2000
>
> **Media:** CD-ROM / DVD-ROM
>
> **Processor:** "Emotion Engine" 294.9MHz
>
> **Memory:** 32 Megabytes
>
> **Online:** Add-on modem and Ethernet ports in the first model; built-in Ethernet connection in the PS Two (smaller console)
>
> **Surround sound:** Dolby Prologic II and 4-channel DTS
>
> **DVDs:** Plays them from the box
>
> **Hard-drive:** Add-on
>
> **HDTV-friendly:** No

Sony Computer Entertainment America

One of the most successful consoles in history (over 100 million units shipped), the PlayStation 2 (PS2) is now past its prime; games in this platform will never look as good as the other consoles—rare exceptions excluded. The PS2 hardware, unfortunately, is simply not fast enough for today's games, which is natural since it was the first of its generation. However, the PS2 had many quality releases during its life—some of them regarded as the greatest games of all time—including *Gran Turismo 3* and *4*, *Virtua Fighter 4: Evolution*, *God of War*, *Devil May Cry 3*, and *Final Fantasy X*. If you want quality releases at an affordable price, the *PS2 Greatest Hits* collection is a surefire way to find them. It's a fact that the PS2 always focused on more mature players (17 and up). The very reason the console was so successful is that Sony tried to make it as "edgy" as possible, as evidenced by the European TV and magazine ads. The PS2 controller, named DualShock2, is among the most comfortable ever designed, well built, and fits hands of all ages. The console itself looks very sturdy and serious, fitting well among high-end home theater equipment. Two different models were released: The early model (PS2) is the most known, while the second (PS Two) is incredibly small and portable. They both offer the same functionality, but the second model is more reliable because it contains redesigned components. There are a large number of titles available for the PS2, although the console is considered outdated by today's standards.

Nintendo GameCube

Year of release: 2001

Media: GD-ROM

Processor: IBM "Gecko" 485MHz

Memory: 24 Megabytes

Online: No

Surround sound: Dolby Prologic II

DVDs: Does not play them

Hard-drive: No

HDTV-friendly: No

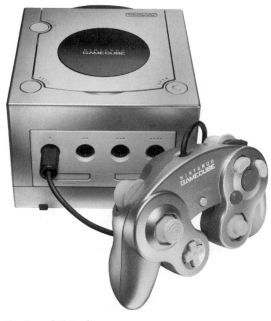

Courtesy of Nintendo

The Nintendo GameCube was always intended as a game console only. It has no DVD drive and cannot connect to the Internet to allow for online gaming. The biggest draw to the GameCube consists of the Nintendo games that you cannot find anywhere else. Graphics- and sound-wise, the GameCube is well ahead of the PS2 but still behind the Xbox (discussed in the next section). Image quality and effects are good if not great, and the console has Prologic II surround sound. Graphics look sharp on an HDTV but may have input lag. Of course, being a Nintendo product, the GameCube excels at kids' games. *Mario* and *Zelda* games can be played by young children, and the controller is appropriately colorful. The mini cube design is also very "cute"—and due to its small form, it will fit anywhere. Notwithstanding the console's core audience (kids), there *are* a few M (Mature) titles for the GameCube —and the most famous of them is *Resident Evil 4*. Keep in mind that a game for the GameCube is not automatically suited for all ages. Lightweight and with a modular cube design, the GameCube is the only console that can call itself kid-proof!

Microsoft Xbox

> **Year of release:** 2002
>
> **Media:** DVD-ROM
>
> **Processor:** IBM Pentium III 700MHz
>
> **Memory:** 64 Megabytes
>
> **Online:** Ethernet only
>
> **Surround sound:** Dolby Digital 5.1
>
> **DVDs:** Needs an add-on remote to play from the box
>
> **Hard drive:** Yes
>
> **HDTV friendly:** Yes

Microsoft Corporation

The Xbox is the latest of the current generation, and it shows. It blows the other two consoles out of the water in every department. Be it image quality or surround sound, the Xbox is better designed and more powerful. It's a safe bet if you don't want to go into next-gen territory. The only features the Xbox lacks are Sony exclusives such as *God of War* and Nintendo's strong titles. Otherwise, it provides solid gaming. Most games are released for all three consoles, but the Xbox versions are usually the best because the platform has the most powerful hardware of the three current-gen consoles (yielding better frame rate, effects, and real-time 5.1 surround sound). Online gaming with consoles was made possible by Xbox Live, a paid service started by Microsoft in 2003. Xbox Live allows Xbox owners to connect to each other and play games together, including voice and text message support. Sony has an online service, but it is nothing like Xbox Live, which means that online gaming with a PS2 can be very cumbersome. The Xbox downfalls are two: the controller and the unit size. The S-type controllers currently sold are a big improvement over the original "Dukes," but they still lose to the PS2 controllers in comfort and finish. As for the console size, it's obvious: The Xbox is *huge*. It's downright scary; be sure to have a lot of space for it in your living room! There are many outstanding games for the Xbox. *Forza Motorsport* is a tour-de-force in racing simulation, as is *Ninja Gaiden Black* in action-adventure. *Conker's Bad Fur Day*, from Rare, is one of the funniest games ever made, and both *Halo* and *Halo 2* combine the very best of console FPSs, single- and multiplayer. Despite being old hardware by now, the Xbox is certainly a very good value—and newer games still look and sound amazing.

Xbox Live Arcade: Giving Arcade Games a New and Improved Home

Arcade games rely on very simple rules. Therefore, arcade games ended up being very short and difficult—requiring manual dexterity, quick reflexes, and intense focus. Still, arcade games are among the most fun types of games available. The display of a "high score" list was a main staple of the arcade industry; player initials and associated scores would be available on the list for all other players to see. Players with high scores would be treated as minor celebrities and earned bragging rights at the local arcade hangout. The whole purpose behind the high score system was ruined after arcade games migrated to home console systems; once the console was turned off, any high scores that had accumulated were lost. (Memory that allowed players to save game information was expensive at the time.) Worse, playing an arcade game at home didn't have the exhibitionist quality associated with a public hangout; who cares what your dog

→

Marble Blast Ultra is just one of the many games available through Xbox Live Arcade. GarageGames

(or even family members) might think about your high score—in comparison to dozens of your peers competing at the local arcade? Sadly, arcade games lost most of their allure with the transition to living rooms everywhere. But Xbox Live Arcade brought some of it back. The Microsoft-owned network reaches every Xbox 360 owner and allows players to download many classic arcade games for only a few dollars. Better yet, Xbox Live Arcade has scoreboards updated in real time—taking good care of high scores. Players all over the world can play together, which is the closest the living room has ever gotten to amusement arcades.

I sent my grandson an email asking if he had heard of Xbox Live Arcade. He hadn't—so I know about something he didn't know about and seem to have some knowledge of "his" area of expertise. I also slyly asked what games he wanted next. He mentioned two. Then I said, "Well, how are your grades?" He was honest and said he had a couple of Cs, so I said, "Well, if you can bring those up to Bs by report card time, I can get you one of the games you want. Straight As will get you both the games you mentioned." Straight out bribery—but I'm only the grandmother so I can get away with it. (Seems better than just being a pushover, gift-giving, granny!)

—Sandy Doell (author, editor, mother grandmother, and gamer)

Microsoft Xbox 360

Year of release: 2005

Media: DVD-ROM

Processor: IBM Power-PC 3.2GHz (3 cores with 2 threads each)

Memory: 512 Megabytes

Online: Ethernet only

Surround sound: Dolby Digital 5.1

DVDs: Plays them from the box

Hard drive: Add-on or in the Premium Bundle

HDTV-friendly: Yes

Microsoft Corporation

The Xbox 360, released in November 2005, is the first next-gen console available to the public. With three fast cores on a single die, its 3.2GHz processor outruns most PC processors, and the 512MB of very fast RAM gives it enough muscle to create some astounding visuals. Being a software maker, Microsoft equipped the 360 with a great interface and gave it services to boot. The new Xbox Live Marketplace is a great way to download movie trailers, game demos, and even full arcade games for Xbox Live Arcade. With an Ethernet connection, the Xbox 360 can stream pictures and music (MP3/WMA) from any PC, which also makes it very adequate as a media server—delivering standard or high-definition content to the big-screen TV in the living room. An interesting accessory is the Live Vision Camera, a USB (universal serial bus) device that allows players to video chat, take pictures of themselves and apply them to game character faces, or have their picture in the scoreboards. The games released as of now vary in quality. Many of the launch titles were very good for launch titles, but they wouldn't stand the test of time. *Project Gotham 3* is one of these; while very enjoyable, it doesn't feel exactly right—having worse tarmac textures than *Forza Motorsport*, for example. Other games in the list are *Gun* and *Quake 4*, rushed ports with lower-quality graphics and frame rate issues, respectively. Outstanding games are *Call of Duty 2*, *Call of Duty 3*, *The Elder Scrolls IV: Oblivion*, *Fight Night Round 3*, *Tom Clancy's Ghost Recon Advanced Warfighter*, *Gears of War*, and *Forza Motorsport 2*.

Sony Playstation 3

Year of release: 2006

Media: BD-ROM (Blu-Ray disc)

Processor: 3.2GHz IBM Cell Processor with 7 additional SPEs

Memory: 512 Megabytes

Online: Wi-Fi and Ethernet

Surround sound: Dolby Digital 5.1

DVDs: Plays them from the box; also plays Blu-Ray discs

Hard drive: Both 20GB and 60GB models available

HDTV-friendly: Yes

The next iteration of the powerful PlayStation brand is the most powerful console of all time. Specialists say that the PS3's Cell processor is 2.5 times faster than the one in the Xbox 360, and the built-in Blu-Ray disc drive may be the next step in High Definition video—reaching 50GB of capacity. Sony is back at the cutting edge of technology—an inversion of what happened in the current-gen console war. With a maximum resolution of 1080p (similar to the Xbox 360), the PS3 may become a contender just by having a Blu-Ray drive—just like the PS2 did with DVDs. The PS3 will be one of the cheapest Blu-Ray players in the market for quite some time; however, the success of this approach depends on whether the winner in the format war will be Blu-Ray or HD-DVD. Two PS3 models are available; the standard version has a 20GB hard drive and no flash card reader, while the premium bundle has a 60GB hard drive and a flash card reader. The PS3 is also online enabled, and Sony will have assembled a network much like Xbox Live—supposedly free of charge. A possible downfall for the console is the price range of $499–599 (way too expensive for a game console), and the fact that the PS3 hardware is very difficult to develop for—with seven coprocessors and the high cost associated with Blu-Ray discs. At least initially, Xbox 360 games will look the same or better than PS3 games due to the more straightforward development process.

Sony Computer Entertainment America

Nintendo Wii

Year of release: 2006

Media: DVD-ROM

Processor: 729MHz IBM "Broadway"

Memory: 88 Megabytes

Online: Built-in Wi-Fi; requires add-on wired Ethernet adapter

Surround sound: Dolby Prologic II

DVDs: Doesn't play them from the box

Hard drive: None—but ships with 512MB of flash memory

HDTV-friendly: Yes—but still no real HDTV graphics

Courtesy of Nintendo

The Nintendo Wii has surprisingly become the most sought after next-gen console in the market. Nintendo ironically said "no thanks" to the ever-increasing graphical requirements of next-gen games, betting instead on a paradigm shift in the form of the Wiimote—a controller that allows players to become immersed physically in the game. The Wii is simply the biggest change in gaming in 20 years, and its impact is being felt all over the world. Gamers can play tennis just as they would with a racquet and shoot bad guys pointing at the screen, much like the old light guns of past systems. The Wii is also very cheap by next-gen standards. While the PlayStation 3 can cost up to $600, the Wii tops out at $250, with a Wiimote, "nunchuk" controller, and *Wii Sports* bundled with the system. While the Xbox 360 is still a great deal, nothing beats the Wii in cost-benefit ratio. Nintendo didn't stop there. Its new Virtual Console functionality allows users to buy NES, SNES, N64, and even Sega Genesis's games online for a few dollars, emulating those machines to perfection. This is a major selling point; retrogaming has been rapidly expanding in the last couple of years, as most in the industry know very well. A special, classic controller is available for virtual console games. Titles include *The Legend of Zelda: Twilight Princess, Mario Galaxy,* and the bundled *Wii Sports*—all top of the line games that stay true to Nintendo's tradition.

Parent Snapshot

Billy Burger

Media Arts & Animation Instructor
(Art Institute of California, San Francisco)
San Francisco, CA

Billy has worked on films (*FernGully 2, James and the Giant Peach*), television series (*Poochini*), over 250 television commercials, and 14 games, and he created and directed his own cartoon, *Racket in the Attic*. Billy has worked at Colossal Pictures, Skelington Pictures, Maverix, Curious Pictures, Morgan Interactive, Spazzco, and Wild Brain.

- Platforms: PS, Wii, GBA SP, GBA, GB Color
- Top Games: *The Legend of Zelda, Mario Kart*
- "The Wii is awesome—but my kids won't let me play it!"

Console Controllers

Let's take a quick look at console *controllers* (sometimes called gamepads or joysticks)—physical interfaces through which players may take control of the game. Computer gamers may use also use controllers, but computer games usually rely on the keyboard and mouse combination.

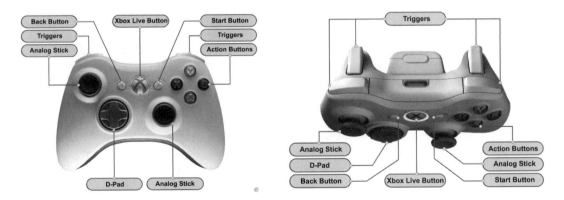

Xbox 360 controller front (left) and back (right), with components labeled. Microsoft Corporation/Annotations by Jason Bramble

- **Analog sticks**—Just like the arcade sticks from the past, analog sticks offer different degrees of movement and varied sensitivities. Current- and next-gen console controllers usually have two analog sticks, which appeared just when 3D games became popular.
- **D-pad**—The D-pad is a digital pad with eight possible directions. They seem very old-fashioned now because of the limited flexibility. Nonetheless, D-pads are still widely used for fighting games because of their precision. Other possible uses include D-pads as shortcuts to inventory menus, different weapon selections (*Doom 3*), and other game-specific actions, such as equipping infrared lenses (*Splinter Cell: Chaos Theory*).
- **Shoulder buttons**—Shoulder buttons are special buttons on the back (or "shoulder") of the controller. The Xbox 360 and both the PlayStation 2 and 3 controllers have shoulder buttons, which are used for secondary functions because they are not very easy to reach. Shoulder buttons are referred to as LB and RB in the Xbox 360 and L1/L2 and R1/R2 (four buttons) on both PlayStation controllers.
- **Face buttons**—Usually named A, B, X, and Y, the face buttons can also be geometric shapes (square, circle, triangle) such as those found on the PlayStation controllers. Face buttons hold a game's main actions and functions. The most important function (jumping, for instance) is always mapped to the A button on the Xbox and Xbox 360 controllers, and to the X button in both PlayStation controllers.
- **Triggers**—There are analog triggers in the back of all controllers (below the shoulder buttons used for precision accelerating/braking or other precision-dependent functions.
- **Option buttons**—The option buttons are used to pause the game or select options while playing the game. On the PlayStation controllers, these buttons are referred to as *select* and *start*—and both the Xbox and Xbox 360 name them <| and |>, which could be interpreted as "back" and "play."
- **Auxiliary buttons**—The original Xbox controller had one white and one black button, known as auxiliary buttons since they had no predetermined functionality. Most controllers have "extra" buttons, which are usually very different from each other. One famous auxiliary button on the PlayStation 2 controller is the "analog" button, which is used to deactivate both analog sticks in order to play original PlayStation games.
- **Vibration**—In 1997, the Nintendo 64 introduced the Rumble Pak, an accessory for the controller that allowed it to rumble in tandem with the action onscreen. It was such a success story that now every current-gen and next-gen console (excluding the PlayStation3) has built-in rumble functionality. Vibration is a veritable hoot to play with, but it can also be turned off in most games if it becomes uncomfortable or tiresome.

Parent Snapshot

Michael John

Game Designer
Pasadena, CA

Michael John is a game designer with over 10 years of experience. He has worked primarily on games for which kids are a large part of the target audience. His credits include the notable character action games, *Spyro the Dragon* (series) for PlayStation and *Daxter* for the Sonμy PSP. Michael also co-authored the "Cerny Method" along with Mark Cerny, which is often cited for popularizing the importance of preproduction in video game projects.

- Family Profile: 5-year old daughter
- Family Playtime: 1–3 hours per week
- Platforms: Xbox 360, Xbox, PS3, PS2, PS, Wii, GameCube, N64, Dreamcast, PC, PSP, DS, GBA
- Top 3 games: *Viva Pinata, Chibi Robo, Loco Roco*
- Memorable Moment: "Sitting with my daughter and taking turns with the controller (although I wish more games had voiceover so that I didn't have to read everything out loud)!"

PORTABLES

The ability to "pick up and play" games is most pronounced in *portable* game systems—platforms that allow for unprecedented convenience and freedom. A large library of games and an abundance of accessories are highly desirable—but battery life, sturdiness, and weight are the primary features that can either make or break a portable game system. The telltale sign of bad portable design is a two-hour battery life. Nothing makes a player's life more enjoyable than a game console that can be taken around the block.

Nintendo DS

Year of release: 2004

Media: Game Card (128 Megabytes max)

Processor: 67MHz ARM946E-S and 33MHz ARM7TDMI coprocessor

Memory: 4 Megabytes

Online: Wi-Fi

Surround sound: No, but "virtual" surround is available

Battery life: Very good—over 10 hours

Sturdy: Yes, but the new version (DS Lite) lost some of its ruggedness in favor of a lightweight, more aesthetic design

Courtesy of Nintendo

The DS is another stroke of genius from Nintendo. Bearing a dual-screen layout (with one of the screens touch-sensitive), the DS proved to be a truly innovative platform—bringing the most creative, left-field games ever to grace a portable. The Nintendo DS is the new darling of gamers everywhere. Being an evolved Nintendo 64, the DS handles 3D games very well for its small form-factor. Super *Mario 64 DS* looks just like *Mario 64* for the Nintendo 64—an impressive feat. The DS also sounds great and feels very well built. While the old model has a characteristic unfinished feel, the new DS Lite is very comfortable in the hands—sharing some similarities with the Apple iPod. Also, certain games such as *Mario Kart DS* can be played via the Wi-Fi connection with up to eight players—and a new web browser is in the works, bringing portable browsing to all DS users. The DS also plays all of Game Boy Advance (GBA) titles, an immense software library readily available. Outstanding games are the *Nintendogs* franchise, *Starfox Command*, *Brain Age* series, *Advance Wars DS*, *New Super Mario Bros.*, and *Metroid Prime: Hunters*.

Sony PSP

Year of release: 2004

Media: UMD disc

Processor: 333MHz MIPS R4000

Memory: 32 Megabytes

Online: Wi-Fi

Surround sound: "Virtual" surround is available instead

Battery life: Weak—around 3 hours

Sturdy: Screen is scratch prone due to lack of protective cover

Sony Computer Entertainment America

The Sony PSP is über portable, very close to what a PlayStation 2 offers. Since both share the same technology, PS2 games consistently show up in the PSP lineup, which ends up defining the platform. The PSP is for people who love home consoles and want to take that same kind of experience on the road. Since the console has a very fast processor and a lot of memory, PSP games such as *Tekken: Dark Resurrection* can easily challenge current-gen console games. However, the PSP is more than a super-powerful portable; it is also a very capable MP3 and media player, having high-fidelity sound and a truly gorgeous, widescreen display. Online connectivity is built in, and a web browser is already available, which makes the PSP more practical than the Nintendo DS (at least for a while). The downfall of the system is battery life. Users will be lucky if they get 4 hours out of a battery; the fact that the PSP uses discs instead of memory cards (like the DS) drains the battery at an alarming rate. The issue is so pronounced that extra batteries and high-speed chargers now flood the market in an attempt to correct the problem. Despite this, many gamers find themselves at home with the PSP, mainly because it brings to portable gaming a very traditional, console-like experience. Important games are *Grand Theft Auto: Liberty City Stories*, *Syphon Filter: Dark Mirror*, and *Lumines*; many other quality releases are expected in the near future.

Personal Computers (PCs)

While console games can be played almost immediately—like a movie on DVD or an audio CD—*computer games* first need to be installed in the machine itself, which takes time and effort. Also, computer games require the latest hardware to run, which means that unless you have a cutting-edge computer, your game will either run slower or look worse than you'd like it to.

Nevertheless, one major advantage of computer games since the advent of the Internet has been online play. Since most computers are equipped with modems and/or a network card, playing with friends online is a breeze. Computer games also tend to be cheaper, and there are often trial or demo versions of games available. On the other hand, playing cooperatively with a friend requires either a second computer, which is cost prohibitive for most families, or that both players scramble in front of the keyboard at the same time. Computers were never good for same-room, co-op play. It's still a great idea to encourage kids to play computer games, especially those that are shipped with "level editing" or "world building" tools that allow players to create *mods* (modifications or versions) of current computer games. Modding—and creating games from scratch through game engines that can be downloaded and run on PCs—is a great way for kids to get their feet wet as game developers (discussed further in Chapter 7). On a sad note, computer gaming seems to be dying out. The competition from current and next-gen consoles is fierce (not to mention online console play), leaving only a few computer-based genres. Right now, many in the game industry are looking for a way to save PC games from eventual extinction.

Computer (PC) Specs

Here's a sample list of PC specs. Compare these to the console and portable specs we discussed in the previous sections.

Media: Blu-Ray/HD-DVD/DVD-RW/CD-RW

Processor: 2.66GHz Quad Core Intel (4 cores)

Video card: Geforce 7950GX2 (1 Gigabyte video RAM—4 times the video RAM of Xbox 360 and PlayStation 3)

Memory: 4 Gigabytes (eight times Xbox 360 and PlayStation 3)

Online: Ethernet and modem

Surround sound: Dolby Digital 7.1

DVDs: Plays them from the box

Hard drive: Yes, 500 Gigabytes or more

Big Stock Photo

Choosing a game platform is always a big decision. Players with money avoid having to choose altogether by buying every single brand and platform type, but most of us have to resign ourselves to purchasing only one of the three major consoles. The first choice you need to make is whether to buy a computer (or use one you already have) or a console. In the current generation of consoles, the system of choice is the PlayStation 2—because it was the first released and could also play the original PlayStation games (backwards-compatibility). The Xbox was the choice of hardcore gamers (early adopters), and the GameCube survived on the sale of kid-friendly games such as *Super Mario Sunshine, The Legend of Zelda,* and *F-Zero GX.*

Next-generation console sales are currently steering toward the Microsoft Xbox 360 and Nintendo Wii. The push has been so intense that many refer to both as the "Wii60," because the systems manage to complement each other rather than compete. Nonetheless, the wildcard in this game is the PlayStation 3, Sony's over-priced successor to the PS2. This time, hardcore gamers might flow toward Sony's system because it promises better graphics than the Xbox 360 (an inversion of what happened in the current generation). However, the low shipment numbers for Japan and the United States, coupled with a delayed release in Europe, put the platform at risk. Who knows if game companies are going to give Sony the same support they have during the last couple of years? In the end, choosing a platform might be a matter of money and personal values. Just make sure that the games you want to play with your kids are available for that platform, and you're set!

RATINGS

The *Entertainment Software Rating Board (ESRB)* is a non-profit, self-regulatory body established in 1994 by the Entertainment Software Association (ESA) that assigns computer and video game content ratings, enforces industry-adopted advertising guidelines, and helps ensure responsible online privacy practices for the interactive entertainment software industry. ESRB ratings are designed to provide reliable information about the content in computer and video games so that you can make an informed purchase decision. ESRB ratings have two equal parts: *Rating symbols* suggest age appropriateness for the game, and *content descriptors* indicate elements in a game that may have triggered a particular rating and/or may be of interest or concern. The ESRB ratings can be directly connected to the Motion Picture Association of America's (MPAA) ratings system. The ratings themselves are very similar:

ESRB	MPAA
E/EC/E10+	G
T	PG/PG13
M	R
AO	X

The ESRB keeps games safe by allowing parents to make informed decisions. It's not a system based on punishment but on *empowerment*. Knowing the kind of content in a game allows parents to participate actively in the whole process instead of being misled by marketing campaigns.

Here's a description of each ESRB rating:

- **EC (Early Childhood):** Content may be suitable for ages 3 and older; contains no material that parents would find inappropriate.
- **E (Everyone):** Content may be suitable for ages 6 and older; may contain minimal cartoon, fantasy, or mild violence and/or infrequent use of mild language.
- **E10+ (Everyone 10+):** Content may be suitable for ages 10 and older; may contain more cartoon, fantasy, or mild violence, mild language, and/or minimal suggestive themes.
- **T (Teen):** Content may be suitable for ages 13 and older; may contain violence, suggestive themes, crude humor, minimal blood, simulated gambling, and/or infrequent use of strong language.
- **M (Mature):** Content may be suitable for ages 17 and older; may contain intense violence, blood and gore, sexual content, and/or strong language.
- **AO (Adults Only):** Should only be played by persons 18 years and older; may include prolonged scenes of intense violence and/or graphic sexual content and nudity.
- **RP (Rating Pending):** Submitted to the ESRB and awaiting final rating. (This symbol appears only in advertising prior to a game's release.)

To take full advantage of the ESRB rating system, it's important to check both the rating symbol (on the front of the box) and the content descriptors (on the back). The ESRB rating icons are registered trademarks of the Entertainment Software Association.

Prior to a title's release, game companies submit a form containing a written description of the game's content along with video footage that showcases that content. The next step involves the collective effort of three raters, who verify the material sent by the publisher. A rating is given if they all agree; if not, additional raters are brought in. A second phase of the rating process starts immediately before the release of the game. At this time, a final copy of the game is made available, and raters actually *play* through it. If any relevant content was missed during the first phase, this second screening process should reveal any problems. If a game is not rated properly, the ESRB has the power to re-rate the game months after it has been on sale.

Parent Snapshot

John Scott G ("The G-Man")

Producer/composer (Golosio Publishing)
Woodland Hills, CA

Scott G is recording artist The G-Man, owner of G-Man Music and Marketing, and co-owner of Golosio Publishing, a music production and licensing firm. You have heard his music in commercials for companies of almost every size and description.

- Family Profile: 15-year old son
- Playtime: Doesn't play with kids (but plays 1–3 hours alone)
- Platforms: Xbox, PS2, GameCube, PC, GB Micro
- "My enjoyment lies in having my son take me through the various programming glitches he finds in games. On one occasion, he got one of the action games to 'freeze' while the score counter continued to rise. He moved to one of the other game platforms to, as he put it, "see if we can reach 100 million points by 3:00 or so.""

GENRES

In film, *genres* comprise certain patterns of theme, setting, and content. For example, mystery often includes the theme of crime and punishment, a criminal, and a character who solves the crime (such as a detective or police officer). Genres in film are associated with the types of stories that are being told. Genres in games, on the other hand, often do not describe the storyline but the style of play (or *gameplay*). As we move through the genres that differentiate electronic games today, you'll notice that not all gameplay involves weapons and warfare. Gone are the days when players could only shoot at demons or aliens. In the video games of today, players can train puppies, make movies, work on their dance moves, and even perform surgery! Let's take a look at a few established game genres.

ACTION

The *action* genre has been the top-selling genre in the United States for the past several years. Part of a broad genre, action games encompass platformer, fighting, racing, and shooting games. All games in the action genre are based on "twitch" gameplay—they focus specifically on quick reflexes and instinctive reactions rather than on reflective thought. Playing action games on a regular basis can significantly improve eye-hand coordination and manual dexterity.

> My oldest son has a number of disabilities. Learning how to play *Sonic The Hedgehog* gave him a tool for enhancing hand/eye coordination. Once I realized this, I didn't mind the fact that the theme music was going through my head day and night!
>
> —Catherine Clinch (associate publisher, *Creative Screenwriting Magazine*)

Platformer

Traditional *platformers* are games that, through a sideways 2D view, have a character progress through different environments collecting items and jumping on top of enemy creatures (who then disappear from view or fall through the world). Platformers involve dodging items and jumping over holes. The term "platformer" was coined after the release of *Donkey Kong*—which introduced the character of Mario, who jumped from platform to platform to rescue his girlfriend from the clutches of the "evil" ape, Donkey Kong. (Interestingly, "donkey kong" was an awkward translation of "stubborn gorilla.") Modern platformers are usually in 3D. They still follow the same basic premise, but now the player has control over a virtual camera that can pan around the character and zoom in and out. The camera puts the action in context, such as finding a better perspective to a dangerous jump, but it can also be a major nuisance if badly implemented. *Super Mario 64* (Nintendo 64) is regarded as one of the most innovative 3D platformers ever released because it managed to bring the traditional Mario style of play (jumping and dodging) to a fully 3D world.

Ratchet & Clank

Platform: PS2
Year of Release: 2002
Rating: T (Teen)

→

Sony Computer Entertainment America

Good platformers aren't easy to find. The transition to 3D hurt them badly; classic control schemes had to be abandoned in favor of still-immature 3D controls. The result? Games that looked great but played badly; being able to precisely pick a "landing spot" for a jump was not easy in the early 3D games!

Ratchet & Clank is one of the benchmarks for 3D platformers. Controls are just as tight as *Super Mario Bros.* in 2D, and the beautiful PlayStation 2 graphics look like they belong to a next-gen system. *Ratchet & Clank* is also a long, deep game, full of different weapons and items and with an extended play time of over 10 hours (long by platformer standards).To top all that, the game also has great voice acting and an inspired production design that brings classic cartoons into the future.

By avoiding the constant jumping of traditional platformers, *Ratchet & Clank* managed to re-create the genre; twitch action (shooting bad guys with cartoon weapons) and puzzles are the deal here. Also, the exploration of different planets (the game's levels) feels very rewarding; this element by itself makes it ideal for teens, since it's a game that manages to be both mentally and physically challenging.

Shooter

Shooters involve weapons or gun battles in general. It is a very basic trait: You might be shooting down a plane, a kidnapper, maybe even shellfish in the depths of the Pacific, but you are shooting *something*. The focus here is not on "what" you shoot but *how* you do it. Factors such as aim, weapon classes, types of enemies, and strategic moves are essential. Shooters may have a bad reputation, but it's worth mentioning that they don't need to contain blood or humans as targets. For example, *Biohazard Battle* for the Sega Genesis featured biological ships that needed to clean a planet of unwanted mutations. The game had absolutely no blood and not a single human in sight. Even a kids' game, *Toontown*, replaces shooting bullets with throwing pies, to humorous effect.

Shoot 'Em Ups

Shoot 'em ups comprise one of the oldest game subgenres. The very first computer game, *Spacewar!*, was a shoot 'em up of sorts. Classic arcade games such as *Space Invaders* and *Galaga* could also be considered part of this genre. Shoot 'em ups can be divided into two classes: vertical-scrolling and side-scrolling. Let's say that the game involves shooting alien spaceships. Vertical-scrolling games show the player's ship topside, moving from the bottom to the top of the screen. Capcom's *1942* is a famous vertical-scroller that focuses on the War of the Pacific during World War II. Side-scrolling shooters do the same thing, only sideways (or horizontally). This means that the ships in the game move from left to right; the *Thunder Force* and *R-Type* franchises were legendary side-scrollers that improved the genre with giant mechanical bosses and multilayered, unexplored planets. However, the last decade hasn't seen many releases, mainly due to the transition to 3D. One of the reasons for the decline of this subgenre is that its perspective doesn't really make use of the 3D capabilities of current consoles, and other genres have taken much of the audience away. Some say that the best shoot 'em up ever released is *Radiant Silvergun*, a Sega Saturn import that was a perfect blend of 2D and 3D graphics, complex gameplay, and epic battles. Copies of the game may go for $200 on eBay!

First-Person Shooter

In *first-person shooters* (FPSs), the player sees the game through the eyes of the player character. The first-person point-of-view (POV) effect is created by showing the weapon and the player character's hands at the bottom of the screen. For that reason, FPSs can offer far greater immersion than other genres. The first known FPS was *Wolfenstein 3D*, from id Software, the same company that created *Doom*. *Wolfenstein* was actually a mixture of 3D (corridors) and 2D (enemy soldiers and Nazi dogs). Later, FPSs would be in the forefront of advances in graphics and sound, and soon they would all be fully 3D. FPSs contain the following features:

Weapon selection (number, different types)

Varied levels (spaceships, temples, underground, jungles)

Challenge (easy, medium, difficult)

Graphics and sound (high detail and surround sound)

Multiplayer mode (split-screen, online)

Today, FPSs are at the forefront of gaming and have spawned popular descriptive subgenres such as World War II (*Medal of Honor* and *Call of Duty* franchises), sci-fi/horror (*Doom* and *Quake* franchises), and even tournament games (*Halo 2* and *Half-Life: Counter Strike*), in which high-level FPS gamers compete professionally for "big money" prizes in televised matches. Most agree that FPS games are more effective on the computer platform because keyboard plus mouse is a more ideal control setup; the combination gives players precision aiming and fine control over movement. However, beginning with *Halo,* developers have been discovering ways to improve the way FPSs are played on consoles (including "sticky aim" settings for analog sticks).

My son and I freaked each other out and nearly knocked ourselves unconscious while sitting in his room late at night in the dark to play *Doom 3* on his computer. Big mistake. He has an elevated loft bed, and his computer is on the desk underneath the bed. We scared ourselves so badly at one point that we both jumped to our feet and banged our heads *hard* on the underside of the bed. Then we couldn't stop laughing and ended up waking my husband and other son, both of whom thought we were idiots.

—Cindi Lash (longtime news reporter and game critic,
formerly with the *Pittsburgh Post-Gazette*)

Half-Life 2

Platform: PC/Xbox/Xbox 360
Year of Release: 2004
Rating: T (Teen)
Half-Life kicked off one of the most entertaining and compelling PC franchises of all time. Developed by Valve Software, the first game in the series took the player community by storm and revolutionized FPSs in many ways—including graphics, style, and story. It was no surprise when *Half-Life 2* was announced for 2004.

→

Valve Software

Half-Life 2 improves on its predecessor, maintaining its tradition of a strong storyline (unusual in FPSs). This time around, the game also has a very advanced physics engine—implementing real-world gravity and inertia into the game itself. One of the guns in the game (the Gravity Gun) is able to grab and hurl objects toward foes!

The key achievement of *Half-Life 2* is not graphics or selection of weapons, but the story. *Half-Life 2* has an engrossing sci-fi plot that narrates the conquest of humanity by an alien race (the Combine) and the Human Resistance movement that fights it. The game effectively follows the tradition of big-time Holly-wood movies such as *Independence Day* and classic books like *1984*. Anyone who still thinks of action games as mindless storylines coupled with flashy graphics will be converted by *Half-Life 2*.

Third-Person Shooter

In *third-person shooters* (TPSs), players can see the characters they're playing onscreen. Ironically, the third-person POV allows players to identify with their characters; rather than looking out through a character's eyes (which focuses the players on the action surrounding their characters), the players observe the physi-cal and personality characteristics of their characters. Not only does this allow for more character development, but it results in more attention being paid to the game's storyline. TPSs still focus heavily on combat and weapons, but there is an added exploratory component that allows for more dramatic possibilities. A good TPS example is *007 Everything or Nothing*, a game based on the James Bond franchise that allows players to move through the game with confidence and ease, making excellent use of Bond's gadgets and vehicles. A new TPS, *Gears of War,* has quickly turned into a benchmark for the genre due to the elaborate set pieces and intense shooting action.

Racing

The feeling of speed is what attracts most players to racing games. Everyone fantasizes about driving expensive exotics on race tracks at ungodly speeds. It's a basic human trait—the thrill of unbridled speed. Racing games give players the setting and the vehicles to experience this exhilaration—safe from real-world consequences. How many teenagers would still take the family sedan for a ride if they had the opportunity to drive a Lamborghini Gallardo in Silverstone, England? How many boys and girls would "drag race" their cars on the streets (a very dangerous and illegal hobby) if they all had access to multiplayer street-races through a game console? Those are the reasons racing games truly serve a social purpose—keeping kids off the streets and allowing their imaginations to run wild in the safety of their homes. Racing games can involve cars, motorcycles, boats, hovercraft, and even air boards, as in *Sonic Riders*. Arcade racers are simple and fast paced, and they may even have a timer onscreen like old arcade racing games. In general, they are less preoccupied with physics and braking distances, focusing on the fun factor instead.

Project Gotham Racing 3

Platform: Xbox 360
Year of Release: 2005
Rating: T (Teen)

Project Gotham Racing (PGR) was a launch title for the original Xbox in 2002. The detailed graphics and arcade physics turned the game into an overnight success, aided by an innovative kudos system that rewarded players for driving with style. Points were awarded for following good racing lines, avoiding hitting the wall, and overtaking opponents, which forced players to be more mindful of their driving *and* have fun at the same time. *PGR 3* is the latest installment, released for the Xbox 360, and the formula has been greatly improved. This

→

Microsoft Corporation

time around, the available cars are even faster, and progressing through the game is more organic and leisurely. This makes the game a great outlet for "speed freaks," since it effortlessly provides adrenalin rushes and all-around excitement to players.

While games such as *Forza Motorsport* punish players for driving badly, making them lose hard-earned money if a car gets damaged (which is like a slap in the face), *PGR 3* uses the "pat on the back" approach, subtly indicating that driving is all about finesse, self-restraint, and road awareness.

Fighting

Performing a few Kung Fu or ninjitsu moves in a console game can be a helpful way of working out aggression and anger. *Fighting* games are perfect outlets for this, and they are incredibly useful for siblings in distress. (Take it from us; we've been there!) Another advantage of fighting games is the focus on the human body. Along with martial arts, fighting games have the human body (or a similar biped form) as the main "character", illustrating the benefits of a healthy and strong body. However, it's important to counsel young kids when they play these games so that they understand that this physical aggression should be left inside the game world. Like platformers, fighting games can be 2D or 3D. Beginning in the arcade era, 2D fighting games made use of a side view similar to *Super Mario Bros.* These 2D fighting games only became popular with the advent of *Street Fighter 2: The World Warriors* in 1991. Having many different settings to choose from (a small village near the Amazon River, a public restroom in Japan, and so on), both players start on each screen corner and fight for a preset number of seconds, usually three rounds of 90 seconds each. 2D fighters use a large number of buttons, usually six. Fighting games also require the use of *combos*, combinations of punches and kicks that connect in a chain of powerful moves. 2D fighters also have a subgenre, *weapon-based fighters*, such as SNK's *Samurai Showdown* and *The Last Blade*, both for arcades and home consoles. 3D fighting games were introduced to the world in 1993 by *Virtua Fighter*, a Sega AM2 arcade game. *Virtua Fighter* had polygonal characters, which added a sense of depth to the battles, and the moves were all based on real fighting styles rather than the use of fireballs or mystical moves such as teleportation. Later, games such as *Tekken* would revert to the fantasy element, but 3D fighters in general remain more reality based (having to obey the laws of physics and martial arts tradition) even if they happen to include monsters and demons in their cast of characters. There are also weapons-based 3D fighters (such as the *Soul Calibur* franchise in which characters may use broadswords, katanas, nunchuks, kendo sticks, and more. The first 3D fighter developed for a home console system was *Battle Arena Toshinden*, which was released for the original Sony PlayStation.

Virtua Fighter 4: Evolution

Platform: PS2
Year of Release: 2003
Rating: T (Teen)

Virtua Fighter 4: Evolution (*VF4:E*) is another masterpiece from Sega AM2. Streamlined and elegant, *VF4:E* focuses heavily on reality-based play with a dozen or so fighters to choose from. Though the number of characters is limited, all of them have very distinctive fighting styles, such as boxing, judo, and even "vale-tudo" (a Brazilian expression that means "anything goes"), popularized by the Ultimate Fighting Championship, a free-form, no-holds-barred tournament.

Since *VF4:E* appears to be very simple, it resembles an empty canvas, making it easy for players to project themselves onto the characters. This doesn't happen as much in a game like *Soul Calibur III*, since humans aren't (yet) able to project fireballs out of their hands and come face-to-face with huge red demons. *VF4:E* offers a more integral experience; players can just be idealized versions of themselves while playing the game! *Virtua Fighter 5* for the PS3, released in 2007, continues the *Virtua Fighter* legacy of excellence.

→

ADVENTURE

Classic *adventure* games put players inside an environment that they are expected to explore; the players must also often put clues together to solve a mystery or unexplained phenomenon. In Chapter 1, we discussed how text adventures involved players typing two-word commands such as "go west," "get knife," "drink potion," and "open box" in order to navigate their way through an adventure story. These text adventures evolved into graphic games that became known for their rich environments. By collecting a clue or solving a puzzle in one area, the player then is allowed to proceed in the game. Adventure games involving several characters also force the player character to engage in dialogue, which involves selecting a single answer from several different choices. *Escape from Monkey Island, Full Throttle, Syberia,* and *The Longest Journey* are some strong examples from the genre. *Indiana Jones and the Fate of Atlantis* allowed the player to play as Indiana Jones alone or joined by non-player character Sophia. The game also had a more action-oriented *wits* mode. Some adventure games can have multiple paths, and others can be quite linear. In fact, one of the big complaints about adventure games was that there was often only one solution to each puzzle, and the puzzles had to be solved in a certain order. This linearity was prevalent in *Myst,* the top-selling adventure game of all time. Another complaint was that the puzzle-solving was fairly unintuitive and arbitrary. For these reasons, the genre began to go into decline during the '90s. However, it looks like it's having a comeback with sophisticated games such as *Indigo Prophecy.*

Indigo Prophecy

Platform: PC/Xbox/PS2
Year of Release: 2005
Rating: M (Mature) Your kids really should be at least 17 or supervised during play.

Indigo Prophecy ® Courtesy of Atari, Inc. © 2005 Atari, Inc. All rights reserved. Used with permission.

Just when the adventure genre seemed to be fading fast, *Indigo Prophecy* emerged to save the day. The product of French studio Quantic Dream, *Indigo Prophecy* has been touted as the first true "interactive movie" of its time, full motion video (FMV) not considered. In *Indigo Prophecy,* the player wakes up inside a diner restroom near a dead body on the floor. Since the main character can't remember how the body got there, he is forced to go out in the world and find some answers.

→

Players can take on the roles of several different characters, and every decision the player makes leads down a distinctly different story path. This mechanism has been nicknamed "elastic storyline" and is an evolution of the branching seen in most LucasArts games, such as *Indiana Jones and the Fate of Atlantis*, although it has a much more dramatic effect in *Indigo Prophecy* since it can greatly alter some of the game's events.

Indigo Prophecy is a powerhouse of story and interaction, and it has garnered much praise in the press for it. The finishing touch is the music by Angelo Badalamenti, who has scored many of David Lynch's films (and the cult TV series, *Twin Peaks*, bringing even more tension and a palpable sense of doom to the table.

My older son does not like violent games, but exploration games. I showed him how to use special god/invisible modes on some FPS game I liked, and he would use this so he could run around on all the levels, find all the secrets, and see how quickly he could collect every item in the level without having to fight. This turned out to be great fun later, since I would play the game and he would be my "navigator," telling me to jump somewhere to get the hidden armor or special weapon, etc. It made for a very fun, cooperative gaming experience before "co-op" became a popular gameplay style.

—Colin Mack (project manager, THQ Inc.)

ACTION-ADVENTURE

Action-adventure games can sometimes be confused with third-person shooters (TPSs) due to the obvious similarities between the two genres. Like TPSs, action-adventure games often involve shooting and collecting. On the other hand, the focus of a TPS is to progress through levels by shooting the "bad guys," while an action-adventure game will require much more puzzle-solving and exploration. A great way to distinguish between both is to pay attention to the way their stories unfold. Action-adventure games will have deeper storylines, while TPSs will try to guide the player through smaller "missions" with simple objectives. The *Tomb Raider* franchise (featuring Lara Croft, one of the first female game heroes) has arguably defined the action-adventure genre. Although archaeologist and explorer Lara Croft gets herself into dangerous situations and must use weapons in order to defend herself, she also spends a great deal of time exploring the environment and piecing together archaeological keys to the mysteries of ancient civilizations. Other strong action-adventure games include *God of War, Ninja Gaiden Black,* and the *Tom Clancy's Splinter Cell* franchise.

We spent hours working our way through the levels of *Tomb Raider* as a family. I usually ran the controller while the kids watched. (They were too scared to play.) [I remember]the excitement I and the kids felt when we finally beat the last level.

—Guy P. Vance (student/customer service representative)

ROLE-PLAYING GAME

Role-playing games (RPGs) are electronic versions of pencil and paper predecessors *Dungeons & Dragons* and *Generic Universal Role-Playing System (GURPS)*. Like adventure games, RPGs often involve deep storylines, but the true focus is on character development. Players often create their own characters and can only advance in the game as their characters gain experience—improving their skills and stats. *The Elder Scrolls IV: Oblivion* for the Xbox 360 is the most recent and talked-about RPG on the market because of its vivid graphics, deep storyline, and rich environments that afford gamers countless hours of play. RPGs represent the deepest genre of all, providing players with entire universes filled to the brim with different fantasy races, classes, magic, and special items. A single game may stretch to over 200 hours of play due to complex storylines and side quests (optional missions that take players on tangents away from the main storyline), and it's not rare to see players crying over an especially moving moment. The main force in RPGs is still the *Final Fantasy* franchise, which began in the '80s, with new installments released on a regular basis. It has been argued that the best RPG of all time is *Final Fantasy VII* for the original Sony PlayStation due to its dramatic and compelling storyline, interesting characters, and balanced gameplay. The game also represented a major jump in RPG graphics, and it is solely responsible for the popularity of the genre in the United States.

I especially remember my children begging to play *Disgaea: Hour of Darkness*. The theme was dark yet humorous, and it had very in-depth characters. There would be dialogues between the avatar and the NPCs that were executed in a lively and animated fashion. When the game played, even when there were no cinematic sequences or cut-scenes, my kids loved reading. My daughter would read all of the female NPC's lines; my son would read all of the male NPC's lines; and I would read the lines of the main character. This became a family activity that was both educational and entertaining. My kids looked at it as if they were watching their favorite cartoon, except they were the characters. I noticed quickly that they formed opinions and preferences about situational circumstances within the game's storyline, and they really immersed themselves in the storyline. The game allowed the player to create an infinite number of customizable characters, and each of my children actively conveyed their desire to be represented as a unique character—detailing the kind of character they would like to be. *Disgaea* eventually became a fond memory of our time interacting as a family.

—Jacques Montemoino (Gideon Games, LLC)

The Elder Scrolls IV: Oblivion

Platform: PC/Xbox 360/PS3
Year of Release: 2006
Rating: M (Mature) Your kids really should be at least 17 or supervised during play.

The Elder Scrolls IV: Oblivion ® © 2006 Bethesda Softworks, LLC, a ZeniMax Media company. The Elder Scrolls, Oblivion, Bethesda Softworks, and ZeniMax are trademarks or registered trademarks of ZeniMax Media Inc. All rights reserved.

Containing 16 square miles of immensely rich and detailed forests and towns. *The Elder Scrolls IV: Oblivion* may be the deepest and most complex RPG ever released. Couple this with highdefinition and the result is one of the best sellers for 2006 in the Xbox 360 platform.

The fantasy-based storyline focuses on the Kingdom of Tamriel, which is at risk following its emperor's murder. Faced with certain destruction, the player begins the search for a viable heir—trying desperately to end the war that ravages the land. This is a very basic description of the storyline; the epic full plot takes the better part of 100 hours. *Oblivion* takes RPGs forward in a most impressive way, with characters displaying human-like artificial intelligence,

→

brilliant lighting, interesting missions, and a "free-roaming" sandbox design that respects casual and hardcore gamers alike.

Oblivion can teach kids (17 and up, of course) all kinds of useful values through in-game challenges involving loyalty, trust, courage, and caution. The lessons learned can be immediately applied to real life. It's not by chance that hardcore RPG players tend to be those who take school seriously; they've learned by playing that life is not a cakewalk—and that nothing short of superior dedication and effort will help them achieve their objectives.

SIMULATION

Simulation games evolved from the "serious" simulation projects that began in the 1960s. All *simulations* are based on real-world rules. Subgenres include vehicle (planes, cars, boats), process (city building, social interactions), and sports/ participatory (tennis, football) simulations. Vehicle simulations are directly related to racing games (discussed earlier in this chapter). Although arcade racing games don't really take into consideration the advanced physics process involved in racing, simulations take physics very seriously. The *raison d'etre* of vehicle sim is to emulate how cars or planes behave in a real-world scenario; most of the fun in these games involves seeing for yourself how fast a Corvette Z06 can take the corkscrew in Laguna Seca, for example. While arcade games allow the player to have fun most of the time, developers know that this fun is secondary to the process they are trying to simulate accurately. Process sims such as *Sim City* simulate socio-economic events such as the growth of a city or the complex dynamics of religion and power. *Sim City*, the progressive game designed by Will Wright in 1989, is the only successful city simulation game; it was the first of a franchise involving three sequels and myriad other derivations such as *Sim Ant* and *Sim Earth*. *Sim City* is so popular that it spawned competitors with titles such as *CityLife, Pharaoh,* and *CivCity: Rome*. The *Tycoon* franchise (*Railroad Tycoon, Rollercoaster Tycoon, Zoo Tycoon*) comprises another set of process simulation games. Sport simulations have always been very popular and trace right back to the video game industry's origin with *Tennis for Two* at the Brookhaven National Laboratory. *Pong* was also a tentative sports simulation. From then on, sports games have been a given in every generation, selling millions of copies. For example, the *Madden* football series helped catapult its developer/publisher—Electronic Arts (EA)—to the top over the years; *Madden '06* (a football simulator) was the best-selling title in 2005. Among the most popular sports for simulations are tennis, soccer, football, basketball, and golf. Sports games are made for all platforms and tend to get outdated very easily because they tend to follow real-life line-ups (which may change in a matter of hours).

Parent Snapshot

Patricia Dillon Sobczak

Administrator (Chapman University)
Mission Viejo, CA

Patricia is a highly educated, curious, energetic person who loves exercise, travel, good friends, good books, Bassett Hounds, and learning. She is married to a wonderful guy and has been the step-mom to his two children for over six years. Patricia is starting a doctoral program and is interested in how playing video games can change leadership behavior.

- Family Profile: two kids, now 21 and 23
- Playtime: 1–3 hours per week with kids (both parents)
- Platforms: Xbox 360, PS3, DS, GB Color
- Top Games: *Madden Football, Tetris, Oregon Trail*
- Memorable Moment: "Beating my son at *Madden Football!*"

Microsoft Flight Simulator X

Platform: PC
Year of Release: 2006
Rating: E (Everyone)

The *Microsoft Flight Simulator* series has a long tradition in the game industry, predating the release of Windows by three years. The first game was designed in 1977 by Bruce Artwick; Microsoft soon bought the rights to it (Bill Gates is an aviation fan) and started releasing semi-yearly versions of the game in the market. Each new version includes more planes, richer scenery, superior physics (and avionics), and a more realistic simulation. As expected, *Flight Simulator X*, the most recent version, leaves all past games in the dust.

→

Microsoft Corporation

Flight Simulator X focuses on both professional pilots and wanna-bes—offering players the complete experience of flying a commercial jet, helicopter, and even gliders. Most real-world airports are included—and other environments (such as Paris, Rio, and Shanghai) can be bought separately as add-ons.

Half the fun in flight simulators is finding new ways to crash. Kids may try to fly very low to the ground or hit another plane in mid-air, just for kicks. When this sort of curiosity is satisfied, kids will then move on to learning how to fly properly; this "task" becomes a personal challenge very fast. Kids will only abandon the simulator if flying normally becomes a chore.

Of course, in dealing with flight simulators, there will always be the 300-page manuals full of useful and not-so-useful information. Believe it or not, some kids are so into mastering the game that they will actually take the time to read these extensive tomes!

Nintendogs

Platform: DS
Year of Release: 2005
Rating: E (Everyone)

Courtesy of Nintendo

Nintendogs is the most successful game released for the Nintendo DS platform. A favorite with kids, this puppy simulation can be mesmerizing. We've witnessed boys and girls alike getting drawn into the world of training, washing, walking, feeding, and playing with their virtual pets—who sometimes become more real to them than their own!

When players first start the game, they have the opportunity to choose a dog (from among several breeds), take it home, and name it. As players accumulate funds throughout the game, more puppies may be purchased from the kennel.

Players can interact with their puppies through the DS's touchscreen and microphone input. The touchscreen is used for "physical" interaction such as

→

petting and guiding, while the microphone allows players to teach voice commands to their puppies—who can be trained to perform up to 14 tricks.

Locations in the game include the player's virtual home, neighborhood (great for walks), dog park (where puppies can be trained to catch frisbees), and the stadium (where puppies compete for agility and obedience). *Nintendogs* also links up to other players' systems through the DS's built-in wireless network, allowing players to exchange puppy toys and other gift items.

STRATEGY

All *strategy* games involve the management of resources, such as food, materials, people, and weapons. There are two variants of the strategy genre that are based on time interval: *real-time strategy* (RTS) and *turn-based strategy* (TBS). The precursors to strategy games are classic board games such as chess. Consider what happens when you're playing these games. In chess, you manage an entire royal court consisting of a king, queen, bishops, knights, castles (rooks), and pawns. Knowing that each of these pieces has a distinct value and set of movement rules, you make certain decisions to move certain members of your "court," depending on the landscape (chess board). You are competing with another opposing royal court, whose members also have the same relative values and movement rules. Imagine that we took a chess game and put it in a 3D digital environment where the board now looks like terrain and the pieces resemble actual human members of the royal court (with the exception of the rooks!)—but we didn't change the rules of the game. We would still be managing resources, but the game would look more real to us. Current strategy games expand this idea further, involving lofty objectives such as building civilizations (*Civilization* franchise), conquering the Roman Empire (*Rome: Total War*), achieving popularity and social acceptance (*The Sims*), or attracting followers and educating a mythic creature (*Black & White*). Most strategy games allow the player to see most if not all of the world from a "god-like" vantage point—just as chess players can see the entire board. The RTS subgenre has gained a lot of popularity due to the challenge of managing several resources at once—often putting its players into an arguably frantic multitasking state. Imagine trying to feed your workers, directing them to get materials and construct buildings—and then discovering that your army needs to advance because an opponent's army is just about to attack the village you're constructing. It's enough to make your heart pound! RTSs often involve a military backdrop—where armies battle for land, commodities, and fuel. The battles can happen in historical *(Age of Empires)*, fantasy (*Lord of the Rings: Battle for Middle-Earth),* or near-future (*Command & Conquer: Generals*) settings. One of the first RTSs was *Dune II,* released in 1989 for the PC and later ported to home consoles. The *Dune* model would later be incorporated into the hugely successful *Command & Conquer* and *Warcraft* franchises. RTS games traditionally have been more enjoyable on computers (and could be considered the last remnants of a PC-centric genre, although the recent *Lord of the Rings: Battle for Middle-Earth II* for the Xbox 360 challenges this trend).

> My oldest son, Dante, and I recently played *Star Wars: Empire at War* together. The game is difficult, and I needed to help my son understand how to pre-plan operations and campaigns and understand the ins and outs of how to use controls, what the controls and icons mean and do, and terms. Even though this is the case, Dante has learned the game fairly quickly and even understands how to play certain levels better than I do. Dante will state that I need to do this or that I'm not doing it right, but it is all in good fun, although it is mind-blowing when he can beat my forces from time to time, and we have only been playing the game for a few weeks!
>
> —Paul Orlando (professor, Art Institute)

The Sims 2

Platform: PC
Year of Release: 2004
Rating: T (Teen)

The wildly successful *Sims* franchise was created by *Sim City*'s Will Wright. *The Sims 2* is the newest installment of the series, which allows players to manage the lives of human characters known as the Sims. This game has been thought of as a "social engineering" strategy game, in which players must balance their Sims' jobs, family life, money, and social lives.

After selling more than 58 million units—including expansion packs—there seems to be no end to the *Sims* franchise. Why is it so popular? The obvious reason can be found in the high degree of identification with the Sims themselves—who represent an endearing simulacra of our own society. As the powerful beings who manage their lives, we decide whether or not to meet their needs, desires, and aspirations—which can lead to some interesting social experimentation. The franchise represents by far one of the most accessible game experiences in history—reaching people of all sexes, ages, and nationalities.

→

Electronic Arts, Inc.

The Sims 2 is also a variation on the "sandbox" school of game design—allowing players to engage in an open-ended and fun experience, while still maintaining long-term objectives for their Sims. With its whimsical "social engineering" flavor, the gameplay never leaves players frustrated or tense. Quite the contrary: *The Sims 2* may cause spontaneous laughs and a serious drive for self-discovery.

Black & White

Platform: PC
Year of Release: 2001
Rating: T (Teen)

Black & White (B&W) is a strategy game that is also known as a "god simulation." Yes, you read that correctly! The game attempts to simulate the kind of

→

Lionhead Studios Limited

choices a *god* would have to make—such as "Should I throw fireballs at that peaceful village since they ignored Commandment 11?" Of course, most choices are simpler than that (like making rain), but others can be very interesting, like educating a mythic creature (a key component of the game).

Like *The Sims* franchise, the player is a powerful being who manages the lives of the game's inhabitants. The gameplay in *B&W* takes part in two different spheres: social (how people believe, fear, and admire a god) and scientific (creatures learn survival skills such as how to feed themselves). *B&W* gives players the chance to make their own decisions and transcend basic human dilemmas such as "Should I eat that cookie now or go to the gym?" In the game, the player "manages" followers, residences, nurseries, farms, and resources (used to build the Temple of Light).

B&W is especially interesting for the examination of good and evil. The game has two "advisors" (a godly figure and a devil) who give the player ongoing contradictory advice. Call it relativistic design, but it sure stirs the neurons in very unexpected ways!

PUZZLE

Puzzle games couple the strategy of tabletop games with the bright colors of video games. The essential puzzle game is *Tetris*. Since that illustrious ancestor, puzzle games haven't changed much, but they still manage to capture a good chunk of the market, especially women over 40. A great example of a modern puzzle game is *Lumines* (for the Sony PSP, which appears to be next in line for the *Tetris* torch). The fast-paced action of traditional puzzle games gets some eye candy, and the electronica soundtrack changes according to the player's actions. Nintendo's *Big Brain Academy* and *Brain Age* series for the DS can also be categorized as puzzle games—since puzzles are used to test players' aptitudes.

CASINO

Casino games are electronic versions of the games found in real-world casinos, such as poker, blackjack, and roulette. They are usually targeted to an older audience and often strive to be photorealistic. These games are also very predominant in online gambling web sites, where people play for real money. In a way, the new Wild West is still the Internet, and online gambling is just another of its faces. Due to the recent resurgence of poker, a networked poker game has been released on Xbox Live Arcade (*Texas Hold 'Em*) that allows players to host virtual poker sessions (without real money involved). This, coupled with the Xbox 360 webcam, will certainly break new ground for casino games.

SURVIVAL-HORROR

The fairly new game genre known as *survival-horror* is unique among game genres in that it defines the story and dramatic elements of the game rather than the gameplay. We've discussed genres such as FPS, RTS, and RPG—none of which describe the setting or story structure of their associated games. A real-time strategy (RTS) game genre describes the time interval (real-time) and the goal (resource management) of the game only—not where it takes place (Rome, deep space) and what sorts of dramatic elements might be involved (romance, military history). Survival-horror, on the other hand, suggests that the game involves classic horror elements (such as ghosts and monsters) and a particular goal (survival). However, survival-horror games could involve shooting, strategy, fighting, role-playing, or even jumping and dodging (platformer)! Most likely the result of the traditional film industry's influence on the game industry, survival-horror games often draw from Hollywood horror movies such as *Night of the Living Dead, The Haunting, Dracula*—and other zombie, ghost, or monster themes. The basic premise is that something very bad and very evil lurks in the mall, town, forest—and you have to survive it. Survival-horror games are all about being forced to survive under horrific circumstances, including limited ammunition, creepy monsters, and broken flashlights. (It's important to note that these games can be extremely graphic!) *Resident Evil* is regarded as one of the first true survival-horror franchises. Even so, it is acknowledged that it borrowed heavily from *Alone in the Dark*, one of the earliest 3D adventure games (which predated the coining of the survival-horror genre); *Alone in the Dark* had a very prominent horror theme, with demons and ancient races reminiscent of Lovecraft mythos. Recently, Hollywood has been taking the inverse route and has made several film adaptations of survival-horror games—including two *Resident Evil* films, one *Silent Hill* adaptation, and the unfortunate bomb, *Alone in the Dark*.

Hollywood Does Games

Hollywood and games have an awkward relationship, to say the least. Arcade games have always been prominent in movies, whether as "extras" or main plot elements. *Tron* was about humans trapped inside a giant mainframe, playing video games from the "monster's" belly.

However, the success of some of the most famous franchises gave Hollywood the wrong idea. Movie execs must have thought that adapting games for the big screen was an easy deal. One of the first blunders committed by big studios was the adaptation of *Super Mario Bros*. The movie, released in 1993, didn't have mushrooms, goombas, or Koopa as a lizard; it was named *Super Mario Bros* but contained absolutely nothing that made the franchise special. It bombed badly—killing other movie adaptations with it.

A much better try was *Mortal Kombat*, released in 1995. This time, studios respected the franchise enough to include most if not all elements that made the game famous. On the downside, the movie ended up cheesier than the game itself. Surprisingly, this is still regarded as one of the better movie adaptations of a game.

Final Fantasy was adapted in 2001, but the fact that none of the game's storylines were used in the movie thoroughly disappointed audiences. While Square Pictures (the motion picture arm of *Final Fantasy*'s game development studio) spent a fortune building a state-of-art computer graphics studio in Hawaii, the box office never reached the $100 million mark—and the game studio's Hollywood dream crumbled months after release.

→

Doom, out in 2005, somehow managed to get rid of demons altogether—subbing them for genetic mutations. Since it was a cheap movie, it must have made the investors' money back, but audiences wholeheartedly saw it as a low quality adaptation, even if it did look a lot like *Doom 3* (at least toward the end, when the POV changed to first-person)!

Perhaps the most successful game adaptation ever was *Silent Hill*, released in 2006. While the script is laughable and most of the story makes no sense whatsoever, the director did hit the nail on the head with atmosphere and overall style. Visually, it was a picture-perfect adaptation, and it received kudos for that.

There are more examples, but the list above should give you a sampling of what Hollywood has done to successful games. (Game adaptations of movies have not fared much better—primarily because the games have been more like movies than games in their own right.) The involvement of Peter Jackson (director of the *Lord of the Rings* trilogy) with the *Halo* movie brings a glimmer of hope to players everywhere. Maybe this time, Hollywood will get it right!

Massively Multiplayer Online Games

In Chapter 1, we discussed multiplayer online games such as *Ultima Online, Lineage,* and *EverQuest.* These games are officially known as *massively multiplayer online games (MMOGs)* and are played by thousands of players online simultaneously in real time. The most successful MMOG is *World of Warcraft,* which contains a subscriber base of approximately 7 million and counting. The MMOG model relies on monthly subscription fees (usually around $10/month) rather than one-time game purchases. The most popular form of MMOG is the massively multiplayer online role-playing game (MMORPG)—an RPG that is played in a massively multiplayer online environment. *Ultima Online, Lineage, EverQuest,* and *World of Warcraft* are examples of MMORPGs. Other variants of MMOGs include the massively multiplayer first-person shooter (MMOFPS) and massively multiplayer real-time strategy (MMORTS) game (such as *Planetside* and *Shattered Galaxy,* respectively). Even the puzzle genre has been transformed into an MMOG; Daniel James of Three Rings Design launched *Yohoho! Puzzle Pirates* after witnessing his girlfriend get hopelessly addicted to *Bejeweled* (a popular puzzle game with the appeal of *Tetris*). James decided to expand the market for puzzle games by creating a rich 2D world where players would cooperatively solve puzzles in order to advance as pirates—doing everything from sailing their ships to sword fighting and even pillaging! *Puzzle Pirates* players even take on their characters' personas by communicating through "pirate-speak" ("Ahoy, matey!"). Being inside an MMOG involves spending copious amounts of time "in character," since the game tries to simulate a fantasy universe. This leads to some players abandoning portions of their real lives in favor of their virtual adventures—resulting in a deeper addiction than playing too many rounds of *Tetris*! MMOGs also contain virtual economies powered by real money—where players can buy, sell, and trade items. MMOGs were initially exclusive to computers—but consoles are now finally powerful enough to run them.

> Our *World of Warcraft* guild is entirely composed of adults (attorneys, pharmacists, financial advisors, senior engineers, etc.). The first time my oldest son led an instance raid in [the game, it was] a fantastic and perfectly smooth instance, and he organized everything very well.
>
> —Donna K. Kidwell (commercialization consultant, University of Texas at Austin)

> One day, my kids and I (just the three of us) captured an entire German army base in *Battleground Europe* against about two dozen enemy panzers and infantry, where most of the enemy players were playing out of Finland. It took us about two hours to pull it off. We had a little air support from the RAF . . . well, a lot.
>
> —Kenneth C. Finney (author, Thomson Learning; instructor, Art Institute)

Toontown Online

Platform: PC
Year of Release: 2003
Rating: E (Everyone)

Toontown Online is the first massively multiplayer online role-playing game (MMORPG) for kids. It was developed by the Virtual Reality Studio, a group inside Disney, and released in 2003 to critical and player acclaim. Disney says that the game reaches upwards of 10,000 simultaneous players in busy hours.

Teamwork, communication, and friendship are essential in the game, since toons must defend the city from "cogs" (evil robots dressed like "men in gray flannel suits") that want to transform Toontown into a gray, cold corporate world. The game is very competent technically, with bright and colorful graphics that look a lot like a TV cartoon. Also, text chats and even screen names are as safe as can be—giving parents much needed peace of mind while their kids play the game.

Toontown Online is a great way to introduce kids to MMORPGs and computer games in general—and it can be downloaded for free. After the trial period expires, the subscription is only $9.99/month.

Disney

MARKET

Common sense says that games are created solely for the entertainment sector. However, this couldn't be further from the truth; entertainment should always be a game's foundation, but there are many additional markets for which games are developed. In this section, we'll discuss entertainment and some other game goals. You might be surprised at some of the non-entertainment-related factors that drive game development.

ENTERTAINMENT

The majority of games are consciously developed for sheer entertainment purposes. There's a huge, multibillion dollar market for games such as *Sonic The Hedgehog, Super Mario World,* and *Final Fantasy,* which focus solely on cool graphics, adrenalin rushes, and/or compelling drama. Why would the industry develop games with anything but entertainment in mind? Of course, there's nothing wrong with games that entertain only. This should always be the starting point. However, games have more to offer than fun-filled moments in front of a TV or computer monitor. Games can teach, socialize, and even heal.

SOCIAL

Games can be used to maintain and expand social communities. Many MMOGs have become meeting places for people with similar interests. Games created for socialization purposes can help communities manage themselves and thrive within an integrated virtual space. Although this functionality has been performed by forums and bulletin boards in the past, game worlds will soon enough become easy to build and maintain, substituting older community spaces as specialized meeting points. The socialization aspect of games can then become the glue that holds people together, whether it consists of classmates or members of a reading group. The game in these cases becomes the interface, a link between people on the same wavelength. In recent years, *Second Life* has become the most popular virtual community; although sometimes marketed as a game, *Second Life* is more of a free-roaming world that can take the form of anything from a performance space to an online education platform.

Teen Second Life is a popular online social community that contains a rich virtual environment. Linden Lab

Parent Snapshot

Rocksan Lessard

Homemaker and student (Art Institute Online)
Barre, VT

Rocksan Lessard is a 32-year-old mother of four children. She is also a part-time student and has a profitable business running in the multi-user virtual environment, Second Life. Rocksan has a background in web design, graphics, and retail.

- Family Profile: 4 kids, ages 9, 8, 7, and 18 months
- Playtime: 1–3 hours per week with their kids (both parents)
- Platforms: Xbox, GameCube, and PC
- Top Games: *Mario Party, Luigi's Mansion, Scooby-Doo: Night of 100 Frights*
- Memorable Moment: "Seeing their faces light up when they beat a level or find an object that they need in the game to move on."

EDUCATION AND TRAINING

Games have an astounding, untapped potential for *education*. Simulation games in particular are educational by virtue of their real-world features. The vehicle sim, *Gran Turismo 4*, is notorious for introducing trigger-happy gamers to the wall in a matter of seconds. While most of this education is "covert" (players don't really notice they are learning), other games teach in more obvious ways. This is especially true in certain games developed for children during the "edutainment era" of the late '80s/early '90s (discussed in Chapter 1), such as *Oregon Trail, Reader Rabbit*, and *Math Blaster*. Classic educational games make no excuses in the teaching department, quizzing and probing the players after introducing new content. They can be effective for younger age groups, but older players avoid them like the plague. MMOGs and other online games can easily turn into virtual classrooms. Instead of talking about a hurricane or showing a plodding VHS documentary, students might log into a game and simply "walk" inside it—exploring the scenario in real time. Perhaps the students could even modify the environment in order to discover the possible causes of a hurricane in the first place. Tying an MMOG or other online environment into the education world would do wonders for the

Sim City has been used in classrooms worldwide to teach urban planning principles. Electronic Arts, Inc.

online distance learning industry (which currently runs on less than optimal threaded discussion-based software); it would also help the MMOG industry segment—where it's getting more difficult everyday for new games to compete with powerhouses such as *World of Warcraft*, which holds over 7 million players captive in its rich, ever-changing 24/7 environment. The virtual community *Second Life*, discussed earlier, is starting to be used to enhance the existing online distance learning platform. Parents who have decided to home school their kids are looking at games to supplement their teaching programs. Even corporations and the government are getting into the act—training employees in various skills through the use of games. A medical game might simulate "patients" for rookie MDs. Flight simulators have been in use for decades in pilot training. On ground level, traffic simulators test for drunk driving and cell phone use—aiding researchers all over the world. Even the strategy game, *The Sims,* is a "social simulator" of sorts—showing kids and teenagers the sophisticated dynamics of relationships. Educational experiences that take place within a game world can provide long-lasting and memorable learning experiences.

Parent Snapshot

Bill Genereux

Assistant professor (Kansas State University at Salina)
Clyde, KS

Bill Genereux has worked as a college teacher, IT director, graphic designer, computer programmer, and U.S. Navy sailor. He has recently started working towards a doctorate in curriculum and instruction, and his research interests are in digital media technologies as instructional tools. He is the proud father of two preschool-aged children who are also beginning to enjoy learning with computer technology.

- Family Profile: 2 children, ages 3 and 5
- Playtime: 1–3 hours per week with his kids
- Platforms: PC, Leap Pad
- Top Games: *Nick Jr.* (online Flash games)
- Memorable Moment: "The first time my daughter saw her favorite TV character Dora on the computer, and she could decide what to make Dora do."

THERAPY AND HEALING

Serious games don't only consist of educational games, but those that focus on healing people through forms of *therapy*. These games can be used to aid in recovery from depression, emotional trauma, complex surgery, and even chemotherapy. A shining example of this is *Re-Mission*, a shooter in which the objective is to shoot down cancerous cells and help the body through chemotherapy. A study involving 375 children diagnosed with cancer proved that, after playing the game, the kids took their medication more regularly and also became much more interested in seeking a cure. *Re-Mission* successfully increased the patients' resolve and hope for the future. Researchers are using virtual reality therapy (VRT) by modifying games such as *Unreal* and *Half-Life* to help people suffering from fear of heights (acrophobia). Patients can take virtual elevators through the use of a head-mounted device (HMD), just like the ones used in fighter jets—and slowly gain control over fear. Even New Age advisor Deepak Chopra has created a game of his own (*The Journey to Wild Divine*), which uses biofeedback as a tool in order to help users take control over their emotional health. These types of games, along with educational use, will clearly be omnipresent in the future.

Fighting cancer is an inside job. In *Re-Mission*, players guide a nanobot named Roxxi through the complex environments of the human body. HopeLab

MUSIC AND RHYTHM

Musical games are gaining ground lately, mostly due to the success of *Dance Dance Revolution (DDR)*. Part of the "Japanese mania" that has crossed the big pond, *DDR* brought a whole different way of playing to U.S. gamers, resulting in a resurgence of musical games. Based on timed movements and rhythm, *DDR* is a favorite among the arcade crowd. *Guitar Hero* (PS2) is a variation on the same theme but utilizes rock music as a vehicle for simplified guitar playing. The game is sold with a big plastic guitar controller; this game is a party favorite, since it combines the "dorkiness" of karaoke with the "coolness" of guitar playing. Let's not forget *Karaoke Revolution*—enough said! There's a very good chance that musical games will be a staple of the Nintendo Wii since the Wiimote can detect movement, and it suits the console's profile very well.

Guitar Hero, with its guitar controller, has breathed new life into music and rhythm games. Courtesy of Casey Maloney and Stephen Millard

EXERCISE AND FITNESS

Games can be used as an incentive for physical exercise as well. The series *Yourself: Fitness* (PC/Xbox/PS2) is a well-thought-out hybrid between a game and an interactive DVD—serving as a digital personal trainer that provides an attractive orientation for stretching and other common exercises. With Sony's EyeToy camera that connects to the PS2, movements are registered by sensors, making its associated games very physical, almost like intense workouts. Nintendo's Wii—with its Wiimote and nunchuk controllers—promises to take "physical gaming" a big step further. Finally, games such as *Dance Dance Revolution* have brought the "exhibitionist" quality back to the arcades, where competing players (usually teenagers, boys and girls alike) participate in dance-offs! There is definitely a physical trend in games; we haven't seen anything yet!

Yourself: Fitness is a game-interactive DVD hybrid that focuses on personal fitness training and motivation. ResponDesign

ADVERTISING AND MARKETING

Advergames are created to help sell products or services. For example, a game where the player fights evil bacteria and microbes could advertise a new, more effective toothpaste, while a Flash-based drag race could show how much faster the new Acura is in a 0–60 mph contest. Advergames are often available on product web sites and are developed to enhance brand awareness, increase Internet traffic, and promote the brand—without boring the audience. Another form of advertising is *recruitment. America's Army*—a groundbreaking recruitment game developed in part by the U.S. Army—is famous for giving teenagers a walkthrough of life in the military. The game is free of charge but emphasizes that teenagers and young adults could have a better life if they enlisted in the Army —a classic marketing technique.

America's Army is a groundbreaking recruitment tool that elevated the image of the U.S. Army. US Army

STORY: *WHAT DO WE PLAY?*

Story in games has a very different meaning than in movies. Game plot lines are not really intended to leave you speechless or to make you feel lost in the jungle. Games are all about purpose and realization; the story must put you *in* the action instead of only allowing you to *watch* the action. Games are definitely not for the lazy! For games, the story serves as a support for the action onscreen. It will provide you with a hero (or heroes), a goal, background info on enemies and bosses, and even "intros" to big sequences in the game. The story fills in the blanks. Here's an example from *Final Fight* (arcade):

Haggar, an ex-wrestler, is now the mayor of a big American city. Since he's an honest man, the gangs decide to kidnap his daughter in order to make Haggar bend to their wishes. As Haggar sees his little girl in the hands of the enemy, his friends

Cody and Guy join him in a quest to free his daughter. If necessary, they will fight every single gang member until they face the big boss himself.

This cheesy plot supports a fighting game. While RPGs such as *Phantasy Star* can be very complex—with events that happen in multiple planets over multiple time frames—other games might have just a hint of a story and nothing else. As discussed in the genre section, puzzle games often manage to have no story at all—but there's always room for change. Good stories provide many dimensions—drawing players into the game universe. This is a very powerful dynamic and can be traced to the fact that humans need to get emotionally involved in order to relate to any kind of event. With the storage provided by DVD-ROM and Blu-Ray discs, games can now give players a fully rendered audio/visual experience, including detailed levels and Hollywood-grade computer graphics sequences (like a feature-length animation), amplifying the emotional connection even further. Games without stories can be enjoyable—but stories have the power to transform games into a rich, dramatic, and immersive art form.

Ms. Pac-Man: The Birth of Game Story Structure?

Ms. Pac-Man was the first game to employ a three-act story structure. MS. PAC-MAN® © 1982 NAMCO BANDAI Games Inc. Courtesy of NAMCO BANDAI Games America Inc.

Even in the early arcade days, games like *Ms. Pac-Man* tried to employ a three-act story structure. As mentioned earlier in this chapter, the player was rewarded with an animated sequence after completing each of the three "levels" in the game. Interestingly, these animated sequences told a (simple) story: Pac-Man and the "soon-to-be" Ms. Pac-Man meet (Act I); they chase each other (Act II); and, finally, Pac-Man Jr. is delivered by a stork (Act III). Each of these types of sequences is now known in the game industry as "cinematics" or "cut-scenes"— story-based linear sequences that players can watch rather than interact with.

GAMEPLAY: *HOW DO WE PLAY?*

Playing games starts with movement—whether it's racing through an alien world to vanquish a parasite (*Halo*), adopting and training puppies (*Nintendogs*), or taking care of the crops and feeding the pigs (*Harvest Moon*). What matters most is how you move—and where you're going. Players *move* with analog sticks. This is the first layer of gameplay.

The second layer incorporates everything else your character can do in a game —whether it involves throwing fireballs, flying, fencing, or talking in another language. This also includes whether the character has special abilities (such as calling for air support). Players *act* with face buttons, shoulder buttons, and analog triggers.

Another layer of gameplay involves *selection*. In FPSs such as *Halo*, for example, players often need to select different weapons. This selection process is a very important part of gameplay. In *Doom 3*, the player has to choose between carrying a flashlight or holding a weapon—having to toggle between the two with a special button. This alters the gameplay dramatically. Players *choose* with the D-pad, shoulder, and face buttons.

The final layer of gameplay involves *how the game plays*. This includes the game's possibilities, difficulty level, and victory conditions (ways in which the game can be won). Players *play* with the controller itself!

Gameplay and story intersect through what could be referred to as "plot points." As an example, let's say your character is roaming through the forest on a dark night and hears sticks crackling nearby. You are carrying a flashlight, which you could use to shine in the direction of the sound. But you could also freeze and wait until the source of the sound moves past you. Another option would be to call out "Who's there?" This situation could be thought of as a plot point or challenge that must be addressed somehow. The fact that you might address it in any number of ways means that you have many choices and strategies at your disposal. Depending on which choice you make, the game may take a dramatic turn and lead down a different story path. As you can see, it's difficult to separate gameplay (which involves choices and actions) from story (which involves situations and drama).

IT ALL BEGINS ON FIRST BASE

In this chapter, you learned the basic vocabulary associated with video games, including ratings, platforms, genres, market, story, and gameplay. We've given you a tour through some of the standout titles in many genres and the reasons your kids can benefit from playing them. We also brought to light many surprising and little known industry facts, giving you even more insight into the transformative power of games.

In the next chapter, we'll take a look at the relationship between you and your kids. Topics will include communication, child development, and lifestyles. We'll also discuss how certain games might be useful for different age groups and how they might help overcome age-specific challenges. Finally, we'll take a close look at how kids of today are different from those of previous generations, including when *you* were a kid!

Part II

The Research

3

You and Your Kids

In This Chapter

- Generations at Large
- Next-Gen Kids
- Game On: Why We Play
- Life or Something Like It
- Your Inner Child Wants to Play

Frequently, the multiple generation gaps experienced by society today make communication and sharing difficult. Values and aspirations usually differ, along with the language to describe them. However, finding a social- and skill-driven common interest just might help close the gap. Perhaps your family used to have Saturday sessions of *Monopoly* or *The Game of Life*. Every family has its rituals, but sometimes finding common ground in the family life of today proves to be a veritable challenge!

In the past, board games and sports were the most common choices for parents who wanted to bond with their kids. Through those activities, parents and kids could spend "quality time" together, slowly but surely building healthy relationships. Although it worked well in the past, kids today are used to MTV, Google, instant messaging (IM), smartphones, legal downloads, and video games; it's no wonder they're more restless compared to earlier generations.

Think of video games as extending the *Monopoly* bond of the past. Games provide a "safety zone" where parents and kids can easily learn and have fun together. Unlike the passive, non-interactive "Nielsen family" TV-watching that reached its peak in the '70s, playing games requires constant communication and cooperation, potentially taking the relationship with your kids to the next level. In this chapter, we'll show you how parents and kids can benefit greatly from playing games together!

GENERATIONS AT LARGE

A *generation* can be thought of as a group of people who share similar social, cultural, economic, and political experiences due to the time in history in which they were born. Those who have come of age during the time of major historical events, such as World War II, the moon landing, the advent of television, and the commercial Internet, tend to display similar values, behaviors, beliefs, and attitudes.

Here are four major generations in the United States that currently play games, along with their approximate age ranges:

1. Silents (65–85 years of age)
2. Boomers (45–65 years of age)
3. Gen-Xers (25–45 years of age)
4. Millennials (under 25 years of age)

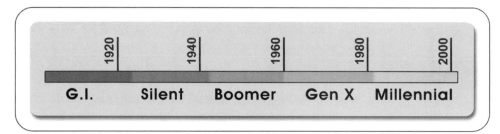

Diagram by Per Olin

SILENT GENERATION: BORN 1924–1943

During World War II, countries such as the United States and the United Kingdom sent scores of young men to the battlefields to fight the threat from Nazi Germany. Those men are part of the G.I. Generation, proud and competent warriors who reached new economic heights with the end of the war. Women of the G.I. Generation, including "Rosie the Riveter," who became the icon of the women's workforce, kept American industry alive during wartime. Too young to be involved in the war effort, the younger brothers and sisters of the G.I. Generation became known as the Silent Generation. While their older brothers and sisters were courageous war heroes and workers, Silents grew accustomed to a mix of comfort and fear—thanks to their over-protective parents and the threat of war. They stayed home while the world was ablaze, afraid of hunger and death. For many Silents, their childhood was cut short—since a world at war was no fun at all.

Illustration by Per Olin

This need for security would later materialize as a need for financial autonomy. This is why Silents are regarded as the perfect "company men" or "men in gray flannel suits," from content 1960s IBM employees to powerful Detroit CEOs. (Sloan Wilson's novel, *The Man in the Gray Flannel Suit,* personified this generation.) Silents wanted shielding from the darker side of life, and they did it through a quiet and steady work ethic. Not surprisingly, Silents are still the generation with the largest financial resources.

A well-known Silent hero is MI6's 007—James Bond—and the very rich and mischievous Thomas Crown from *The Thomas Crown Affair*. Both are suave, cultured characters carrying deep emotional wounds—who could also be cold-blooded and ruthless if necessary. Even Superman, who poses as "mild-mannered" Clark Kent—who looked like he walked out of the pages of the book, *The Man in the Grey Flannel Suit*—could be considered a Silent Generation icon.

BOOMER GENERATION: BORN 1943–1961

The Boomers were born at the tail end of World War II and enjoyed the monetary gains of a nation that won the war. They had plenty of time to have fun and to rebel against the "square" Silents and G.I. heroes.

Boomers believed in free love, free will, and alternate models for society. Boomers said yes to sex, drugs, and rock and roll—and then proceeded to shake the country politically like no generation before them. From the genius of Steve Jobs to the experimentation of Timothy Leary, a core Boomer belief was that the world needed them, and that they would revolutionize the way we live our lives.

Illustration by Ian Robert Vasquez

In a way, they have succeeded, not necessarily due to large-scale revolutions but because of "smaller" ones, such as the invention of video games and the proliferation of computers. Also, time gave Boomers a whole new perspective on rebellion and the defiance of traditional standards. Life taught them that, to fight the system, they had to be part of it. That's how Boomers became part of businesses everywhere.

In the late 1970s, Boomers started laid-back companies out of garages and single-room apartments. Imagine their surprise when such companies became big-time corporations such as Apple, Compaq, and Microsoft! Others focused on the stock market, becoming powerful Wall Street types. Known as "hippies" as they came of age, during the 1980s Boomers transformed into the hard-working and driven "yuppies" (young urban professionals).

Boomer heroes are rebels such as Dennis Hopper and Peter Fonda in *Easy Rider* and both Robert Redford and Patrick McGoohan (playing government agents fighting "the system" in *Three Days of the Condor* and *The Prisoner* television series, respectively).

GENERATION X: BORN 1962–1981

Born when the birth-rate reached an all-time low, Xers were forced to witness the disintegration of the American Dream and the social unrest that followed, having no alternative other than to fend for themselves. Xers also had to deal with high divorce rates, a low birth rate, a crumbling school system, and a sharp rise in crime. If you're part of Generation X (both the authors of this book are!), growing up was not often "easy." The term "latchkey kid" was coined during the Gen X era, since many parents (whether single or married) were members of the work force, and some children came home after school to empty homes. Television's "after school specials" were a new source of entertainment for these children, but the family animated features so popular today were practically nonexistent then. (In fact, Disney almost shut down its animation studio during the '70s.)

Films such as *Rosemary's Baby*, *The Exorcist*, and *The Omen* reflected society's increasingly negative attitude toward the nuclear family—shown in a continued drop in the birth rate and rise in the divorce rate. Later, "slasher" horror films such as *Nightmare on Elm Street* and *Friday the 13th* reflected the angst of a generation of largely unattended, "hurried" children who often had to grow up too quickly. Horror became a best-selling literary genre—and Stephen King became one of the top-selling authors of all time during this era.

Angry at the world, their parents, and society in general, Xers were known to have bleak points of view, illustrated best in a literary genre known as "cyberpunk" (popularized later by *The Matrix Trilogy*) that focuses on near-future, technologically driven universes where law and compassion are nonexistent. The *Mad Max*

Big Stock Photo

series is another example of a post-apocalyptic future, another big chunk of the typical Gen X frame of mind. On the other side of the spectrum, Boomer John Hughes discovered how to "speak" to the angst and disillusionment faced by Generation X through films such as *Sixteen Candles, Pretty in Pink,* and the X classic *The Breakfast Club.*

On the positive side, Generation X is the very first generation to come of age during the advent of personal computers and was the first to make use of the Internet as a commercial tool as they entered young adulthood. Unlike the Boomers before them who railed against the technological control when coming of age, Xers have learned that technology can make life more interesting, and they proceeded to adopt every new gadget as one of their own. This was the case with Laserdiscs (precursors to DVDs, released in 1978) and the audio CD, introduced by Phillips in 1982. Generation X was the first generation to take video games very seriously as players, while Boomers were the first to become professional game developers. Both generations are responsible for rescuing the game industry from the crash of 1983–1984.

Finally, while Xers were characterized as slackers—since they didn't trust existing social structures at all—they eventually proved the world wrong by engaging in cutting-edge fields such as biotechnology, software development, neuroscience, and Internet startups such as Netscape, Yahoo, Amazon, and eBay. Achievements like these transformed the so-called "Lost Generation" into one of the most innovative and daring generations of the 20th century. Xers fueled new technology with their individualistic mindsets; these latchkey kids had grown up to be innovative entrepreneurs.

Heroes for Xers are Max, the ex-cop from the *Mad Max* trilogy, John Rambo (*First Blood* and Rambo II and III—Vietnam veteran), and the captain of the *Millennium Falcon,* Han Solo.

MILLENNIAL GENERATION: BORN 1982–2002

Millennials are sometimes referred to (erroneously, in our opinion) as Generation Y, which intimates that they are simply an extension of Generation X. Far from it, the Millennial generation represents the complete opposite of the generation that came before it. About the time those "Baby on Board" placards began to appear in the backs of station wagons (SUVs, rather), we began to see the birth of this new generation that has risen to 80 million—outnumbering Boomers (60 million) and completely eclipsing the Xers (a mere 35 million). Contrary to popular belief, put forth by assumptions of the generations before it, kids today take fewer drugs, have less sex, and engage in less crime. At the same time, they have more homework, do better in school, and *spend more time with their parents!* Let's face it: Most parents today dote on their kids like never before. While "latchkey kid" was coined during the Gen X era, both "soccer mom" and "helicopter parents" (those that "hover" over their kids) came into being during the age of the Millennials. (We don't have a term yet for children born after 2002 who represent our newest generation, although the "working title" has been the New Silents.)

In film, the Millennial era began with the release of *E.T.* in 1982 and continued on with films focusing on the positive aspects of parenthood, such as *Three Men and a Baby* and *Look Who's Talking.* Disney's animation studio was saved—first with *The Little Mermaid,* followed by *Beauty and the Beast* and *The Lion King.* Pixar, starting off as a small animation studio that created shorts for specialized audiences, began to hit it big with blockbusters such as *Toy Story, Monsters, Inc.,* and *Finding Nemo.* Even during the opening weekend of the long-awaited and hyped Bond film, *Casino Royale,* it was difficult to move through the maze of children in the theater; not surprisingly, it was *Happy Feet* that topped the box office (two weeks in a row)!

Unlike the more individualistic, entrepreneurial Xers, Millennials are more teamwork oriented, focusing on social networks such as MySpace and instant messaging (with sometimes upwards of 500 names on their buddy lists!) to coordinate their social lives. Boomer parents might notice that their Millennial offspring live in

Big Stock Photo

the "Age of Aquarius," a superior form of mankind in which women have the same rights as men, everyone speaks from the heart, and people work collectively to achieve common goals. (Not only do women have the same rights as men in the Millennial era, but girls appear to be leading in all areas—socially, scholastically, and creatively.) Xer parents, most of whom rejected this collective ideal when coming of age in the '70s, are watching their kids taking ownership of these utopian beliefs. Millennials, surprisingly enough, are showing all these traits and more:

- Millennials believe in structure (instead of fighting against it).
- Millennials play together cooperatively. There's still room for competition (as seen in *Halo 2*), but even a typical Gen X "lone hero" style game such as *Doom 3* has a co-op mode where friends can kill demons as a team.
- Millennials communicate within large social networks. They make heavy use of email and use cell phones capable of instant messaging (such as T-Mobile's Sidekick 3) to keep tabs on friends and family 24/7.
- Millennials don't care much about privacy. Their helicopter parents have maintained transparency in the home, and Millennials are not uncomfortable sharing their personal lives with the world (MySpace, YouTube).

■   Millennials are more conservative. Statistics point to an all-time low on teenage pregnancy, school violence, and drug use. They are also currently the *most* religious generation in the United States!

The origins of this generation are quite interesting. They were wanted from the start, being welcomed into the world by loving and protective parents during a time in U.S. history when the birth rate rose most dramatically. Millennials came to the world as "blessings," and the trust their parents have invested in them is having a direct effect on the way Millennials trust the world. This is a generation that wants to improve the way we live our lives, not revolutionize it.

Millennial heroes are the siblings from the *Spy Kids* franchise and, of course, *Harry Potter*—sociable and "smart" kids who thrive in complex environments. Generation X and Millennials have been depicted very differently by the media. A 1990 *Time* cover referred to Generation X as "laid back, late blooming, or just lost?" Overshadowed by the baby boomers, America's next generation has a hard act to follow." A 2000 *Newsweek* cover referred to Millennials very differently: "God, sex, race, and the future: What teens believe."

A Cultural Shift

A paradigm shift is currently happening in U.S. culture, fueled by the Millennials, the oldest of which are just beginning to take part in being *creators* rather than only *consumers* of entertainment culture. As parents, most of the entertainment you've been seeing on the market has been developed by Xers and Boomers rather than Millennials. The issue here is that not all generations are truly in touch with the voice of the youngest generation. But we are starting to see an interesting shift—most obviously shown in the transition from primarily "lone hero" single-player games, involving characters such as Lara Croft (*Tomb Raider*) and Gordon Freeman (*Half-Life*), to games with strong multiplayer modes (such as *Gears of War*) or those heavily dependent on in-game relationships (such as *World of Warcraft*).

Saturday is game day; each of the older children gets to play with mom or dad for an hour.

—Rocksan Lessard (homemaker and student)

Every Friday night, it's pizza and a new console game to check out. Then we wrap it up with a *Warcraft 3* match or two.

—John Hight (Director of External Production, Sony)

NEXT-GEN KIDS

By definition, parents and kids are always from different generations, which can make the parent-child relationship and communication efforts more complicated. How can you successfully interact with your kids if the values you hold dear are seen as old-fashioned? How can you truly communicate if you don't share the same lexicon? The challenge of parenting is more than a fight for what's right. Parents who make it a priority to understand how their kids are different than they were as children will ensure that the inevitable generation gap remains as small as possible.

SPACES

The way our houses are organized has changed a lot in the last 20 years. Most parents are still attached to 1980s room divisions, such as those found in their family homes. We believe that, in order to connect with their kids, parents need to update their concepts of how spaces are used in modern homes.

"Retro" Space Division

In the past, the living room was a family domain—the place where family members played board games together, had parties, and watched TV. Depending on the era, the living room might also have been the father's sole domain—at least for a while. Some households had a separate room, known as a "family room," that contained a pool table or ping-pong table and even an arcade machine or two, but this was more common with wealthier families. Similarly, some families opted to have "play rooms" for the kids; the alternative was to wade through a sea of toys!

If the family had a personal computer, it would often be located in the home office, usually part of the parents' "territory." The computer was bought so that the parents could use spreadsheets and word processors such as Excel and Word. Kids had to sneak in to use the computer; perhaps that's why parents started buying kids their own computers in the '80s.

Finally, if children were lucky enough to have a TV set of their own, it would be a small one. Their bedrooms would also have a stereo and maybe a game console like the Nintendo Entertainment System (NES). Kids would commonly have friends over and play video games in their bedroom, away from the "seriousness" of adult life.

With puberty—and possibly as a consequence of this "segregation policy"—kids started to forbid parents from entering their rooms. Bedrooms had become protected spaces—parent-free lairs where the usual rules did not apply. The unfair "ownership" divisions between the living room, parents' bedroom, and kids' bedroom became a rift between parents and their kids, expanding the generation gap even further.

This was the story with most Silents and Boomers—and their Xer kids. But the relationship between most Millennials and their parents is helping to change all of this . . . for the better.

The 21st Century Space Division

The future is here . . . sort of. Although houses still have the same basic layout, the rooms themselves have been greatly upgraded. Technology has radically changed the very basic foundations of family life.

Take the living room, for example. Living rooms today have transformed into home theaters equipped with widescreen HDTVs, Dolby Digital surround setups, and at least one game console. The PlayStation 2 and Xbox started the trend, but next-gen systems such as the Xbox 360 have an even firmer grasp on the territory. From "family gathering place" to "family entertainment center," living rooms have merged with technology and in the process have become a fully democratic space— in line with Millennial beliefs.

The living room is now the place to watch crystal clear, high-definition content with family and friends. Most families gather around for movies on DVDs (now even HD-DVDs) and standout TV series such as *Heroes* and *Lost* rather than arcade racing on the Xbox 360, but the fact is that people are watching TV together again, a habit that most deemed dead just a few years ago (the never-ending popularity of *The Simpsons* notwithstanding). This is also one of the reasons moviegoers are becoming increasingly reluctant to go out; who in their right mind would leave home, find a parking spot, and feed the family overpriced food (not to mention the price of the movie itself) just for big screen entertainment that's inferior to what they have at home?

Game-wise, the living room is now the official gaming space of the house. As many as four people, parents included, may simultaneously go online for a round of old-fashioned warfare in *Call of Duty 3*, or a group of friends may spend hours on *Madden 07* in glorious high-definition. Parties are planned around *Guitar Hero 2* (a game that includes a functional "toy" guitar that puts players in the skin of wild rock stars), and many parents have moonlighted as race car drivers on the challenging tracks of *Gran Turismo 4*. Game consoles seem to have abandoned the bedrooms for good!

As for the home office, chances are high that now all kids have their own computers, not counting mom and dad's laptop. Siblings can play *Age of Empires* against each other instead of being forced to go solo, and every person in the house has access to the same amount of information through broadband wireless Internet connections.

Bedrooms themselves are now sleeping and studying places, rather than the former "caves" where teenagers hid, listening to concept albums and blocking out the rest of the world with large-sized headphones. Computers help kids do their homework and school assignments, fulfilling a promise made in the mid-1980s, but bedrooms are in no way dominated by them. The relocation of most game playing and movie watching to the living room has resulted in the end of closed doors—an unforeseen bonus.

Of course, not every house is networked, and not every console has a spot close to the house's main DVD player, but the above description fits the changes we have been seeing during the last few years. There is no going back: Houses are quickly turning into integrated, not segregated, living spaces. This is in part due to Boomer and Xer parents growing tired of being alone—and also because Millennials like to stick around and just *be* with their parents. Unlike Xers, Millennials don't feel the need to run away, not on a day-to-day basis, and maybe not before they get married. U.S. market-research company Twentysomething Inc. has reported that 65% of all college graduates now move back with their parents after graduation!

The living room is your best bet to spend quality time with the kids inside the house. It's a place where they feel comfortable and where they can bring friends or rest after school. It can easily become the family home's heart and soul by allowing everyone to have fun at the same time.

> My oldest son (Dante, age 7) and I will play *Star Wars: Empire at War* for about an hour each night after his homework is done. We limit the time, and we only play this game together—although he does play *Lego Star Wars* by himself on his laptop.
>
> —Paul Orlando (Professor, Art Institute)

Although I've always enjoyed games, I probably wouldn't have had as much time to continue playing them as a mom if my sons had not also been interested. That's why I happily stepped into the game review gig at my newspaper several years ago: because it offered an opportunity to explore an exploding industry and to be knowledgeable about a pastime of interest to my sons and their friends. Frankly, as a parent and consumer, I also felt it was important to be knowledgeable about games in order to educate myself about what I thought was appropriate for their consumption—just as I would do for a film or other form of mature-themed entertainment. We monitored and restricted the amount of time they spent on games at home, and we balanced that time with other activities. But our family also has had a lot of fun over the years playing, challenging, teasing each other, and discussing aspects of games before I wrote reviews. And now that my sons have reached those know-it-all teen years, I suspect that my game-reviewing duties and gaming interests are the only thing about me that they find remotely worthwhile.

—Cindi Lash (longtime news reporter & game critic,
formerly with the *Pittsburgh Post-Gazette*)

Like too many people, I work long hours that really cut into family time. For a while, it was my job to review games. I intentionally chose family and kids' games to review, so that we could all play games together and then write reviews together. The kids got their names on actual reviews (check out The Zoo's reviews, at GamersInfo.net) and I got to spend some of my work time with the kids. Even now, we still occasionally review games together.

—David Ladyman (Publications Manager, IMGS, Inc.)

Parent Snapshot

Colin Mack

Project manager (THQ Inc.)
Agoura Hills, CA

Colin has worked in video game production for 12 years. He began as a programmer, and he has worked as a technical director, producer, and production management positions since then. Currently, he is the lead production manager for the *WWE* and *UFC* games at THQ.

- Family Profile: 2 boys, 10 and 17
- Playtime: 1–3 hours per week with kids
- Platforms: Wii, Xbox 360, Xbox, PS2, PlayStation, GameCube, N64, Dreamcast, Saturn, GBA, GBA SP, Game Boy, Game Boy Color, DS, PSP, PC
- Top Games: WWE wrestling games, Wii Sports
- "I like to give my kids the opportunity to 'help dad' with work. I always have them review their new games for me, keep me updated on what the kids at school are playing, and get them involved in helping prepare feedback on games in progress that I review."

The Living Room: Rules of Engagement

Since the living room is a coveted area, every effort must be made to ensure that it's not transformed into a war zone. The following are several "rules of engagement" that should be followed if at all possible:

- **Avoid "the living room is mine" mantra.** Your kids need to feel welcome in the living room. They need to see it as part of their own space in the house. If they feel like they're trespassing, they will migrate to a friend's house. Being selfish about the space *will* make your kids avoid your presence.

- **Equip your living room with technology as well as aesthetics.** Make sure you have an attractive and well-equipped living room. Ask for your kids, help: What kind of AV equipment should we have? What kind of sofa do you like? Be sure to include them in the decision-making process; it will make a big difference in the long term. Of course, not everyone has money to spend on interior decorating and AV equipment. It's understandable if you can't afford anything fancy!

- **Find a different room for "tough talks."** The living room should be a place for fun and understanding. If you need to discipline your kids in any way, do it in the privacy of their bedrooms. It's more respectful if you keep discipline a private matter, and you want to make every effort to avoid associating the living room with "tough talks."

- **Reach common agreements when deciding how to use the room.** Try to avoid making unilateral decisions regarding how and when to use the living room. Invite your kids to discussions, and spend the time necessary to reach a common agreement. Find out how to integrate everyone's needs so that you can share the good times. That's the best way to have your kids in there while also respecting your rights as a parent.

- **Allow your kids to improve the room.** Give your kids a chance to "redecorate" and make the living room a true "family room," perhaps suggesting color schemes, comfortable chairs, and functional game storage furniture. They might even want to use some of their allowance to "chip in" for a new game console or a higher quality DVD player. Let them add value to the room; their sense of ownership will strengthen the bond between you and help develop their autonomy at the same time.

- **Celebrate their passions in the living room.** Your kids may be fans of *Halo*, the movie version of *Lord of the Rings*, or a new TV show on Nickelodeon. Music-wise, they might crave live concerts or be fledgling musicians

$\rightarrow$

themselves! Celebrate these passions with "launch marathons" for games, trilogy parties for movies, weekly family rituals (perfect for TV shows), and mini music performances accompanied by the piano, guitar, or your child's instrument of choice (or even karaoke if everyone just wants to sing). Your kids will feel truly appreciated if you recognize and celebrate their passions.

We wanted to buy only one game console if we could help it, and my grandson often visits with friends. I wanted them to be able to play their favorite games, so I asked him which console he'd prefer we get. He wanted the Xbox 360 so he could play *Call of Duty* online—which was great because that's the one we wanted for its media sharing capabilities anyway. I don't know if I would have actually asked my kids or grandkids what kind of furniture they wanted me to buy for our media room, but I did take their needs into consideration. We're still furnishing that room—but some big soft cushions or beanbags are going in there (because they seem to love lying on their stomachs on the floor), along with easy care carpet and upholstery. I don't want to have to be too concerned over spilled drinks; I want them to have fun in there, not feel like they have to be careful all the time.

—Sandy Doell (author, editor, mother, grandmother, and gamer)

REMEMBER: GAMES ARE NOT THE ENEMY

Now that the living room is once again the heart of the house, some parents have suddenly realized that there's just no way of stopping their kids from playing games. They see them playing games after school, on a Saturday morning (instead of watching cartoons), and even late on a Sunday night, with a group of friends and boxes of pizza lying around. Video games may have been popular since the mid-1980s, but next-gen systems, with photorealistic graphics and booming sound, somehow feel more threatening than Mario and Luigi ever did. When limited to the bedroom, games could be contained or even ignored; on a 60-inch television screen in the living room, they seem to be capable of swallowing up the whole house!

Parents might feel like they're giving in to the enemy. "Why should I allow my kids to have the living room for themselves? They're just wasting time." These fears are perfectly natural. Every new technological age is met with full acceptance from the younger generation and fear from other areas of society. The process was exactly the same with the advent of cinema in the early 1900s and television in the '40s. Early technologies are usually seen as unregulated, revolutionary—and sometimes downright dangerous. Parents often fear that new types of entertainment will have their kids throw values and beliefs in a trash can somewhere and then proceed to live an empty, sad life. Remember the prejudice against TV in the late 1950s? What about young adults and their Walkman portable players, seen as instruments of rebellion in the 1970s? Somehow, human beings always have trouble trusting *new* technology—unless they're under 20, that is.

Parent Snapshot

Guy P. Vance

Customer Service Rep
Tacoma, WA

- Family Profile: 5 children, ages 21, 19, 18, 7, and 2
- Playtime: 4–6 hours per week with kids
- Platforms: PS3, PS2, GameCube
- Top Games: *SpongeBob: Bikini Bottom, City of Heroes*
- "Every night is game night if we aren't watching a movie together. We don't schedule a weekly event, since the systems are always on!"

Parent Snapshot

Aaron Marks

Composer/sound designer/parent
Fallbrook, CA

Practically falling into the game industry over 10 years ago, Aaron has amassed music and sound design credits on over 70 online casino games, a dozen touchscreen arcade games, 20 class II video bingo/slot/keno machines, two class III video slot machines, eight CD-ROM game projects, a PlayStation 2 title, a Dreamcast game, and numerous other multimedia projects. He also sidelines as a writer of game audio interests for *Game Developer Magazine, Gamasutra.com,* and *Music4Games.net.* He is the author of *The Complete Guide to Game Audio* (an expansive book on all aspects of audio for video games) and primary author of the upcoming *Game Audio Development* (part of Thomson's *Game Development Essentials* series). Aaron continues his pursuit of the ultimate soundscape, creating music and sound for various projects.

→

- Family Profile: 16-year-old daughter
- Playtime: 1–3 hours per week with kids (both parents)
- Platforms: Xbox, Wii, N64, PC, GB
- Top Games: *Wii Sports* (bowling), *Excite Truck*, *The Legend of Zelda*
- "We play games so much that having one night set aside to play would be silly!"

DEVELOPMENTAL GAMING

Different ages have different needs. As children grow, select areas of the brain require certain stimuli in order to reach their full potential. Guided by the research of two classic practitioners of developmental psychology, Erik Erikson and Jean Piaget, we have determined which games might be appropriate for each age group. Although both Erikson and Piaget have similar beliefs, we concluded that Erikson is more didactic and detailed than Piaget. For the sake of simplicity, we'll focus on Erikson's concepts in this book, but we do recommend that interested parents read Piaget's theory. You'll find that he also has a very interesting (and more progressive) take on the subject.

Erikson's stages of psychosocial development consist in a description, step-by-step, of the development of human beings from birth to death. It is especially useful because of its minimalism. They are as follows:

1. Infancy (birth–1 year)
2. Toddler (1–3 years)
3. Pre-schooler (3–6 years)
4. School-age (6–12 years)
5. Adolescence (12–18 years)
6. Young adult (18–30 years)
7. Adult (30–60 years)
8. Late adulthood (60–death)

Each stage has different goals and outcomes. We'll focus on Stages 1 through 6 in this book. Curiously, if you think about these stages, they are not very different from levels in a game (the many "stages" a player has to go through in order to beat the game). In an RPG, when a player succeeds at any kind of challenge, be it killing a monster or finding special items, experience points are awarded, allowing the character to rank up. In a way, we also "rank up" in life: We get to drive a car on our

16th birthday (if we have a driver's license) and win bonuses at the office for good performance!

Infancy (Birth–12 Months)

Infancy is all about *trust*. Through parents and other adults, the infant learns to trust in the world. It's important to give the child a lot of attention; there's need for constant and reliable care. This age might define how well a child is able to fit in. Since kids are still getting used to their senses, it's difficult for them to isolate the other four and focus solely on vision by way of a television screen; that's why video games cannot be recommended at this age. Sensory toys such as fur animals that make funny noises are certainly more appropriate!

Toddler (1–3)

Here the focus shifts to *autonomy* versus *doubt*. Toddlers want to explore, but a question arises: Does Father approve? If so, toddlers will develop a sense of pride and assertion. If not, they may never fully believe in themselves. Here, we'd rather be conservative again and recommend that parents avoid games until the next phase. In order to explore virtual worlds, kids first need to explore their own—traditional learning toys such as Lego will be a lot more instructive and fun.

Pre-schooler (3–5)

The pre-schooler stage marks the beginning of *initiative*. This is when children learn to start something new, to give the world something to think about. Since these can be both positive and negative enterprises, parents have to navigate the muddy waters of good and evil by providing their kids with the basic values that allow us to choose between the two. However, while kids need to learn to be responsible, they shouldn't have to deal with premature guilt trips; beware of excessive punishment and shaming!

This is the age in which electronic gaming really starts. Games for solo play (unsupervised) should consist of simple image and sound exercises, focused more on developing symbolism than winning or losing. Vocabulary should also be of prime importance at this time, since the brain is more than ready to absorb new words. As children get older (4+), buy them an inexpensive portable game console such as a GameBoy Advance and see how they react to some Early Childhood (EC) titles. They might seem simplistic but are indeed useful to introduce a child to gaming. Last but not least, you could also have them sit on your lap while you play a game about the time they reach 5 years of age. Try that only if the game in question has no violent content! If the game is cartoonish or more arcade-like (involving "twitch action"), young children will surely find a way to appreciate it; the game will greatly help in the development of fine motor skills, and they might beat you after a couple of tries!

Franklin the Turtle is an EC (Early Childhood) game that's appropriate for pre-schoolers. The Game Factory

School-age (6–12)

Most of all, school is hard work. So no wonder the main characteristic of children at this stage is *industry*—the ability to start and finish projects. If rules and standards didn't really matter in the earlier stage, this one has kids doing their best to "do it right" and be the best. It's the very beginning of *competition* and the feelings of pride (for a job well done) and inferiority (if your volcano is the least impressive experiment in the Science Fair).

While pre-schoolers can deal with twitch action games, school-age kids have, for the first time, the patience and skills necessary to play more sophisticated games. They still have a hard time differentiating between the reality of a game and "real life," but the capacity to learn the rules and reach interdependent goals is there for the first time.

This is usually the age where most kids really start to enjoy games. Avoid anything too realistic, since kids this age can't really understand it; you might think they do, but they don't. All other games rated EC, E, and E10+ are welcome, and even some 3D fighting games (rated T) shouldn't be a problem.

Kingdom Hearts 2 is an appropriate game for school-age children. Disney

Adolescence (12–18)

Everyone who goes through adolescence comes out with scars. Adolescence is the very first time we have to face the question of *identity*: Who are we? We need to figure out who we are, all of a sudden, and it's not easy or pretty. Moreover, adolescence marks the birth of *critical thinking*. Kids become knowledgeable in their country's history and geopolitical place; they learn about death and might develop spiritual and/or religious beliefs around it. It's also the age of puberty, which adds much-anticipated pleasure and drama to their lives. Adolescents like to plan, strategize, execute, and achieve. "Mini-adults," they are like alpha versions of games, where everything is there (feature-complete), but nothing works quite as expected.

Here, the love for strategy and role-playing games is born. Adolescents might also develop a taste for horror and science fiction in games. First-person shooters (FPSs) also start to get popular with kids around this age. Teenagers have wildly different levels of maturity, so it's tough to guarantee that they all will be able to deal with certain topics. For example, two different teenagers might have an opposite reaction playing *Grand Theft Auto: San Andreas*. One might become more violent, and the other might cease to be violent at all. The rule of thumb is to know your teenagers. Some of them will be more than able to deal with sex and violence in games, while others might need constant supervision and guidance. Older

Fight Night Round 3 **is an appropriate game for adolescents.** Electronic Arts, Inc.

teenagers will be able to stand on their own, but beware of 13–15-year-olds who see themselves as "more than ready"! Even sci-fi fantasy games like *Gears of War* require a degree of maturity—that's why they're rated M!

Young Adult (18–30)

Now that kids are starting to leave home later (sometimes in their 20s), it's appropriate that we mention this age group. Young adults are taking their first steps towards independent life; they are learning about serious relationships and money the hard way. While this stage is difficult to define, it is certainly a quest for some of our earliest objectives in life—a career, money, healthy relationships, and general lifestyle choices. The fact that most of these are shallow is just a testament to their young age—real (and deeper) objectives become part of their lives after 30.

Some early young adults might go for sex and violence without a second thought since they can clearly see the difference between a game and real life; it makes the game that much more interesting. This happens because young adults use gaming for cathartic purposes; life gives them so many responsibilities and pressures that an escape valve is needed from time to time. Don't worry if your kids have seemingly extreme tastes; unless something more complex is going on below the surface, these are just symbolic representations of the added challenges they now face. Standout M-rated titles are *Dead Rising* and the upcoming *Halo 3*, both for the Xbox 360, while PlayStation 3 has *Resistance: Fall of Man*.

God of War II is an appropriate game for young adults.
Sony Computer Entertainment America

Next, let's take a look at what motivates your kids (and everyone else) to play video games!

Parent Snapshot

Travis Ogurek

Parent and student
Depere, WI

- Family Profile: 8, 6, 2, 3-months
- Playtime: Both parents play 1–3 hours per week with kids.
  Platforms: PS2, PC, PSP, SNES
- Top Games: *Kingdom Hearts, SSX Tricky 3, Tony Hawk's American Wasteland*
- Memorable Moment: "The first time my son was able to beat me, even though I was trying my best. That was an eyeopener!

GAME ON: WHY WE PLAY

Nobody is forced to play games. We do it because it's fun, like playing soccer on a sunny day, and figuring out "whodunit" in a mystery novel. *Fun* is the core of every single game ever invented (well, the good ones). But games are more than just fun. They're compelling, engrossing, frustrating, challenging, and rewarding. In a way, games are a lot like life itself.

Why do people play games? In 1981, Thomas Malone explained the motivation for gaming in terms of fantasy, challenge, and curiosity. In short, we play games for the experience. For example, let's say you go back to the 1970s in a time machine and get to choose between watching a Pink Floyd concert *live* or a film version inside a three-projector Cinerama screen in the heart of Hollywood. Which would you pick? Most of you would probably go for the live concert. Now why would anyone prefer to face lines, crowds, smoke, and unhealthy noise levels instead of safe, state-of-the-art sound and picture? For the *live* experience!

Experience is being there. It can be a memory from Mars like in the film *Total Recall* (from Philip K. Dick's story, "We Can Remember It for You Wholesale"). It can be fighting the Strogg in *Quake 4*. It can be going to the market and having trouble finding lactose-free milk. Experience is going through an event (in real time) that happens to us. We are the central characters—and we remember every second of it.

In order to create these experiences, games resort to all sorts of strategies. Game companies now hire Hollywood film composers to write the score and professional screenwriters to polish once cheesy game dialogue. Human-like characters are painstakingly modeled by artists, programmers make sure everything does what it's supposed to do, and game designers try to make the game compelling and fun. The collective effort of all these forces shapes the game, which, in turn, determines the kind of experience you'll have playing it.

There are countless different ways of experiencing games. Here are just a few:

- Exploration
- Competition
- Cooperation
- Escape from reality
- Bending reality
- Learning new skills
- Passing time
- De-stressing
- Socializing

Let's analyze each one of these.

EXPLORATION

Exploration is an innate instinct in most intelligent species. A mix of curiosity and basic necessity, exploration is a skill that's necessary in order to survive new environments. Games have loads of exploration in them: You need to explore a dungeon in order to locate a rare item; a whole game is based on jumping from planet to planet in search of new weapons (and money, of course). Exploration is directly connected to expansion, since it's the only way—other than force-feeding players new levels in *Pac-Man*—to allow for growth and discovery within the game. If you don't do any exploring, you might as well put down the game.

Tomb Raider (Anniversary edition, shown) involves a great deal of exploration. Eidos Interactive Ltd.

Dungeon Siege was pretty fun. The boys demanded to be the warrior and the wizard, which left Dad with the good old elf/archer woman. Well, it turns out the kids are ninja looters; so we'd be fighting a bunch of goblins, and suddenly Dad (the elf archer) is fighting a bunch of goblins all by himself . . . because the warrior and wizard are apparently busy rifling through all the treasure chests. *But* the fun little lesson was that *Dungeon Siege* gave out XP based on your personal kills—so pretty soon Dad was an 8th level archer, and the boys were still 3rd/4th level. Suddenly *everybody* wants to be an elf/archer because an elf/archer seems pretty cool!

—Brian Reynolds (CEO, Big Huge Games)

Why is exploration so enticing? Well, it's a major source of pleasure for human beings. We love the thrill of the unknown, the joy of learning about new things. After all, this is one of the reasons we put up with long check-in lines, bland plane food, and a foreign language; we want to explore Paris, find out everything about the city, and come back to tell the tale. We feel more alive than ever when in a foreign country; our brain buzzes with new information—images, sounds, even the way the air smells. Of course you can't smell a game character—a positive feature if you ever need to meet up with Orcs or the Pooh Monster. Whether they feature Indiana Jones or Lara Croft, good games go a long way toward providing the most incredible worlds and creatures to satisfy the explorer inside us, giving players access to locations both mysterious and lush, real or imaginary, around the world and beyond.

COMPETITION

If Darwin was right, the only reason we can write this book (and you can read it) is because millions of years ago, *homo erectus* somehow evolved into *homo sapiens*. Evolution spared no organism in the planet; from fungi to Nessie (the Loch Ness monster), every species had to fight for survival until only the most prepared and capable were left alive. This evolutionary process defined the world we live in today—and will certainly define the world of tomorrow.

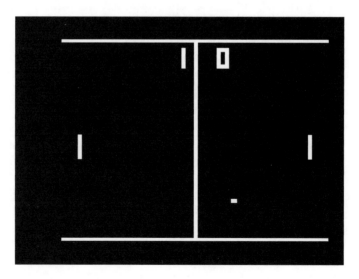

The first commercially successful arcade game, *Pong*, involved two-player competition. Pong® screenshot courtesy of Atari Interactive, Inc.

But evolution is competition, right? Yes. And competition in all forms and shapes has fueled games since the very beginning. Competing is still hard-wired in our genome; we might be very civil with our boss at work, but we absolutely *need* to frag dozens of opponents in *Halo 2*. In reality, we are always competing against ourselves, but the existence of opponents—as opposed to the predictability of computer-controlled ones—gives us the arena to truly test our might. Games allow us to do this in constructive ways; no one gets hurt, no windows are broken, no light sabers are damaged. For example, instead of ripping somebody's arms off in gladiatorial Rome, you can steal their flag from under their noses in *Call of Duty 3*. Instead of crashing a Ferrari Enzo drag racing in Malibu—like a Gizmondo executive did in 2006—you can win an online race in *Test Drive Unlimited*. We love to play games because we love competition.

> I have really enjoyed playing *Chicken Invaders* with my son the most. The Christmas version was a lot of fun during the holidays. If he starts losing, he will shut the game down and restart. I cannot win!
>
> —JoAnna Almasude (instructor, media arts & animation; Art Institute Online)

COOPERATION

After competition, another die-hard instinct is cooperation. We might have been savages against the other tribe, but we still loved our family dearly. Some hunted, and some gathered, but all cooperated toward the common goal of staying alive.

Games allow us to cooperate with friends and family instead of repeatedly beating them in *Mario Kart*. We have the choice of working together as a team, of strategically uniting efforts to face a shared enemy. Cooperation, in contrast to competition, has not always been present in games. The rise of cooperation in games goes hand-in-hand with the rise of the Millennial generation; modern kids like to share, and due to their insistence, now most games have team or "co-op" mode.

Puzzle Pirates involves crews of players who solve puzzles in order to explore and pillage. *World of Warcraft* promotes the existence of guilds, allowing willing priests to join parties if they feel the need for adventure. (Priests can heal injured warriors, so everyone in the game likes them.) We have always had the need to form a group—to belong and to care. Now we can do the same in games, where the risks are nil and the rewards (such as marriages, extra income, and new friends) are extraordinary.

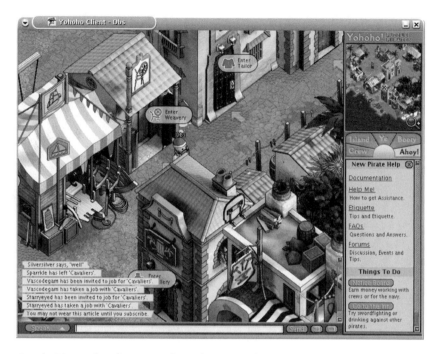

Puzzle Pirates involves team-based cooperation. Three Rings Design, Inc.

ESCAPING REALITY

Life sometimes isn't fair. Worse yet, life has no pause or reset button! Situations at home, school, and work can be difficult to deal with at times, and they can be particularly challenging for your kids. Unlike illegal drugs and alcohol, games can be very helpful in this time of need. Although the best games are filled with obstacles that need to be overcome, they also provide a tangible, fun-filled reality that can easily serve as refuge. Almost all players have fled to their favorite games in order to deal with the challenges of real life. Simulation games might allow us to test out scenarios that we haven't had experience with in real life, whereas a fantasy role-playing game (RPG) might allow us to escape into worlds and characters that might only exist in our imaginations. We can become doctors, lawyers, artists, musicians, poets, dragonslayers, magicians, superheroes—and even super villains!

Players can immerse themselves in fantasy characters such as knights in *Neverwinter Nights 2.* Neverwinter Nights™ 2 screenshot courtesy of Atari Interactive, Inc.

Occasionally, some players get a little too wrapped up in highly immersive game worlds at the expense of some real-world activities. Most of us don't take such extreme measures; we use games as temporary shelters from the harshness of life, as warm, safe places where we can rest our minds, regroup, and reassess our resources. After a few minutes or a couple of hours, we'll be ready to take on the world all over again.

All forms of entertainment have helped us escape into fictional worlds, whether fantasy novels, radio dramas, Saturday morning cartoons, comic books, or family films. *Harry Potter* is still one of the top-selling book series of all time, which shows that children haven't given up books completely for video games. But active role play has been a powerful form of escapism. Generations of kids have escaped into their backyards or bedrooms, acting out "make believe" stories on their own or with friends. Just one generation ago, structured role-playing games appeared in the form of *Dungeons & Dragons*, in which kids often sat around a dining room table while temporarily living in a world of elves, mages, dwarves, and orcs. With the power of video games, especially role-playing games (RPGs), kids can immerse themselves in a fantasy world with rich visual and audio effects capable of rivaling imagination itself.

BENDING REALITY

"There is no spoon." No one can forget the moment when Neo miraculously *bent* a metal spoon in the first *Matrix* movie. In context, it taught Neo that real life couldn't be altered by his mind, but because he was in fact in the Matrix, he could do just that. The exhilaration felt by the audience during that scene is also one of the reasons games are so popular.

Bending reality during a race in *San Francisco Rush*. Midway Games

A racing game such as *San Francisco Rush* has "larger than life" ramps that can send your wanna-be Camaro careening through the air, to the top of a high-rise. It's a great feeling, even if we all know that Beetles don't really fly and were certainly not made to hit ramps at 120 mph. This is "game thinking" at its best; while still based on reality, a good game will change it just enough to make it fun.

Time tricks are also part of a game's arsenal. From the slow motion of *Need for Speed: Carbon* to a full VCR-like rewind in *Full Auto*, games never let time stand between you and the lap record. Even old games such as *Populous* had a button to pause time, if you ever felt the need.

LEARNING NEW SKILLS

Skills can be divided into two categories: useful and not so useful. Learning how to fly a 747 can be useful, while we all agree that learning how to fly the *Enterprise* is not very useful! Let's say you've read the manual, played through the tutorial and, after 200 hours of flight, you've learned how to fly both. Does it matter that the *Enterprise* is science fiction? How's the difference to your brain—the one muscle that you really exercised during those 200 hours? There's no difference, but the sense of accomplishment is there anyway. You feel good; unconsciously, you realize there's nothing you can't master.

Taking on the role of a movie mogul in *The Movies.* Lionhead Studios Limited

Those are the effects of learning a new skill, be it making scrambled eggs or bungee-jumping. The very best games are those that give you a chance to learn a new skill. It can be as simple as jumping from one platform to another without falling, or as sophisticated as managing the electricity that powers Manhattan. Sometimes, learning something theoretically is not compelling enough and can feel "incomplete." With video games, you have the chance to immediately *apply* what you've learned. For example, *Microsoft Flight Simulator* has plenty of pre-set flights that may put you in a World War I plane during a storm or force you to land a damaged jetliner at Chicago O'Hare under strong winds. Since this "training" is still fun, it's seen as a challenge, and that makes the learning effective and addictive. Games attract players by *covertly* teaching them new skills that they can immediately apply to situations; players are compelled to take the time and effort to learn, often because they want to "master" the game itself. Kids soon become aware that learning takes time and effort, and they eventually apply this sort of patience and diligence to skills they learn in real life.

PASSING TIME

While Millennials are usually good students, they are growing up during a time in which multitasking is an almost essential part of daily life: juggling Google searches, quick IMs, 30-second YouTube video clips, and more. The younger you are, the more likely you might be to need something, anything, in order not to go nuts with downtime. Millennials are not like other generations, who would be more than happy to read *The Inquirer, People*, or *Mad Magazine* at the dentist. Millennials need to be entertained; while waiting, an old magazine simply won't do!

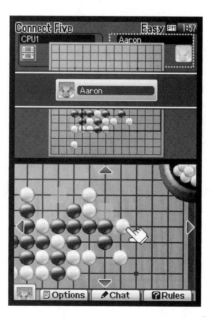

The variety of card, board, party, and puzzle games in the *Clubhouse Games* (*Connect Four,* shown) collection allows time to pass quickly. Courtesy of Nintendo

There's nothing worse than waiting, and kids are just not as patient as adults are! In fact, the only time one of the authors of this book remembers ever being bored was as a child of 10 during one long summer weekend. Perhaps there were no new books to read or games to play! Games *will* fill your kids' time, guaranteed. Yours, too! The next time you find yourself waiting in line or sitting in a waiting room, try playing a puzzle game on your cell phone. If you happen to have a portable game system such as a DS or a PSP, try playing *Clubhouse Games* or *Lumines*. These games are not replacements for book reading, but they do help keep your mind engaged using pattern recognition, quick reflexes, strategic thought, and even a bit of mathematics.

Games can make spare time into exercise for your mind, your fingers, and your feelings. Hours will go by like minutes, and you'll find your mind moving from "x number of errands" to "how do I reach this next objective?" Through the magic of games, dead time comes back to life—with a vengeance.

> We have a TV in the van, and we can hook up the game consoles to it. We go on trips to gain a closer relationship with our kids—and the game can sometimes help.
>
> —Jim Greenall (animatronics designer/fabricator/puppeteer)

De-Stressing

Modern life can be so chaotic that relaxation might sound like an unlikely proposition. Unless we practice yoga on a regular basis, we often only envision true relaxation in the context of an island in the Pacific or the coast of Brazil! Relaxation is just not very common in the networked world in which we choose to live.

At the end of a work day, most of us can find ourselves exhausted and moody. Our minds might be running on fumes, and thoughts will escape any attempt at arranging themselves in logical order. It's like a core meltdown in one of those big sci-fi spaceships, but worse; nothing works, and all the engineers have gone to sleep. At times like these, we all need to sit back and "de-stress."

De-stressing is loosening up without shutting down. Instead of meditating, try playing a slow, immersive RPG like *Final Fantasy*. Instead of vegetating in front of the TV, try doing some laps in *Gran Turismo 4*. Just for the hell of it, allow yourself to float to a simpler, less demanding, world.

Games can help you deal with the anxiety and nervousness of modern life. By attacking the corners with your Maserati, you avoid nagging your kids. By strategizing a massive Viking invasion, you avoid being eaten alive by stress. If you need proof, go out now and buy either a Nintendo DS with *Nintendogs* or a Sony PSP (which doubles as a media player) with *Lumines*. If you play them just a little bit

Playing *Nintendogs* is a great way to de-stress!
Courtesy of Nintendo

every day, you'll see for yourself how games can free your mind from the "mess" we call life.

Ironically, the Millennial generation is recognized as having the most stress of any generation that has come of age in the United States during the past 50 years. The reasons? More homework, greater peer pressure, less privacy, higher college entrance requirements (often involving hours of community service), and elevated expectations for academic, athletic, and creative success.

SOCIALIZING

We are all social beings. When left alone, human beings will eventually crave having someone else to talk to and have fun with. It's written in our genes. In the past, games weren't very good for socializing; with a maximum of two players, there wouldn't be much social variety. Later on, when the Nintendo 64 added four controller ports, four-player gaming sessions became the norm, and whole weekends could be spent chatting and playing *Goldeneye 007*. Still, four was all the variety you'd get.

A major appeal of massively multiplayer online games (MMOGs) such as *World of Warcraft* is that large numbers of players can socialize with one another. World of Warcraft® image provided courtesy of Blizzard Entertainment, Inc.

With the advent of broadband connections and more modern consoles such as the PlayStation 2 and Xbox, online gaming finally became a reality to console owners. This meant that no one would ever have to play alone again; friends, enemies, and competitors became reachable; and, most importantly, players were able to chat with the use of voiceover IP (VoIP), discussed in Chapter 4, "The Social Game").

Socializing is a very strong reason to play a game; it might be the strongest of all in MMOGs, in which players might log in just so they can meet up with friends instead of actually playing the game, in stark contrast to the "lone gamer" cliché propagated by the media.

All those factors give games much more purpose and usefulness than you might expect. The preconception of games as simple pastimes doesn't apply anymore; games have gained much-needed complexity and depth (while remaining easy to use) and consequently have become a major cultural force. Games wouldn't be where they are today if they were only gadgets or toys.

Your kids play games because they enjoy most, if not all, of the features described earlier. They have learned from infancy how to use the very best that games have to offer, simply because they were born during the supernova-like expansion of the Information Age. Although it may not be immediately obvious, we are in reality living lives that most people would certainly have deemed science fiction a mere 10 years ago.

Now that you know *why* we all play games, it is high time that you grab a chair and join in. Nothing will make your kids happier than to share the games they love with you.

A Word of Caution

Some mistakes have dire consequences. Others have no consequences at all. The three examples below can make or break the relationship between you and your kids.

1. **Avoid preferential treatment**. If children grow up feeling as if they're being treated unfairly, they may never fully trust their parents and will have difficulty trusting others. They will also have less respect for the parents, relying instead on sophisticated ways to "con" both parents to get what they want.

2. **Some parents utilize the "do as I tell you, not as I do" philosophy, which is disastrous for children.** They will eventually notice the hypocritical behavior and simply stop listening or even asking for advice. It also fuels a deep mistrust of other authority figures, since (in the eyes of a child) people seem to never act as they say, especially those with power. Kids believe in parents who live by their words, and there's nothing they desire more than to fully trust their parents.

3. **Simply showering kids with consoles and games is not the same as being parents.** Using gifts to trigger positive behavior from children could eventually be recognized as a "buyout" rather than generosity. Gifts are a priceless opportunity to reward your kids for goals and achievements—not a chance to feed some warped "gaming habit."

Video games are an evolution of physical and board games, from sports to chess. They are tools of modern times; use their power wisely, never selfishly, and always with your kid's well-being in mind.

Parent Snapshot

Jim McCampbell

*Department Head, Computer Animation
Department (Ringling School of Art & Design)
Sarasota, FL*

Jim began his career as a graphic designer. After working for years as senior art director for several advertising agencies, he began doing computer animation in 1986, working for several film and video production companies with national clients. Since 1995, Jim has been teaching at Ringling School of Art & Design in Sarasota, Florida where he is head of both the Computer Animation and the Game Art & Design programs. He also owns Peculiar Pictures Inc., a Sarasota-based 3D animation production business specializing in animation for film, broadcast, and video games.

- Family Profile: two children, ages 16 and 12
- Playtime: 1–3 hours per week with kids
- Platforms: Xbox 360, Xbox, PS2, GameCube, N64, Genesis, PC, PSP, DS, GBA SP, GB Color
- Top Games: *Atari Battlezone* (actual arcade game purchased in 1980, still in mint condition), *Coleco Telstar* (purchased new in 1976), *Gears of War*, *Ridge Racer 6*
- "Games supply a common ground where adults can communicate with kids, all in the framework of having fun and/or learning something. It also lets you challenge them and (OK I admit it) 'trash talk' them a little: 'Nobody beats Daddy at *MooMoo Farm*!!!'"

LIFE OR SOMETHING LIKE IT

Maybe you're an old-school gamer, or maybe you have nothing but contempt for video games. In either case, we bet you are a proud parent, and you want to be able to relate to your kids. It's as simple as that. For teenagers in particular, life consists of three main activities:

1. Sleeping
2. Eating
3. Socializing

Diagram by Per Olin

Let's see how these three elements play out:

1. You can't be part of their lives while they sleep.
2. You can have meals with them. Families go out to restaurants, sit at the dining room table, or plop themselves down in front of the television set. The latter, of course, doesn't stimulate much interaction; although the family does get to share an entertainment experience, this is done in a passive rather than an active way. There's nothing wrong with dinnertime TV; it is just probably not the best place to dine on a regular basis. Most families can't afford to go out to dinner regularly, although a once-per-week family "pizza night" has been a tradition with some (especially when Chuck E. Cheese and pizza video arcades were a popular option). The dining room table has been the most traditional setting for family meals. This can be good and bad. The ideal is that the dining room table allows families to tighten bonds through conversation. But some families tend to use the dining room table as a battleground for arguments. The dinner table can become a double-edged sword.

3. You can talk to your kids about relationships. They might tell you about a romantic interest at school or that dating is too complicated. Sorry, but we have to break it to you: Teenagers aren't the most trusting species on the planet (and boys are more secretive than girls). There is a chance they will talk about such intense feelings as love and rejection with you, but don't expect it.

Facing this scenario, many parents feel that they can only be tyrants or providers in the eyes of their kids. What else, they ask? How can I have a meaningful presence in my kid's life if we seem to value and enjoy opposite things? You guessed it. Games represent a traffic-free, seven-lane freeway to your kids. Since games are such a huge part of most kids' lives, you can use them as powerful channels of interaction and communication.

Let's say you have a young boy who is afraid of the dark. While you are both playing *Super Mario Bros.*, your kid might one day, out of nowhere (and without a single question from you), say exactly how he feels while trying to progress through Bowser's Lair. The dark and scary, dungeon-like castle will bring his fear afloat, and because your kid feels comfortable playing, he might blurt it out in the same breath as he says "I hate this boss." This is a very basic example of how games can "unlock" your kids!

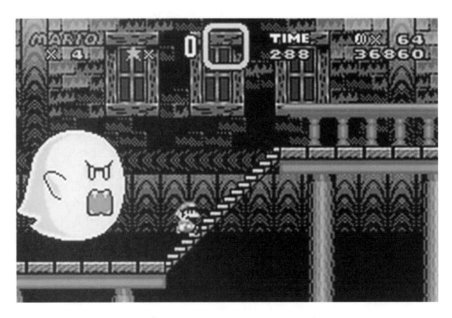

Mario navigates through a dark castle in *Super Mario Advance 2*. Courtesy of Nintendo

Through games, you'll have a chance to become much more than a parental figure. If your kids trust you enough to fight alongside them in a game, they will trust you to stand by them in real life. Suddenly, your kids will no longer be judgmental sphinxes, condemning or absolving you as a parent, but children happy to be with the most important person in their lives . . . you.

Parent Snapshot

Denice McLaughlin

Parent/student
Elgin, TX

Denice is a mom, costumer, and a gamer. Her family of four all game together, and they run a blog called GamerParents (http://gamerparents.blogspot.com). Their main game right now is *World of Warcraft*. All four of them play!

- Family Profile: two children, ages 10 and 13
- Playtime: 7–9 hours per week with kids (spouse plays 4–6 hours per week with kids)
- Platforms: Wii, N64, Genesis, PC, DS, GB Color, GB
- Top Games: *World of Warcraft, Wario Wii, Mario*
- "I think that a family that 'games' together is closer. I talk with our kids about things I myself would never have talked about with my parents. I feel we have a good trusting bond."

HOW TO APPROACH YOUR KIDS

Let's investigate methods of approaching your kids to begin playing with them. Even if you're already a very "cool" parent by any standard, you might need an "approach technique." Creating a game-specific relationship with your kids is not automatic; they need to desire it themselves and not feel like they're being thrust into it as if it were an obligation. Following are some methods that will help you establish that first connection.

Games are a way in, especially these days when my son tends to be pulling away from Dad, the authority figure. To get to his level and to need his help in playing and understanding a game gives him the power in the dynamic and, therefore, allows him to open up to me.

—John Francis Whelpley (writer-producer, Skibberrean Productions, Inc.)

If You Have Never Been a Gamer . . .

This is tough. Games have never been part of your life, and now you've decided to play them with your kids. At first, this kind of situation seems very daunting and scary. Most parents fear being seem as "losers" by their kids since they might lack the dexterity necessary to play certain games. Don't worry; there's a surefire way to turn your "noobness" (from "newbie" or "noob," which is what hardcore gamers call those with no gaming experience) to your strategic advantage. All you have to do is approach your kid and say: *"Hey, what are you playing? (pause) Do you think you could teach me? (pause) This looks like a great game!"*

Simple, eh? By admitting you have no experience, you give your kids a chance to teach you something. From their side, this feels like one chance in a million; it's a very special event by all accounts. From your side, it takes the competitive edge away. It gets even easier if you pick a game that doesn't rely on twitch reflexes, like an adventure, strategy, or role-playing game (discussed in Chapter 2, "Games 101"). Even five-year-olds can teach you something new —if you care to ask them!

If You Played Video Games as a Kid But Haven't Touched Them Since . . .

Quoting *Pac-Man*'s ghost names and the virtues of *Enduro* on the Atari 2600 will get you nowhere with Millennials. Unless they are truly hardcore, which means they will know and appreciate old consoles, you might get resistance, a few giggles, or just looks of confusion. Still, there's a way to use this exact perception to your benefit.

Tease them—as jokingly as humanly possible—that some old arcade game is better than *Soul Calibur III* or *The Legend of Zelda: Twilight Princess.* Try to strike a deal with them: You will play modern games only if they play the old classics anthology with you. You can easily buy them for the PS2, Xbox, or as Live Arcade games on the Xbox 360. Half-an-hour each, one hour each, or maybe even half-an-hour of classics versus one hour of modern gaming; it doesn't matter. The goal here is to reach a fair deal, where all parties are 100% satisfied, and stick to it.

After a few months of being "exchange game students," you and your kids will hopefully begin to respect each other a lot more. You will learn to speak the same language. And, as the final touch, your kid will always want to show you the newest, coolest games on the market. If you show honest interest, they will gravitate toward you and seek you out to play games with them. Mission accomplished!

I have four children. The youngest two are my biological kids, but the older two are from my wife's previous marriage. I grew closer to my oldest two by primarily being myself, which included a love of cartoons, games, and toys. Playing electronic games afforded me a way to interact and learn about them. I quickly discovered that my oldest daughter is very confrontational and blindly investigates problems, whereas my son was more analytical and preferred to think rather than rush headlong into an implied obstacle. Through gaming I was able to develop a loose profile of the sorts of personalities I was dealing with, and I was able to develop a personalized method of communication with each. Five years later, my stepchildren have dropped the "stepfather" title and really see me as a friend and a father figure.

—Jacques Montemoino (Gideon Games, LLC)

If You Are a Hardcore Gamer . . .

We're sure some of you hardcore gamer *parents* are reading this book. Being this sort of gamer is actually tricky when it comes to parent-child relationships. Some hardcore gamers might play games with their kids from the very beginning and have a terrific relationship with them. Others, however, will see kids as distractions to their gaming and might avoid mixing "parenting" with "gaming." Here, things may go wrong.

For those classic console gamers, we know how you prize your collections, especially your rare skeleton Sega Saturn. Make sure you protect your valuable game consoles if you're concerned about your kids accidentally destroying them, but remember that your kids are much more important than any hard-to-find Japanese import.

Yes, it might sound inconceivable, but hardcore gamers as parents can be very damaging to their kids; they might put them down and tease them, among other minor forms of harassment. We've seen kids resent their parents when treated this way, while playing games or even playing catch.

If you want to challenge your kids, fine, but do it in a healthy way. Let them win from time to time; it will help boost their egos and improve their skills. Of course, you can still show them who is boss, but the trick is to use balance. Providing a challenge is not the same thing as being annoying, and it's certainly not the equivalent to being cruel. Use all this ferociousness on Xbox Live; that's where it belongs . . . not at home.

Also, your kids might always be casual gamers at best. Pushing them will not make any difference; accept the fact that your kids might not turn out just like you. If you have a tricked-out PlayStation 3 in the living room, there's no shame in sharing the screen with a Nintendo Wii. Acceptance is more important than skill, and surely leagues beyond gaming preferences!

Being close to your kids has never been easier if you're a hardcore gamer yourself, but remember that the opposite can also be true.

> I bought the Wii this year in order to have a closer relationship with my daughter, who is now 16 and spends little time at home. Having the Wii gives us a great excuse to spend some quality time together doing something without the "lectures."
>
> —Aaron Marks (composer/sound designer/parent)

> My oldest and I chat in-game and find it a very good environment to simply talk together in. The family participates in Wii polls and has a great time debating the latest Wii issue. Games are a large part of our family activities and a key component to how we stay in close relationships with our kids.
>
> —Donna K. Kidwell (Commercialization Consultant,
> University of Texas at Austin)

TIME TO PLAY!

Now you're ready to play. The first step in having a nice gaming session with your kids is to carve out time for it. We know how hurried and stressful our lives can be at times; that's why you'll need to schedule time for gaming, at least at first. This might sound silly, but it's the only way you'll stop the madness and have enough time for them.

Illustration by Ian Robert Vasquez

Now it's time to think about the game itself. You'll have to figure out whether you want to play *with* your kids or *against* them. Co-op play can be very fun, and it's recommended for younger children, while competitive play might be more suitable for the daring teenage mentality. Pick a game beforehand and, if possible, create some excitement around it. This is supposed to be a treasured event, not a boring appointment with your kids!

> I use video games to help my oldest son think for himself, not just follow what other people do. I often ask him why he does a certain action and help him reason through things.
>
> —Jennifer Anderson (tech support rep)

Be sure to have controllers for everyone, and make sure you know beforehand *how* to get everyone to play. Avoid leaving some waiting, since the "chair dance" will distract them from the game. Once everyone is settled, dim the lights and pump up the volume; this is as important as that Disney cartoon they have seen 20 times in a row. Another good tip is to go through the game tutorial with everyone, so that all of you have the same information. (When we say "game tutorial," we mean the tutorial that's available through the game itself. This does *not* involve reading the manual aloud to your kids, which could make them want to run out of the room and find a TV show to watch.) So, to make it easier:

1. Pick a time. Have at least two hours reserved for playing.
2. Gather your kids.
3. Distribute the controllers. Be sure everyone can play at the same time.
4. Dim the lights and pump up the volume.
5. Start the game. Be sure it is appropriate for everyone.
6. Have fun!

If you're playing with more than one kid, you might notice during the session that one sibling might pick on another, or that maybe two will pair against one (usually either the youngest or the oldest). Try to keep the competition within the game; if someone says something like "you suck!" or similar personal criticism, try to show them that no one wins a game by making aggressive remarks, and that these can actually take everyone's concentration away. They will soon notice that talking trash does indeed eat away at their performance!

As a final note for this simpler gaming session, remember that the goal here is to make your kids feel comfortable playing with you. Everything else—including winning or losing—is secondary. Congratulations on your first step connecting (or reconnecting) with your kids!

Discussing the programming aspects of games almost always leads to other topics. In the past year or so, conversations between me and my son have touched on these subjects:

- The economics of multiple platforms
- The marketing of products to various demographic and psychographic groups
- The competence of helpdesk personnel
- The possibility of extending computing power exponentially
- The influence of music on mood
- The pre-judging of games based on their names and/or graphics

—John Scott G ["The G-Man"] (producer and composer; Golosio Publishing)

Parent Snapshot

Chris Lenhart

Network technician (NATO)
Geilenkirchen, Germany

Chris Lenhart is a 34-year-old father of three daughters and a graduate of the Art Institute. Currently in Germany finishing a contract with NATO, he plans to move back to the states to look for work in the game or film industry.

- Family Profile: 3 daughters—ages 9, 7 and 4
- Playtime: 1–3 hours per week with kids
- Platforms: Xbox 360, PC
- Top Games: *City of Heroes*, *Fight Night Round 3*, *Oblivion*
- "My oldest daughter plays *Project Gotham Racing*. I told her I would never let her win—so when she did beat me, it would be for real. Well, she finally did—and she was very excited. Great to see!"

TIME OUT

For many reasons, you don't want your kids playing eight hours of games every day. This most certainly will take away time from other valuable pursuits—sports, homework, reading, and socializing. We believe that three hours a day is more than enough even for hardcore gamers, especially for children. On the other hand, teenagers 16 and up and young adults might play for over four hours at a time, or

Illustration by Ian Robert Vasquez

more on occasion; they do this because they might have spent days without playing (you probably know their lives can get as busy as yours), and they may feel the need to relax and/or unwind. Also, if they're playing online games that involve other players, many teenagers consider this part of their social time—where they can reconnect with friends, whether to compete in quick racing matches or engage in role-play as part of a guild.

It's healthy to balance gaming with other complementary activities such as reading and learning how to do searches on the Internet. Gamers do much more than play games; they research technology, learn programming, read reviews of their next game, participate in online forums, and follow the latest news. These activities take a lot of skill, and this is why you should help your kids find their way around the Internet; once you teach them how to make positive use of it (the best way to write emails, how to find game and console reviews, etiquette for forums), you'll never have to worry about them again. This is a much better way to deal with the potential "danger" of the web; if you entrust your kids with freedom, they trust you in return.

Choosing and buying games is another important topic that will help regulate their playing time. We recommend a firm policy here; it's too easy to buy three or more games per week and end up not playing any of them. You don't want to teach your kids to spend all that money solely on games, either; it can become an expensive habit once they start working and making their own money.

We suggest that you give them one new game per month, regardless of good behavior, and let them buy two other used games with their own money. Here are the advantages of this strategy:

- It gives your kids a sense of safety; they know you support their decision to play games.
- It teaches them the need for research. It will soon be clear that if they only get one new game per month, it's essential for them to choose a great game instead of a bad one.
- The two used games allow them to have some independence and invest in their own hobby. Of course, you'd still need to approve the games they buy.
- Three games per month adds up to 36 games a year, the beginning of a nice game library. And it's not hard on the wallet, either, with $60 for the new game and at most $30 for the used ones (likely $15 for each or even less in the case of older releases).
- A limited number of new games forces your kids to actually play them to the end, which is much more beneficial than sampling a level or two and moving on to the next one.
- If they finish the game quickly, you can always sell it on eBay (best value but could take some time) or EB Games (lower trade-in value but immediate).
- And finally, make sure their new game is full of unlockables and hidden content. A game like that can last months instead of hours inside the console.

Save Money with GameFly

An alternative to purchasing games is GameFly, a rental service similar to Netflix (in which the consumer pays a basic fee for unlimited rentals). The service is by mail only (no downloads), but it's as speedy and reliable as Netflix and, since you can keep the game as long as you want (no late fees), it's a great way to save some money and try out new games at the same time. The most affordable plan (~$13/month) only allows for one game at a time. (The next step up—two games at a time—is priced around $22/month.)

Parent Snapshot

John Francis Whelpley

Occupation: Writer-Producer
(Skibberrean Productions, Inc.)
Location: Ventura, CA

John is a single father of a 16-year-old surfer son who loves video games. Working as a writer-producer for 30 years, John was raised Catholic and now plies his trade mainly in science fiction. He comes from a large Irish-American family.

- Family Profile: 16-year-old son
- Playtime: 1–3 hours per week with son
- Platforms: Xbox 360, PS2, PC
- Top Games: *Tony Hawk IV, Medal of Honor*
- Memorable Moment: "*Medal of Honor* got us not only into a 'watch my back, I'll watch yours' camaraderie, but it also allowed for my son (who wants little to do with Dad these days) to talk about history, sacrifice, what his grandfather did in the war, and why war and evil persist within the human condition."

Parent Snapshot

Steven Herrnstadt

Professor Art and Design, Iowa State University
VP of Business Development, Micoy Corp.
Ames, IA

Steven Herrnstadt has contributed to over 60 international and national exhibitions and papers in Moscow, Barcelona, and Australia. He owns a U.S. and a Japanese patent. While a project manager at EAI, he developed projects for the Smithsonian and Adler Planetarium.

→

> Steven has been teaching in computer graphics since 1981 in the areas of digital media, computer game development and design, modeling, rendering, and lighting.
>
> ■ Family Profile: Children 26, 23, 19
> ■ Playtime: 1–3 hours per week with kids
> ■ Platforms: PS2, PS, Genesis, PC, NES
> ■ "Games have changed so much since I last played them with my kids. Now that they are 'adults' and away from home, I am starting to play online multiplayer games to keep in touch and team up with them. We play 'side by side' but from a distance, as it were."

PLAYING SMART

If you begin to have weekly or even biweekly gaming sessions with your kids, you might see it as the best possible result brought on by this book. We agree that playing video games with your kids can be very fulfilling and certainly fun, but this is still far from the mountain top. There's a whole new level to reach within these gaming sessions.

Another way of gaming with your kids is actually not playing, but being in the same room. This is made possible when they trust that you won't disturb their playing. Hopefully, they will *want* you around when they play! You might be working on the laptop while they battle monsters onscreen, but your kids will know you can hear them and might want to talk. Whether they want to or not, their playing can unlock the unconscious in some ways, loosening their tongues, in other words. It will be common for your kids to "blurt out" things they wouldn't usually say aloud. This can be an excellent time to engage in conversation and efficiently deal with possible problems or questions.

Topics that may arise:

■ A teacher they don't get along with
■ A child at school that they "hate"
■ The difficulty of working as part of a team
■ Fear of getting hurt in sports
■ Self-image issues; feeling "ugly" or "dumb"
■ Early romantic interests or "crushes"
■ Trouble with reading
■ Dealing with frustrating challenges and obstacles
■ Bragging about how much better they are at the game than their brother/sister/friend

It's a long list, and it's by no means complete. The technique was partially developed by Anna Freud and Melanie Klein (1961, 1987) and came to be known as "play therapy": therapy through games. The theory behind it is that children will talk more easily and candidly if they are focused on a game or other immersive activity, granting the therapist access to their unconscious. Play therapy is not really therapy in the traditional sense. The official explanation is available on the BAPT web site (British Association of Play Therapists) at http://www.bapt.info/: "Play Therapy helps children understand muddled feelings and upsetting events that they haven't had the chance to sort out properly. Rather than having to explain what is troubling them, as adult therapy usually expects, children use play to communicate at their own level and at their own pace, without feeling interrogated or threatened."

> My kids and I have been playing video games together since they were old enough to hold a controller. Even when they were older and I was with my second wife in Ohio, the older kids and I would meet online every night to play *City of Heroes* together.
>
> —Guy P. Vance (customer service rep)

> A game is something we can play together, and it has become a great topic of conversation.
>
> —Patricia Dillon Sobczak (Administrator, Chapman University)

We're not advocating that you become a pseudo-therapist for your kids, but talking to them (or better yet, *listening* to them) during a gaming session can bring you a lot closer, and it will certainly help in dealing with complicated topics. This is gaming put to 100% efficiency!

YOUR INNER CHILD WANTS TO PLAY

As you can see, games can be a safe pathway to your child's inner universe. Gaming is the conduit between pre-schoolers and young adults, kids and parents. By utilizing the tips in this chapter, you will maximize the already significant potential of games, along with your relationship with your kids. More than having "game night," the tools introduced here can bring your family closer, all ages included. Remember—it's never too late to learn how to have fun together! In the next chapter, we will investigate the socialization aspects of games with particular emphasis on helping you take your first steps into the exciting world of online multiplayer gaming.

4 The Social Game

In This Chapter

- Interaction
- Communication
- Relationships
- Gaming Side Effects
- We're Gonna Need a Bigger Playground

While for a few decades interaction in games was confined to two players, it has now expanded to fuel a new social phenomenon. Instead of two siblings scrambling to compete in front of a 14-inch TV, there are now thousands of simultaneous players in the same virtual universe feuding for fame, money, items, or natural resources—or all of the above. The scope of games has expanded, too; a "single-player" approach can no longer suffice, since the focus has dramatically shifted from individual to group. Welcome to the 21st century!

Social psychology is the study of why and how individuals react to social interactions. In multiplayer games, social interactions are everywhere, from a rude Guild Leader in *World of Warcraft*, a Mustang driver going against traffic in *Forza Motorsport*, or a teammate covering you while you take the enemy flag back to your base. Through concepts developed by psychology, sociology, and semiotics, we are now able to have a better grasp of the mechanics behind the countless social interactions—found in both offline and online multiplayer games.

According to Webster, *socialization* is defined as (italics are ours):

1. The *adoption of the behavior patterns* of the surrounding culture.
2. The act of *meeting for social purposes.*

Although the game rules are obvious, and players get punished if they ignore them, social rules *cannot* be ignored. In order to preserve the social order, games employ a variety of mechanisms that range from booting players from a match to banning them forever from a server, common in PC games. On the console side, Xbox Live allows *player feedback* to be uploaded to Microsoft's servers, making unruly players *personas non grata* on an individual basis. (If you submit a negative feedback rating, the system will avoid putting you and that player in the same game from then on.) This and other features are directly related to the new possibilities brought about by connected, global gaming networks.

INTERACTION

Players engage in different forms of interaction with other players. The ways in which players interact depend on a number of factors: space (in-game, real-world, and physical space) and prior relationships between the players (peer or hierarchical). Let's take a look at a few types of interaction and how they all play a part in the way games are experienced.

A Society Ruled By . . . Rules

Game rules are based on millions of lines of code—not that different from social "codes of conduct." Unfortunately, we need these rules in order to co-exist in relative peace with the other six billion human beings on the planet. But rules are not bound to large social groups only; they also apply to our family and friends. Even the best of friends will end the friendship if a major rule is broken. Conversely, most of the events in a game are nothing more than an approximation of the social interactions of real life, and more than the code itself, they carry social rules of their own. There's a very good chance that we invented "play rules" in order to better understand (and cope with) the real ones!

IN-GAME, REAL-WORLD, AND PHYSICAL SPACE

Real-world interaction might include cursing your performance in a game; pleading with another player to tell you how to open a locked door; or even voice-chatting about current world events. Even though this might take place in-game, its context belongs to the real world. As a result, this kind of interaction breaks the fourth wall and takes away from the "being there" feeling traditionally associated with games. On the other hand, immersive (in-game) interactions occur within the context of the game; they depend on what's happening inside the game world itself. In a fighting game such as *Soul Calibur*, for example, punches and kicks can be considered forms of interaction! In a puzzle game such as *Lumines Live*, you make your opponent's playfield smaller by solving your side of the screen faster, thereby sending a clear message to your opponent.

Illustration by Ian Robert Vasquez

Interaction can happen within the game universe (in-game) or in the physical space in which the game is being currently played (such as in the living room). A good example is when you are playing a game with at least one other player in a physical space such as your living room, but you're also playing with other players online. Interactions in the physical space might consist of high-fives, pats on the back, and even pillow fights! Not surprisingly, purely physical interactions like these often depend on in-game events, and the performance of some players within the game (in-game) will sometimes affect their behavior in the living room (physical space).

PEERS AND PARENTS

When parents play games with their kids, they often have a tendency to steer toward a friendlier, more casual mode, putting hierarchy aside. This can work by diminishing the distance between parents and their children, but it can also undermine parental authority by bleeding into non-game situations. It might feel like you and your kids are pals while playing games, but this isn't the case in reality! Always preserve the parent-child dynamic; just soften it slightly. This will make your kids feel safer (even if they might say otherwise), while also allowing them to fully enjoy playing with you.

We know you love your kids, but you are not their pals! Illustration by Ian Robert Vasquez

In peer relationships, often a dominant child "takes over" and becomes the effective leader. First seen in primates, these leaders became known as *queen bees* for girls and *alpha males* for boys. It's common to observe peaceful playing when all agree on who the leader is; however, if the leader is challenged, arguments and fights might take place until balance is reached again. No one can guarantee that playing will always be peaceful, but we can nonetheless make sure that our kids are ready to face this challenging social landscape. Through talks and real-life examples, such as the way parents behave in similar situations, our children can learn more effective ways to deal with the teasing and fighting typical of these scenarios.

> I always enjoy spending time with my daughter, but as she gets older, she'd rather spend time with her friends instead. Luckily, I'm considered one of the "cool" parents on the block because I love to play video games, and there's always a crowd of kids over. Now that we've added the Wii, our house is even more popular. It's great to see the kids having clean fun, joking and laughing, and enjoying the experience. Plus, we get to make fun of them when they get too goofy.
>
> —Aaron Marks (Composer/Sound Designer/Parent)

COMMUNICATION

Games have only recently been considered part of communication media. Even though one-way communication mechanisms such as broadcasting (radio and television) have been considered media for decades, we feel that games are much more powerful communication media, especially since they all have the potential for multi-way communication through online and LAN-based play. For *media*, let's look at another set of definitions, courtesy of Webster (italics are ours):

1. A means or instrumentality for *communicating*.
2. The *surrounding environment*; "fish require an aqueous medium."
3. An intervening substance through which *signals can travel as a means for communication*.

Video games satisfy all three definitions, yet they weren't traditionally regarded as media. Electronic games were pigeonholed early on as toys, not necessarily as a means of communication. They were also considered more of a "loner's pastime," without any connection to other human beings, even though 2–4 player games have been around for decades.

Today, things have changed. More than ever, games are recognized as ideal platforms for communication, integrating the features of the telephone (voice), television (images), and networked computers (shared applications). Far from the solitude of playing alone in a dark bedroom, online games are capable of giving players the experience of real, live communication with human beings. Let's take a look at the many ways you can communicate in a game.

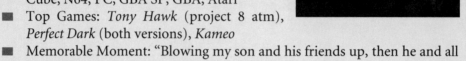

Parent Snapshot

Tommy Smith

Student/parent (Art Institute Online)
Ridge Farm, IL

- Family Profile: 14-year-old son
- Playtime: 1–3 hours per week with his son
- Platforms: Xbox 360, Xbox, PS2, Wii, Game-Cube, N64, PC, GBA SP, GBA, Atari
- Top Games: *Tony Hawk* (project 8 atm), *Perfect Dark* (both versions), *Kameo*
- Memorable Moment: "Blowing my son and his friends up, then he and all his friends teaming up against me to blow me up!"

INFORMATION EXCHANGE

One of the most basic uses of communication is the exchange of information. In games, this can happen in many different ways:

The redesigned headset for Xbox Live—this time, with wireless technology. Microsoft Corporation

- **Voice over IP (VoIP):** Chat!
  Most modern consoles allow for voice conversations between gamers. Both in-game chats and private chats are available; the system is very similar to a telephone conference. The in-game chat (a voice channel) is especially interesting because it allows everyone to talk at the same time. Common uses for VoIP are better coordination for team-based games and the sharing of strategies and cheats among players.

- **Text messages:** Type!
  Text messages are common in massively multiplayer online games (MMOGs). Some players can't use VoIP (due to accessibility issues or lack of VoIP functionality), so they are forced to rely on text to communicate with other players. Since text can't carry intonation and other subtle cues present in speech, misunderstandings can become a problem.

- **Body language and gestures:** Act!
  MMOGs make body language-based communication possible, with preset movements easily accessible through the game's interface. *World of Warcraft* contains all kinds of interesting gestures, conveying fear, courage, mockery, and even flirting. The animation is still somewhat stiff, but the idea of using body language inside a game is very enticing. When body movements, voice, and text work together, players can fully become their characters.

- **In-game markings:** Tag!
  Some game universes can be altered in simple ways by players, allowing them to leave visual messages; an online multiplayer first-person shooter (FPS), for example, might allow players to "write" by shooting bullets at a wall. This is just one of many ways players can leave their marks in the game world.

- **Character personalization:** Customize!
  Another way to transmit a message is to have customized costumes and items. In *Forza Motorsport*, the in-game customization tools give players the ability to write on their cars with the use of basic shapes. Multi-user environments such as *Second Life* allow player-designed costumes to be uploaded to the game and worn by their avatars.

- **Web forums:** Post!
  Most games have official forums that, although outside the game, represent a hub for communication among players. Microsoft's Xbox.com hosts forums about every single game in their catalog and also includes Xbox Live's *gamertag* and other details, such as *gamerscore* and games the player is currently playing, in each player's posts. Player forums are the perfect place to ask questions, complain, form clans (organized teams that play against other teams), and request support from the developers.

Parent Snapshot

Brian Reynolds

CEO (Big Huge Games)
Timonium, MD

A 15-year industry veteran, Brian Reynolds is recognized as one of the industry's most talented and productive game designers. Honored by *PC Gamer* magazine as one of 25 "Game Gods," Reynolds has masterminded the design of an unbroken stream of hit strategy games, including the multimillion-selling *Civilization II, Alpha Centauri*, and *Rise of Nations*, as well as such new games as *Rise of Legends* and *Catan Live*. Highly regarded for his mastery of the art of programming, Reynolds' dual specialty gives him the substantial advantage of being able to bring his own visions to life. He has built a reputation for finely tuned strategy games. As CEO of Big Huge Games, Brian concentrates on the creative side of the company, devoting most of his time to hands-on development of new game concepts and prototypes.

- Family Profile: Two boys, ages 11 and 9
- Playtime: One hour every now and then (with his kids, who get to play one hour per day if they're "good" and have all their work done)
- Platforms: Xbox 360, PC
- Top three games: *Marvel Alliance, Lego Star Wars*
- "[My kids] got to about level 45 [in *World of Warcraft*]. They'd be getting instance expeditions together and doing reasonably well at it. Obviously, at ages 10 and 8 (at the time), there was a limit to how well they were going to do, but it taught them a few useful social lessons."

NEGOTIATION

Playing games with other human beings will always involve a lot of negotiation, such as what to do about team killing, how long the match should be, and which map should be chosen. Every time multiple interests are at stake, negotiation is necessary. In games, this usually happens when players on a team decide to "go solo," ignoring the rules of the game to the point that the experience of others is affected.

World of Warcraft **party enjoying the view.** World of Warcraft ® image provided courtesy of Blizzard Entertainment, Inc.

In a game such as *World of Warcraft (WoW)*, a *noob* (new player, or *newbie*) might attack every monster on a path, attracting a lot of unwanted attention to the party. More experienced players will have to negotiate with the feisty noob to ensure that the new player behaves as part of the team. More than anything, it's in everyone's interest to have the noob as an asset. However, if the player does not cooperate, other players will be forced to either kill the player on the spot every time (a last resort in a game such as *WoW*) or report him to the Game Master (GM), a god-like player who rules over limited areas of the game world.

Negotiation can also happen between human players and non-player characters (NPCs). Although very limited in scope, artificial intelligence is still not sophisticated enough; negotiations take place with the use of multiple answers for the NPC's questions, special items (which might evoke a certain reaction from the NPC), and pressure from a group of players (which can alter the NPC's behavior based on the number of players in a group). Player-NPC negotiation is still in its early stages, but the presence of human players in all MMOGs more than makes up for it!

Team Killing (TK)

Team killing involves turning against your own team in game modes such as *Team Death Match* or *Capture the Flag*. Team killers might decide to "have fun alone" and begin arbitrarily killing members of their own team instead of their enemies. Some might engage in team kill for kicks or perhaps because they don't really like being on the team.

Most players abhor team killing because it makes enjoying the game experience difficult. In a multiplayer game, eight or more people depend on a server to host the matches. Everyone accepts most of the default rules, but some of them can be *negotiated*. Team killing is usually very easily disabled by the host, but curiously, people insist on leaving it active in the game. Despite the fact that some players decide to vent their frustrations this way, servers still leave team killing "on" by default! Why? The way we see it, players want to give the potential team killer the choice of being part of a team or not. They want these players to face a moral dilemma every time they play the game!

Curiously, some developers feel that players who don't play by the rules (such as TKers) actually help inject reality into the gameplay mix. Many feel a game has more balance, unpredictability, and real-life elements due to these troublesome individuals.

MISUNDERSTANDINGS

Remember those old 2D side-scrolling fighting games such as *Streets of Rage* and *Final Fight* (where you and a partner could fight common enemies and rid the streets of thugs, gangsters, and crime lords)? These games were both evolutions of *Double Dragon*, which pioneered simultaneous co-op play and the "beat 'em up" subgenre, and their attempt to solve the rising crime wave through more violence was an absurd proposition that had a lot to do with comic books from the '80s (like *The Punisher*) and the Charles Bronson franchise, *Death Wish*. Beat 'em up games traditionally allow for co-op play: you and friends can rid the city of crime together, fighting the baddies on the same screen. Sounds straightforward, right? Well, sometimes your teammate becomes an "accidental enemy." This is usually caused by misunderstandings during play. Let's say you are clearing the left side of the screen and your friend is taking care of the right side. Suddenly your friend loses a target, invades *your* side of the screen, and lands a punch on you. Your friend didn't do this on purpose, and part of you knows that, but you punch him back anyway.

With co-op fighting games, making enemies out of friends could happen 8–10 times per game, usually due to a misunderstanding. The first move is always an accident, but it can lead to a real fight that bleeds into the real world. Despite the fact that your friend is sitting right next to you on the couch, and you can speak freely at any moment, it's often difficult to understand what would motivate your friend to punch you instead of the enemy! Another issue here is that players can get so immersed in the game experience that they've got their minds in "cyberspace" even when they're sharing physical space with their friends and co-players.

In Xbox Live, trash talk is as ubiquitous as players under the age of 15. Anything can instigate conflict: bad performance, team killing, disrespecting the rules, not talking to anyone, talking too much, not speaking English, or even singing during team play. Can you imagine playing with people from all over the world (all languages included) with only a low-quality voice connection between players? Chaos ensues.

Games will always contain a lot of misunderstandings. Since the game is already a complex activity, it's very easy to misunderstand the "people on the other side of the screen" and get angry at them. With games, communicating properly has turned into a major challenge, and the fact that most multiplayer games are in real time doesn't help.

Players today are learning a new form of etiquette, just as people had to learn a certain *netiquette* to send emails or participate in chats in the early days of the Internet. Team players should follow certain protocols so that they work with and not against each other. The truth is that we need to learn how to communicate in a *much more effective way* to play games online, a "feature" of gaming that many didn't foresee 10 years ago.

COOPERATION

As discussed in Chapter 3, "You and Your Kids," one of the reasons for playing games together is cooperation. Now let's tackle how cooperation works in-game and in real life. Cooperation feels great because it's an expression of one of the most elevated human traits, camaraderie. Fighting together for a common goal is among the most incredible human experiences, resulting in a sense of purpose. Even if defeated, the effort is enough to transform those who fought together, as we've seen before, from the battlefield to the Olympics.

In games, cooperation is now second nature since most games are built with it in mind. *Gears of War,* for example, features a *hot-join* co-op mode that allows a friend to jump in right in the middle of a single-player campaign. Clear examples of cooperation within a team can be found in team-based FPSs such as *Halo 2* and the *Call of Duty* series.

Gears of War has a robust co-op mode. Epic Games

I've noticed that my son is likely to take a chance on trusting players in team play, yet not be overly disappointed or even very surprised if they let him down. "You can always find another partner and start another game," he says. In that regard, he's teaching me about patience, since I would be extremely annoyed if things like that happened to me.

—John Scott G ["The G-Man"] (Producer/composer, Golosio Publishing)

Other kids come over and play games with my son all the time. They seem to like the road race style games the most outside of the shooter games. What is remarkable is that there is very little fighting over who gets to play the game. If it's a good game, they like to be spectators as well.

—John Francis Whelpley (writer-producer)

COMPETITION

Online gaming is often rough, unnerving, and not for the faint of heart. Matches involving upwards of 40 players can be frantic, even chaotic, and might induce a testosterone overdose (regardless of gender)! Imagine a 40-person gladiatorial match occurring every two seconds; that's the scope of most online games. Competition has always fueled gaming, and with online multiplayer games, its effects are much more visible.

Resistance: Fall of Man has amazing graphics and 40-player multiplayer madness. Sony Computer Entertainment America

The need for competition is not as bad as it seems. We owe to competition most of the technological advances now seen in cars and computers. Sports (America's favorite pastime) would involve mere physical exercise without the goal of winning. For more detail on why competition is so prevalent in games, see Chapter 3.

Games enhance the drive for competition in several interesting ways:

- **Safety:** Car racing, gun fights, even football are much safer (and saner) within a game. Of course, when you opt to play a sport with a game console, you lose the physical exercise. At the same time, it'll be that much harder to break an arm or a leg! The sole exception is the Nintendo Wii, because the Wiimote allows for a certain degree of movement.
- **Accessibility:** There are many accessories on the market that allow the physically disabled to play video games. Accessories can be mouth-controlled, voice-operated, or can rely on a simplified controller in order to allow virtually anyone to play a game, regardless of physical limitations.
- **Available competition:** Pro football players can't expect to play against one million other football players during a single lifetime. Gamers can. The addition of online connectivity brings an almost unlimited supply of opponents, many much more skilled than gamers themselves. The variety in competition allows for games of all skill levels, and it makes it easier to set up large matches.

■ **Visibility:** If we are on top, we want people to know that! We want them to see our performance, live. Modern games allow that through the miracle of the Internet. *Project Gotham Racing 3* has Gotham TV, a "channel" that broadcasts races live, 24/7. This is a major boost to competition since it rewards the best drivers with instant celebrity status.

Competition might seem harsh and sometimes rather intense, but it can also be very positive if at first confined to the game world. Knowing how to deal with competition in-game translates to more success in real-life competitive situations, allowing kids to become the best at what they love.

> There is always a sense of friendly competition between my kids and their friends—seeing who can get further in the game or who has the "better" character in a RPG. For our family, video games are a social time, spent with both family and friends.
>
> —Guy P. Vance (customer service)

> My daughter enjoys being competitive with the other kids and likes that I "helped" her get good at the games. Nintendo 64's *Waverace* was one of our favorites!
>
> —Aaron Marks (composer/sound designer/parent)

Parent Snapshot

JoAnna Almasude

Full-time faculty, Media Arts & Animation
(Art Institute Online)
Florence, SC

JoAnna is a professional artist and has been exhibiting her work internationally for over 20 years. She also teaches college-level art courses online and onground. Born JoAnna Pettit in 1964 in Marietta, Ohio, JoAnna grew up on a farm in southeastern Ohio before studying art at Marietta College, Ohio University's School of Fine Arts, and then in London. After graduating from Ohio University in 1993 with a Masters of Fine Arts in Painting, JoAnna traveled to Morocco with her husband Amar (originally from Nador, Morocco), working with him on projects dealing with the language of the indigenous people in North Africa, including the creation of a computer program that brought the formerly unwritten language of Tamazight to print. She traveled extensively in Morocco and

→

researched the culture, politics, and condition of the Moroccan people. While there, JoAnna began her current fine art series about the people of Morocco. JoAnna and her family currently reside in Florence, SC.

- Family Profile: Children ages 11,15, and 18
- Playtime: 1–3 hours per week with kids
- Platforms: PC
- Top Games: *Chicken Invaders, Robot Arena, Feeding Frenzy, Ricochet*
- "My son always wants to be the winner!"

ARGUMENT AND DEBATE: ENGAGE!

Almost every time a group of people discuss issues such as "what the best map is" or "which combination of skills results in a stronger character," they're debating or arguing extremely common communication modes.

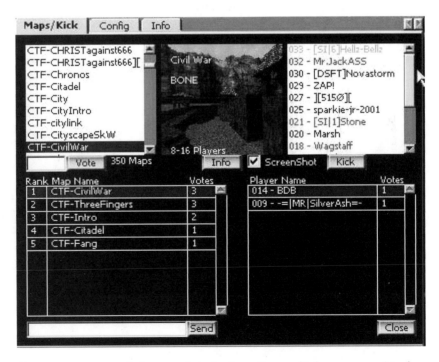

Players can vote on their map of choice in online multiplayer games (mod from *Unreal Tournament* shown). Epic Games

During in-game chat, game-specific arguments can occur, but debates about current events might also pop up in games that might have nothing to do with the topics. As a result, it's also feasible that, through chats and text messages, we hear about new topics and takes on subjects we might not have considered. Have you ever heard something said in-game and immediately rushed to a computer to Google it? Games spread knowledge through argument and debate.

Violence and Aggression: Deal with It

Let's face it: People get angry. It's a human trait, portrayed from Greek mythology to the latest blockbuster from Hollywood. The problem is that, when people get angry, they might also get violent. Games have an amazing (and seemingly ignored) ability to function as an escape valve for such extremes of emotion. The official name for this phenomenon, as put forth by researchers Feschbach and Singer in 1971, is the *catharsis theory*. We've seen it time and time again: A young kid is really angry at something (or someone), but after just half-an-hour of gaming, he's calm enough to talk about it. By *acting* on his anger (instead of just watching violent TV), the kid releases the tension he has gathered inside. Of course, *social learning* theorists would indicate otherwise: Some researchers speculate that gaming teaches antisocial behavior to kids, showing them the ways of violence and disregard for human life. What have you observed? Do your kids calm down after some frantic onscreen action? Or do they try to replicate what they see?

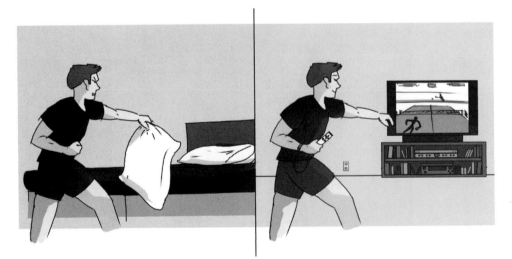

Linden Lab

More often, the catharsis theory stands correct. Until now, no other method has been able to address this anger in such an effective way. Anger and frustration are feelings that can bottle up inside us, often because we can't necessarily address our anger when we're ready to; perhaps the person we're angry with is not available, or perhaps we don't have enough time for a lengthy talk. In situations like this, games allow those feelings to be expressed immediately (in a safe environment), much like the classic "cushion punch," "stomping rug," or even "primal scream" advice of the 1970s. The release of negative feelings into a game world protects both the individual and society.

Games and Emotional Health

When children are experiencing anger or sadness, some games can be used to teach them to deal with their feelings in a constructive manner. Here are a few tips:

1. Choose a *single-player game*. If you choose multiplayer, you might end up mistreating other players.
2. Pick a simple first-person shooter (FPS) or action game. Killing monsters in *Doom* or *Quake* might make you feel a lot better. For kids, many games display "cartoon violence" (such as *Ratchet & Clank*), which is kid-safe. On the other hand, a slower-paced game such as the role-playing game (RPG) *Oblivion* is also known to calm people down. Puzzle and other "mental" games also engage the left side of the brain, helping you to keep your emotions in check.
3. Unleash your anger *in-game* only. In an FPS, you can destroy objects and defeat enemies. In a racing game, keep your lap times as low as possible by balancing speed with precision. Focus on the perfect driving line, speed, and braking—pushing your car to its limits. And always try to avoid the temptation of throwing the controller at the wall!
4. Focus on perfecting your game by switching from "impulse-release" to "impulse-control." Attempting fast laps in *Gran Turismo 4* puts you in a different mode, where using your energy in a controlled way becomes a priority. This will convert your anger into usable energy and then channel it into an achievable objective. Mastering a game will also inject a sense of accomplishment into the situation, which can immediately turn your mood around.

Public opinion constantly demonizes video games. It has been that way since *Death Race* in 1976 (inspired by the cult sci-fi film, *Death Race 2000*), the very first violent game—almost immediately banned from arcades due to its subject matter, which involved running over "stick figures" in the road to gain points. Some assert that games influence kids negatively, making them more violent and less apt at school. Of course, dozens of studies have attempted to make that connection. This might remind you of public opinion on violence in both music and television programs popular in the '60s and '70s—only *games* are now the "new media" focus. A Danish report published in 2003 entitled "Playing with Fire: How Computer Games Affect the Player" *(http://resources.eun.org/insafe/datorspel_Playing_with.pdf)* contains a very interesting distinction between the various schools of thought found in the scientific community.

Active User Theories

Active user theories (AUTs) focus on the user experience. They include semiotic, anthropological, and sociological studies. In short, AUTs study subjects in their own environments and make careful observations on what kinds of experiences the subjects seek and their participation in these experiences. AUTs assume that *it's the individual user who defines the impact and strength of the media.*

Active Media Theories

Active media theories (AMTs) give media the power to transform users. According to AMTs, *certain media have palpable effects on users, regardless of user interaction.* AMTs study subjects in laboratories, and because they look at games from the outside, AMT researchers usually lack enough knowledge of the games they attempt to study.

The AMT that best applies to gaming is the catharsis theory (mentioned earlier in this chapter), in part because it may be the only AMT that actually takes the user experience into consideration. AUTs, on the other hand, have the benefit of looking at gaming without any kind of prejudice, allowing them to dive into the true potential of the media. Researchers and sociologists in particular have been writing innovative books on the topic with exponents such as Steven Johnson (*Everything Bad Is Good for You*) and James Paul Gee (*What Video Games Have to Teach Us About Learning and Literacy*) leading the pack.

This is just the beginning of the *real* research on the impact of games. We understand that an AMT approach is, at most, inadequate to deal with games since they are part of interactive media and have changed drastically in the last few years. We believe that AUTs are most capable of measuring the results from gaming, since they focus on the way players (including parents and children) deal with games instead of assuming that each individual has no critical ability whatsoever and, even worse, supposing that subjects behave naturally while being observed and analyzed inside a laboratory environment. Modern AUTs point out that there is no causal connection between violent behavior and games.

RELATIONSHIPS

Many types of relationships are formed during games. Let's look at the journey that might be taken by new players starting out in a multiplayer game. What types of relationships can be formed as players take that "long journey from noob to elite"?

STARTING OUT AS A NOOB

When you play a game for the first time, you are known as a *newbie* or *noob*. Being a noob isn't easy. All kinds of things happen to noobs, from being *hunted* (noobs are easy to beat) to teasing and abuse from veteran players. This is nothing new: Human beings have traditionally participated in hazing and heckling new recruits as rites of passage. There are moments in a game when you haven't the faintest idea how to play or what to do. That's what makes you a noob: You lack the basic knowledge of the game world's rules and strategies, and you have little to no experience within that world. Nevertheless, since no one is ever an elite player in the very beginning, being a noob is nothing more than a passing phase.

Everyone starts out as a *noob*. Illustration by Ian Robert Vasquez

In highly competitive FPS games such as *Halo 2* and *Counter-Strike*, closed clans have no room for noobs. In fact, they actually require tough *auditions* for any players who wish to join them! This kind of hardcore gaming, fueled by kids with a lot of time on their hands, might make some games very unfriendly to noobs. Playing *Counter-Strike* for the first time can be traumatic, to say the least.

The best bet for noobs is to find training grounds inside their game of choice. *Halo 2* has "practice" zones where inexperienced players meet and get better together, away from the preying eyes of the skilled. Not surprisingly, this mixture between a noob island and a mentoring program is the most effective way to get better in an FPS.

Best Noob Survival Practices

1. **Know your game***: Before you attempt online play, learn the basic rules of the game in single-player mode. Save yourself the burden of having to learn complex rules and movements with 15 other players screaming at you.

2. **Practice***: When you feel comfortable with the basic rules and gameplay, it's time to play the online version, but only in practice mode at first, preferably with other noobs who will empathize with you.

3. **Respect the rules:** This goes without saying, but some people get into an online match and decide to play their own version of the game. It just makes everyone mad; your creativity can be better used elsewhere.

4. **Announce your status:** If you are a noob, say it aloud to others. Warn them of your "noob" status. You'll be better treated.

5. **Apologize if necessary:** When needed, say you're sorry: If you team kill by accident, apologize immediately and avoid that player for the rest of the match if possible. You don't want others to misunderstand your action—thinking you TK'd on purpose. Later on, do your best not to injure that same player *again*!

6. **Be polite:** Saying "good game" at the end of a match is a sign of nobility between gamers. When necessary, ask about the rules. Always focus on teamwork. You'll go far if other players see you as someone who can take orders; that is, until you start giving them!

Basic FPS Vocabulary

Even if you're a noob, it's important to have a little knowledge of slang commonly used in multiplayer games. Here are some need-to-know words:

1. **Owned:** In games, you either "own" or "get owned." So if someone killed you with a headshot, you got *owned*. On the other hand, if you somehow managed to kill someone with a pistol (a weak weapon in most games) you just *owned* them . . . badly. Similarly, *owns* is a synonym of *dominates*. Someone might say their team *owns* or that the M1 Garand in *Call of Duty 3 own all.*
2. **Camping:** The habit of staying in the same place during the whole game, killing enemies as they show up, is known as *camping*. The word is kind of old-fashioned nowadays, but a sniper who doesn't move will be called a *camper*. Be warned: Campers are traditionally associated with noobs; you'll never leave your noob status behind if you camp.
3. **Spawn killing:** When someone dies, they need to *respawn* in order to get back in the game. Most games have defined spawn areas, and it's not hard to figure them out. *Spawn killing* (or camping) involves going to these areas and killing other players as they respawn. Being pigeonholed as a spawn killer is not a good idea; this also guarantees perpetual noob status.
4. **Teabagging:** The act of *teabagging* is jokingly used to humiliate players in certain games (usually FPSs). A player gets teabagged when the opponent repeatedly crouches up and down over their dead body, usually right after killing them. It's a move designed to tease, humiliate, and challenge all at the same time. (Chances are, your kids will have no clue why teabagging is known outside of the game world as an obscure sex act, but you can Google it anyway.)

We play cooperative games, where we play on the same side against the enemy. This sometimes includes my wife playing on our side, as well. Usually she drives a truck to take the three boys to the battle. Sometimes she commands a transport ship to move us when we are in tanks. I'm usually the commander, and the boys learn about discipline and following orders, while also figuring out how to convince Dad to use their great ideas. Other times, one of them will be in command of a mission. It develops their problem solving skills, as well as showing them how to make logical and sensible arguments. They sometimes learn that mistakes can be costly (in a safe environment), but indecision can sometimes be even costlier. They learn how to take responsibility for their decisions. The online aspect of the games also teaches them interpersonal skills—especially when they witness some of the bad behaviors of the cheaters, *griefers*, and trolls.

—Kenneth C. Finney (Author/Instructor)

Even though *SOCOM: Navy Seals* is rated for mature players, I allow my oldest son to play online . . . when I am online with him. I make it a point to explain to him that the online gaming community is relatively unsupervised, and it is an environment where fellow players can and often do exhibit poor and/or inappropriate social behavior. Most of the players that fall within this category are only behaving in this manner as a direct emulation of substandard adult behavior and/or as a way to freely interact with a social community in a way that they feel cannot be monitored or regulated by their own parent, therefore assuming they will suffer no consequences for their inappropriate behavior. My son is usually very reserved and prefers not to verbally interact with other online players unless he is addressed personally, but he revels in the idea that pitted against human adversaries he can self-evaluate his own ability to compete and gain validation as a competitor.

—Jacques Montemoino (Gideon Games, LLC)

Parent Snapshot

Cindi Lash

Longtime news reporter and game critic, formerly with the Pittsburgh Post-Gazette)
Pittsburgh, PA

As a news reporter for the *Pittsburgh Post-Gazette,* Cindi covered regional and breaking news for the local news department, but she also reviewed games and wrote about game development for the arts and entertainment department.

- Family Profile: Two sons, ages 14 and 18
- Playtime: 4–6 hours per week with kids (spouse plays 1–3 hours per week with kids)
- Platforms: Xbox 360, Xbox, PS3, PS2, Wii, GameCube, N64, Genesis, PC, PSP, DS, Game Boy Micro, GBA SP, GBA
- Top Games: *Guitar Hero II*, NHL 07 (360) or *NHL 2K7* (PS3), *Elder Scrolls IV: Oblivion or Gears of War*
- "As my kids get older, we have had some trash-talking, and I have quickly and firmly jumped in to dial it back. I keep our game systems in our family and game rooms, where I can clearly hear what is being said and can step in if/when I'm not comfortable with what I'm hearing. Setting standards and consequences upfront, and enforcing them if they are broken, also has been effective. The game goes off immediately when the conduct lines are crossed."

My son is an achiever and would prefer to use a voice system, such as ventrillo, over typing. He is facile with chat systems but prefers to use voice when he can. We have stressed etiquette and respect in all game interactions, so the kids are all trained to say "please" and "thank-you" just as they would in real life.

—Donna K. Kidwell (commercialization consultant)

We are in a guild, so the kids can chat online with *guildees*. Online gaming has improved their typing skills. (And they are polite!)

—Denice McLaughlin (parent/student)

LEVELING UP

Eventually you'll cease to be a noob and graduate to player with some experience. Things get a lot more comfortable when no one screams at you any more. Now, your challenge becomes *not calling anyone else a noob*. Let's face facts: The only reason this sort of heckling still exists is that ex-noobs take their newfound skills and experience and proceed to treat new noobs the way they used to be treated. If people would just grow up and be more accepting, this behavior would slowly disappear. Here's hoping that, as the average gamer gets older, courtesy and respect will become more common in multiplayer games.

Contrary to what some believe about video games, there can be some good interaction with others that perhaps will only grow. With games such as *Guitar Hero*, online play, and the entire Wii system that ask for more interaction, the lonely kid stuck in a chair playing a video game is a thing of the past.

—Tommy Smith (student)

THE FRIENDS YOU MAKE

One of the greatest things about the multiplayer game experience is that many friendships can begin and be nurtured throughout play. Playing together is already something that friends do, so the game environment makes the formation of new friendships that much easier. Friendship can occur in two different ways.

Online-Bound Friendships

Online-bound friendships are those that began and continue to remain online. This is especially true of friendships formed through Xbox Live, consisting often of nothing more than a gamertag, an icon, and a recognizable voice through a headset. Online-bound friends might evolve into real-life friends, but it is a lot more common for them to remain online only, since most people live in distant locations throughout the world.

A "friends list" on Xbox Live. Microsoft Corporation

We have activated the Xbox Live account with *Tony Hawk, Smackdown vs Raw*, and a couple other games. My son has made several Xbox Live friends and speaks to them frequently when he can through the headset.

—Tommy Smith (student, Art Institute Online)

My oldest son plays *World of Warcraft* habitually and has for some time now. He has friends as far away as Australia and plays with them every night as if they were buddies just next door.

—Guy P. Vance (customer service)

My job involves a lot of massively multiplayer online games, and so the kids are interested in those games. But they don't get involved with other players. They're not mature enough to handle relationships with adults; it wouldn't be good for them or fair to the adults (who reasonably expect a competent partner in adventure, not a 10-year-old newbie).

—David Ladyman (Publications Manager, IMGS, Inc.)

Real-World Friendships

Some *real-world friendships* (those that are formed in the real world) can extend into the online world. For example, high school or college friends might start playing together online. Some couples have been known to play massively multiplayer online games with each other on separate computers in the same physical space! One of the authors turned a real-world acquaintance into a friend by extending the relationship online.

> When other kids come over to play games, they often take turns and watch [each] other, often using "cheats" to perform outrageous stunts for mutual amusement.
>
> —Greg Costikyan (CEO, Manifesto Games)

> When other kids come over, they focus on competitive and long game play. They try to beat the game in one sitting.
>
> —Joseph Welsh (student)

Even though Luis and Paulo were part of different circles in high school (Luis hung out with the brains, while Paulo hung out with the "bad boys"), they discovered one day that they were both car aficionados and were addicted to the racing game *Need for Speed*. Luis and Paulo found a way to play the game online and started racing against each other on their PCs after class. Even the "bad boys" Paulo hung out with discovered that Luis was "cool" because they also liked the game, and they all became friends. The story is a perfect example of a friendship that goes online and, through gaming, becomes deeper and more meaningful. Co-workers go through the same: They see each other at work, exchange nametags, and later meet online to play together.

> When friends come over, they sit next to each other on the couch or floor playing their individual handheld games, sometimes showing each other what just happened in their game or asking each other for tips.
>
> —Rosanne Welch (freelance writer/college instructor)

> The other kids come over to play on our dance mat. My daughter enjoys the interaction and social skills that develop while playing games with other children. It helps her learn discipline and develop social skills.
>
> —Dennis J. Jirkovsky (instructor)

> My son has most of the current platforms and a large TV, so his friends are over here a lot to play games!
>
> —Patricia Dillon Sobczak (administrator)

Many times I come home and there is a room full of kids. Some hate to lose and never want to pass the controller. Others talk tall and think they can't be beat, and some don't want to try for fear of losing. But they all have fun . . . and whine when it is time to stop!

—Travis Ogurek (parent and student)

On occasion, we will host a *Wii Sports* competition and invite friends over. It's a very active event that's usually followed by popcorn and a movie. Everyone has a wonderful time.

—Donna K. Kidwell (commercialization consultant)

Parent Snapshot

Gordon Walton

Game Developer/Studio Director
(BioWare Austin)
Austin, TX

Gordon Walton has been authoring games and managing game development since 1977. Prior to BioWare, he was Vice President, Executive Producer, and Studio Manager at Sony Online Entertainment in Austin, working on an unannounced product and *Star Wars Galaxies*. Gordon was also Vice President and Executive Producer of *The Sims Online* at Electronic Arts/Maxis, and he held the same position for Origin Systems managing *Ultima Online*. Gordon also served as Senior Vice President and General Manager of Kesmai Studios, where he oversaw the development of several MMOGs, including *Air Warrior* and *Multiplayer Battletech*. Gordon has owned and managed two development companies and was development manager for Three-Sixty Pacific and Konami of America, Inc. He has personally developed over 30 games and has overseen the development of more than 200 games.

- Family Profile: Children ages 8 and 6
- Playtime: 1–3 hours per week with kids
- Platforms: PS2, GameCube, PC, DS, GBA SP
- Top Games: *BattleFront II, World of Warcraft, Bejeweled*
- "When other kids come over and play games, their behavior can be best described as 'cooperative strategizing.'"

The entire neighborhood wants to have sleepovers here. Sometimes, we have five or six kids in the house—and that's not for a party! They love the Wii!

—Denice McLaughlin (parent/student)

We have many games and game machines, so we get lots of kids over to play games. This is in Japan, where the DS is king of the industry—so typically all the kids bring their DSs with them and compare their progress in the current popular games they all own, taking turns playing each others' games. Then other groups split off, mostly to play party-type games in groups of four on the GameCube in the kids' room—or single-player or one-on-one games on the Xbox 360 in the living room. They also like to watch me play the "grown-up games" or "American games" on the 360 more so than playing those games themselves. I think this is partly because they find many of the games I play intimidating, but also because it's apparently great fun to laugh at an adult when he loses/crashes/dies in a video game.

—Colin Mack (Project Manager, THQ)

Parent Snapshot

Jim Greenall

Animatronics designer/fabricator/puppeteer
Simi Valley, CA

Jim is a 40-year-old father who builds animatronic characters for the entertainment industry and puppeteers them as a member of the Screen Actors Guild. In his home, he has an original *Pac-Man* cocktail table that has been modified to include several other *Pac-Man* games. He also has an original *Rip-Off* game that was one of his favorites when he was a kid.

- Family Profile: Four daughters: Julia (17), Jamie (14), Allyson (12), and Amelia (8)
- Playtime: 1–3 hours every 3 months
- Platforms: PS, GameCube, DS, 2 full arcade machines (*Pac-Man / Rip-Off*)
- Top Games: *Mario Party 5*, *Mario Kart: Double Dash*, *Muppet Racing*, *Tetris* (2 players), *Bomber Man* (4 players)
- "When the cousins come over, the games come out!"

Parent Snapshot

Janet Wilcox

Author/instructor (UCLA Extension)
Los Angeles, CA

Janet Wilcox was the voice of E! Network's *Hollywood & Divine: Beauty Secrets Revealed* and AMC's *Nicole Kidman: An American Cinematheque Tribute.* Janet also played opposite Brian Benben in the movie *Mortal Sins* and opposite Susan Saint James in *Kate & Allie.* As a writer, producer, and director, Janet worked on major promotional campaigns for HBO and also promoted programs on The History Channel. She directed promo segments with Keith Carradine for the HBO series *Deadwood.* While at HBO, she also directed segments with celebrities such as Jerry Seinfeld, Martin Mull, Colleen Dewhurst, William Petersen, Kate Capshaw, Sugar Ray Leonard, Sam Kinison, and Gladys Knight. Janet received her master's degree in communication from the Annenberg School of Communication at the University of Pennsylvania, and she has taught "Sources of the Modern Cinema" with Amos Vogel, one of the original founders of the New York Film Festival. She also taught at Marymount Manhattan College, Heyman Talent, and the SAG Conservatory. Janet currently teaches a studio voiceover class at UCLA Extension in Los Angeles. She is also writing a book, *The Game Is Never Over: Winning Strategies for Voiceover.*

- Family Profile: 16-year-old son
- Playtime: Doesn't play games with son
- Platforms: Xbox, PS2, GameCube, Dreamcast, PSP
- "When friends come over and play games, there's 'macho talk' when someone scores and so on. Sometimes, one kid will play alone while friends do other activities. My son has *Guitar Hero,* and his friends like that, too. There is a lot of cheering when they play games together."

ENEMIES AT THE GATE

Why would anyone play a game with an enemy? There's a chance that you might make "enemies" while playing online games, perhaps players that you've accidentally injured or killed in a game, or players who are just plain obnoxious and love crashing their cars into everyone in their vicinity during *Test Drive: Unlimited.* You would most likely make a note of the gamertags of any annoying players and try to avoid them at all costs.

Crash in *Test Drive: Unlimited* Test Drive® Unlimited Courtesy of Atari, Inc. © 2006 Atari, Inc. All rights reserved. Used with permission.

However, players are sometimes forced to play on the same team in online gaming situations due to automated player matching. It's also possible for new teammates to appear at a moment's notice. A sworn enemy can become a teammate instantly! In order to understand enemies a little better, let's first separate them into two classes: short-term and long term.

Short-Term Enemies

Short-term enemies come and go. It sounds obvious, but keep in mind that a single team-kill can turn you into an enemy. However, if you stop team killing and proceed to score against the opposing team, your teammates will forgive your blunder—and you might be among the top players. All of this can happen in a matter of minutes! Since your exposure to most players doesn't last more than a few hours at most, the chances that someone will take issue with you for the long term are low. If players are offended by you, they will simply provide negative feedback (by submitting a player review, for example), and that will be it.

Long-Term Enemies

Long-term enemies are rare in games. The only viable way to make a long-term enemy is to bump on the player constantly and *at the same time* launch insults and provocations. It sounds like hard work. This kind of situation might be more common in competitive tournaments, where the people are more or less the same and the stakes are high. It's still unlikely to happen since competitive play implies professionalism, but we won't rule it out completely. Gaming is just not a very good platform to create enemies; the workplace or schoolyard is much more appropriate!

Despite the cursing, complaints, and high stress level of multiplayer games, enemies aren't really all that common. Short-term enemies are all over the place, but we can't consider them enemies in the true sense of the word. Long-term enemies, on the other hand, are a reality only with the few immature players who participate in tournaments, and the phenomenon is rare enough not to affect most players. You'll make a lot of friends with online multiplayer games, not enemies!

> My kids use matchmaking to find opponents for competitive play or set up hosted games with friends. They typically play with friends on one team and AI [artificial intelligence/NPCs] as enemies.
>
> —John Hight (Director of External Production, Sony)

WHEN THE DISCIPLE IS READY, THE MASTER *MIGHT* APPEAR

It's common today for tutorials to appear at the first level of every game as an update to the old instruction manuals that no one ever reads. Those tutorials usually have a mentor figure, a character who explains the game to the new player. The mentor has prerecorded lines that guide the player through button configurations, rules, complex movements, and some basic gameplay. However, interaction pretty much stops there. The mentor is a nonplayer character (NPC), and NPCs can't ask customized questions or leave the tutorial and step into the game itself. This is precisely why players sometimes feel lost in a newly acquired game. Some games make the mistake of getting "hardcore" immediately after the tutorial, which makes things very difficult for new players. MMOGs, especially, do this a lot, giving players plenty of opportunity to get killed early in the game. Besides a tutorial, how can a noob be helped? Can the noob get some in-game help at all?

Not surprisingly, developers have come to the conclusion that no experienced player will help a noob just for the pleasure of it. If they are going to do it, they need some kind of incentive. This is the origin of "mentoring programs," a developer-sponsored practice that attempts to give noobs some support in their early days

Orientation Island in *Teen Second Life.* Linden Lab

through the game. The idea is to make *babysitting* an interesting activity for experienced players: They can make money doing it, receive items made by the noob as a gift, and maybe even be healed if the noob in question is a priest. What matters most is to keep the noob useful and the experienced player interested in the noob's well-being.

Games that include this functionality are *World of Warcraft, StormReach,* and *EverQuest II.* Even the multiuser virtual environment (MUVE) *Second Life* contains Orientation Island, where noobs are isolated from the other players so that they can build their skills undisturbed.

On a darker note, noobs can sometimes be threatened or tricked by not-so-nice mentors—official or otherwise. Some might force noobs to work for them in some way or make needed items. This can sometimes be seen as a form of virtual slave labor, and it's certainly not supported by developers. This isn't the rule, but it does happen, and it might be the reason mentoring programs aren't available as much as we'd like them to be. As in real life, good mentors are hard to find. The fact that games now include this kind of relationship is just further proof of how relevant gaming can be to both gamers and non-gamers from a sociological perspective.

AUTHORITY FIGURES

Authority figures in-game have changed somewhat in the last decade. When Gen Xers (now being replaced by Millennials) were a major force in games, story lines usually involved either being an authority figure or rebelling against one. Being a team player was never a primary Xer personality trait.

With Millennials on the rise, it's no surprise that modern games have players as members of a team, with a benevolent "captain" who usually gets killed midway. Millennials are more interested in the coordinated effort of a team, while Xers trusted themselves and no one else.

As an example, *Quake II* (released in 1997) had a single marine fighting on his own terms against the Strogg. *Quake IV,* released eight years later, ditched the rebelliousness in favor of a being "just another marine" (of course, a mean one still) with no gripe against his superiors. He was happy to be part of the team and following orders.

Every multiplayer game that calls itself "modern" requires extensive team play. Multiple character classes allow for a variety of skills (all balanced), and most objectives simply cannot be achieved with a team full of lone wolves. The trend is confirmed as traditional Xer game modes such as *death match* give way to less self-absorbed, team-oriented modes such as *capture the flag* and *team death match.*

THE NEEDS OF THE MANY

Most early games contained a limited number of players: one or two! Four players were out of the question, and only college students could play huge multiplayer games. Today in the age of Xbox Live and the PlayStation Network, games can contain any number of players.

Psychologist Abraham Maslow devised, in 1943, one of the first hypotheses for the hierarchical relationships between basic and advanced human needs (in ascending order: physiological, safety, love/belonging, esteem, and self-actualization). Maslow's Hierarchy of Needs soon became a standard in measuring how human beings fill physiological needs and thus can move toward utilizing their full potential.

As gamers grow out of basic arcade action (not that there's anything wrong with that), they tend to become more curious—in an educational sense. The second compartment (top to bottom) includes learning, growing, and achieving something. Good games have a foot set firmly here. The very best games in history manage to include the first compartment qualities for the duration of the game, constantly challenging players to become faster, more intelligent, and more advanced versions of themselves: Creativity, spontaneity, and problem-solving have long been proven side effects of gaming!

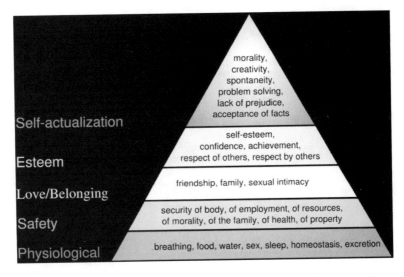

Maslow's Hierarchy of Needs. Courtesy of J. Finkelstein (Wikipedia Commons)

If you look at Maslow's pyramid, you'll see that the need to belong, to love, and be loved is a cut above anything physical; in order to love and care, human beings must clear the two lower compartments of the pyramid, named "physiological" and "safety." If we were to translate that into gaming, we can see clearly that some games are, in fact, much more physiological than others, like twitch platformers and FPS. Those games speak to our animalistic side, allowing it to relive the thrill of the chase or the rush of escape. As gamers have these needs fulfilled, they start to move toward social gaming. Yes, that's compartment #3, from top to bottom. Interestingly enough, to belong and to care fit perfectly with online gaming.

Let's take Maslow's model and create another hierarchy that shows how a player might rise from focusing only on intrapersonal (self) needs to the needs of a much larger group (eventually, humanity itself). If we agree with Maslow that love/belonging and esteem are extremely important in personal development, we need to take a closer look at social development. Note that the base of our Social Hierarchy of Needs hierarchy is intrapersonal (single person), followed by interpersonal (two people), team (small group), community (large group), and world (everyone). Let's see how these social needs can be mapped onto multiplayer games.

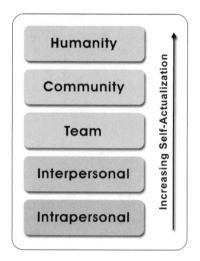

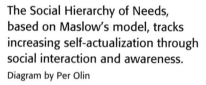

The Social Hierarchy of Needs,
based on Maslow's model, tracks
increasing self-actualization through
social interaction and awareness.
Diagram by Per Olin

Single-Player

As you might expect, single-player games always focus on one individual and can be played by one individual only. Still the most common type, single-player games are the easiest (and cheapest) to develop. Single-player adventures are also the best for immersion. A single-player game has the capacity to focus only on the player's needs, such as self-preservation, avoiding the loss of lives, and mastering the game. These motivations are common in single-player puzzle and classic arcade and adventure games, where the player is faced with a constant stream of enemies or must complete a series of objectives that don't involve other characters. Developers avoid focusing only on intrapersonal concerns, creating an "artificial" social environment by including NPCs whom the player learns to care about. On the other hand, if the NPC in the game only acts as an opponent (as in chess, for example), the player will focus only on intrapersonal needs. Games like these are known as *zero sum* games, which means that both "players" have opposing needs, and that only one player can win the game. As we move into more cooperative game modes, we begin to see *non–zero sum* games, which can be much more complicated to play.

Fable is a single-player role-playing game. Lionhead Studios Limited

Two-Player

Two-player games have been available from the very beginning with *Spacewar!*, the first computer game. Their *raison d'etre* was purely technical, but it soon became clear that games were a lot more fun if you could play against a friend or a sibling. Today, some games still avoid online play and include support for two players only—a limitation that is increasingly seen as a fatal mistake by reviewers, players, and publishers. Our Social Hierarchy of Needs shows that interpersonal relationships are a step above intrapersonal. If a two-player game is co-op (such as *Streets of Rage*), the interpersonal element comes into play. If one player is being attacked by many street thugs at once, the other player will rush to his aid. Of course, many two-player games are not cooperative and are strictly competitive. In this case, we jump back to an "intrapersonal" focus.

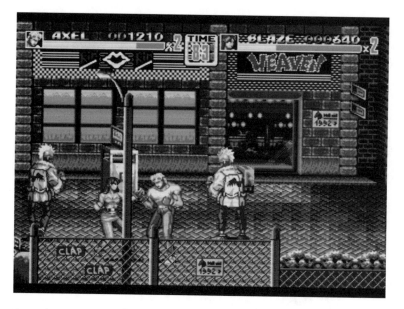

Two-player co-op action in *Streets of Rage 2*. © Sega. All rights reserved.

Three-Player

Games developed for the arcade platform were initially the only ones that contained a three-player mode. For some reason, developers thought that three was a safe player count for co-op play, and many '80s classic beat'em ups having support for this awkward mode. Three-player only games are a rarity now.

Final Fight supports three simultaneous players. © Courtesy of Capcom USA, Inc.

Four-Player (and Multiples of Two)

The rule for game developers usually was that if your game supported more than two players, you'd go the distance and double that. That was especially true at home, where four-player–capable consoles started to appear by 1996. (The Nintendo 64 was the very first one.) This was the origin of the "multiples of two" tradition: 4-player, 8-player, 16-player, etc., and it was the beginning of organized team play. An early example of an eight-player game was *Daytona USA*, which allowed eight friends to participate in the same race through networked arcade cabinets. Having four players allows for teams of two. This is a major jump in interactivity and social dynamics, since team play and competition can occur in the same game. This was the big change brought about by the successful *Goldeneye 007* for the Nintendo 64. Games that involve four players on two teams move players into the "interpersonal" section of our Social Hierarchy of Needs, and games involving six or more players on two or more teams move players up to the "team" section. Players will thus find themselves focusing on their partners' needs, whether it's only one partner or a small group of partners. Games that involve four or more players with *no* team configuration bring us back to "intrapersonal" needs.

The *Mario Party* franchise (*Mario Party 8* shown) focuses on four-player gameplay.
Courtesy of Nintendo

Small Groups and Teams

Cliques are subgroups that are often first seen in classrooms but never really disappear from the social landscape. Even offices have cliques; we might get older, but most of us still need to feel that we belong to a social group, people who behave and think like we do. The best way to understand cliques is to compare them to animals that travel in packs (such as wolves or lions); members of a particular pack are not necessarily blood relatives, but they become a new type of "family." In games, cliques might mutate into clans, guilds, or parties. These small group formations are not identical but follow the same principles: a leader backed by many supporters with different, complementary functions. Cliques play together constantly, perhaps daily, and rely on the leader for direction and strategy. It's important to mention, though, that general multiplayer matches don't really contain cliques unless the game supports a sturdy clan system (as in *Halo 2*, in which players can form parties with their friends and play against other clans). In small groups, players are always focusing on the needs of the "team"; however, "intrapersonal" needs sometimes come into play, especially when each player is still ranked individually.

Battlefield 2142 has small groups as teams. Electronic Arts, Inc.

Large Groups and Communities

Large groups contain more than 64 players. In order to keep a game with a high number of players (64 to 300+) enjoyable, hosts commonly resort to LAN (local area network) parties. The easiest way to understand the concept of a LAN party is to imagine a basic gathering of friends and then add one networked PC for each guest. By the way, while online games have thousands of players and make use of VoIP, multiplayer games played on LANs will always have direct communication between players, since everyone is on the same room!

The Lord of the Rings: The Battle for Middle-Earth is one of the few real-time strategy games that is played at LAN parties. Electronic Arts, Inc.

Large groups are the sweet spot for competition and communication. Online gaming can be a little impersonal since you'll never see most of your adversaries face to face, but large group gaming counters this with the power of the human element. A mix between a tournament, a party, and an all-night game session, LAN parties give people some of the old-fashioned pleasures of playing with a bunch of friends in the same space, but on a much larger scale. Groups of this size move from the "team" definition into the "community," where there might be several teams that focus on meeting the needs of the community in different ways.

Global Scale

The top rung on our Social Needs hierarchy contains the "world," or "humanity." MMOGs, games that involve thousands or even millions of players, fit into this category. Each individual player might need to protect or fight alongside an entire race of people (or even the world of players in the game) rather than only being concerned about a large group, or community. Some MMOGs involve player-versus-player interactions, team-versus-team interactions, and co-op play against enemy NPCs. It's possible to have so many NPC enemies in the game that all the players must cooperate with each other in order to vanquish the "enemy race."

Worlds at war in *EVE Online.* CCP Games

Parent Snapshot

Greg Costikyan

CEO (Manifesto Games)
New York, NY

Greg Costikyan is CEO of Manifesto Games (www.manifestogames.com), an online retailer of independently created computer games. He has designed more than 30 commercially published board, role-playing, computer, online, and mobile games, including five Origin Award-winning titles. Among his best known titles are *Creature That Ate Sheboygan* (board game), *Paranoia* (tabletop RPG), *MadMaze* (first online game to attract more than one million players), and *Alien Rush* (mobile game). His games have been selected on more than a dozen occasions for inclusion in the Games 100, *Games Magazine's* annual round-up of the best 100 games in print. He is an inductee into the Adventure Gaming Hall of Fame for a lifetime of accomplishment in the field and won the Maverick Award in 2007 for his tireless promotion of independent games. He also writes one of the most widely read blogs about games, game development, and the game industry (*www.costik.com/weblog*).

- Family Profile: Three kids, ages 18, 15, and 3 (daughters 18 and 15)
- Playtime: 1–3 hours per week
- Platforms: Xbox, PS2, GameCube, Dreamcast, Genesis, PC, GBA, NES, SNES, N-Gage, 3DO
- Top games: *Arc the Lad, World of Warcraft*
- "My kids interact socially with other players online through role-playing and trading. My older daughter is also captain of a *Puzzle Pirates* ship!"

Communities and the World Outside the Game

In the game industry, communities form around manufacturers and platforms, such as Xbox 360 or Nintendo Wii, because consoles are not compatible with each other. Community can also be thought of as a geographic *region*. In this case, we have the American, European, and Japanese gaming communities.

→

Regional communities are platform-agnostic since markets can host many different platforms with various degrees of success. Regional communities can also exist within a single country: The West Coast and East Coast have communities of their own within the United States. News travels fast in communities, and chances are the members of the same community can better understand each other since they share a similar reality. Since the advent of the World Wide Web, the world has been brought together as one. It's still an incomplete process, but we can already see changes in some strata of society. Gamers are perfectly positioned in this regard. Being a tech-savvy, high-income group, gamers are lucky enough to enjoy the benefits of this global world before other sectors of society. During a console launch like the one for the PlayStation 3, consoles travel the world to better paying markets. Internet forums light up with reports, first impressions, and questions. Players join games online, chat, and leave their marks in online rankings. The gaming world almost has a mind of its own. Similar to moviegoers, gamers have policy-changing power and demand the very best from both electronics and the game industry. The technological revolution brought by high-definition DVDs (HD-DVD and Blu-ray), next-gen consoles, and top-of-the-line PCs is helmed by gamers worldwide.

Parent Snapshot

Jennifer Anderson

Tech support rep/student
Wichita, KS

Jennifer Anderson is a 31-year-old mother of two children. She has played video games for most of her teen years and adult life. She and her husband both play games at night. They encourage their children to play role-playing games as a way to teach them to think about their actions before doing them.

- Family Profile: Two boys, ages 12 and 6
- Playtime: 4–6 hours per week (parents and kids)
- Platforms: PS2, PC, DS
- Top Games: *Ultima Online, The Sims, Sim Zoo*
- "My oldest loves to talk with people all over the world. I think it's given him better confidence."

GAMING SIDE EFFECTS

More then clinical or educational benefits, games allow us to transcend our limitations. Games can be thought of as lucid dreams in disguise, alternate realities where we can be what we always wish we were. In more ways than one, gaming sets both mind and body free.

WHO NEEDS LIMITS?

Life requires limits, mostly because the human body has physical limitations. We are educated from birth to know our limits and respect society's wishes. However, a life full of limits might hamper an individual's drive to greatness. Somehow, we must learn that success is also about *breaking those limits*. It's a paradox of modern living: two conflicting messages repeated throughout our lives. Luckily, games give us some tools to navigate the paradox and make the best of it.

Illustration by Ian Robert Vasquez

Game universes are known for the sheer immensity of rules, values, challenges, and freedom. The whole point of creating a game is to carve a universe out of imagination and dreams, a high-tech playground where children and adults can be whatever they wish to be. The reason for this is simple: Without room for experimentation, it's very hard to gauge our hearts' desires and goals. We need the space to be silly so that we can make good choices in life.

In the past, either kids were able to experiment in real life, with the occasional dire consequences (drugs, car accidents, pregnancies), or they didn't get to experiment at all. Through games, most of these experiences can be had inside the virtual environment, with parents close by in case of need. Remember *Super Mario Bros?* Didn't you love how high you could jump? Didn't you stare in awe at the TV the first time Mario went down the green tubes? Those very basic game mechanics were somehow meaningful to kids worldwide; they were windows of opportunity to their own imaginations.

Exploring the limits of a game gives everyone know-how on complex systems, *their* limits, and how to break them. It's essential knowledge, now that the world has become a networked mass of silicon, media, and entertainment. Exploration also teaches kids more about themselves, since self-reflection is essential if you want to find out why you like a game and how you like to play it. Metaphorically, when kids play games they are in reality playing with their own inner worlds. Everybody needs limits, but there's nothing like escaping into a world with limitless *possibilities* once in a while!

EMPOWERMENT AND EQUITY

Real life (RL) is anything but equal and fair. Inequality is all over the place, from famine in Africa to early adopters in Southern California. Our planet might be small compared to others, but it's surely immense on a human scale with so much history, culture, and diversity. It is surprising that we are not in worse shape than we are.

In order to be truly happy, human beings need to feel that they have some measure of control over their lives. As long as the introductory price is paid (~$250 for the Wii, $300–400 for the Xbox 360, $500–600 for the PlayStation 3), game consoles allow everyone to be equal inside the game world. Games give players a glimmer of hope when their lives are entangled in debt, complicated family relations, and demanding relationships. Games give everyone a chance at greatness, and practice for real life so that, when the time is right, people will know what to do.

Being able to match your opponent's might and skill is a great way to feel empowered, countering limited, low-key everyday life. Getting some power back, even inside a game environment, is enough to inspire us to higher and more daring flights.

Everybody wants super powers (*City of Heroes*).

Parent Snapshot

Catherine Clinch

Associate publisher
(Creative Screenwriting Magazine)
Los Angeles, CA

Catherine Clinch has written for television series such as *Hunter, Jake and the Fatman, Miami Vice, True Confessions, Knight Rider, Hart to Hart, The Love Boat,* and *Foul Play.* In the downtime between assignments, she did stand-up comedy and was a regular performer at LA nightclubs including The Comedy Store, The Improv, and The Playboy Club (where she was conspicuously over-dressed). Eventually, she gave up the glamorous life of entertaining drunken audiences in smoke-filled rooms to become a wife and mother of three. Through her involvement with the WGAw Women's Committee, Catherine

→

helped develop programs that sought to put an end to discriminatory practices in the workplace. During her two-year term on the WGA Board of Directors, her attention turned toward defining the role of the writer in the international marketplace amidst emerging technologies. Catherine has taught screenwriting and communications theory courses at Loyola Marymount University and California State University Dominguez Hills. She has pioneered the field of distance learning for the entertainment industry, teaching the first fully accredited university online course in screenwriting for CSUDH in 1995. Also for CSUDH, she partnered with professors from USC and UCLA to create an online program in Entertainment Industry Technology. Catherine wrote, produced, and presented more than 200 hours of live interactive television for the educational series *American Society & Television* and *Mass Media & Society*. Her latest venture is Nuclear Family Films, an independent production company dedicated to putting the family back into family films. She currently serves as the associate publisher for *Creative Screenwriting Magazine*.

- Family Profile: Three boys, ages 20, 18, and 15
- Platforms: PS2, PS, N64, GB Color
- "My oldest son (who has multiple disabilities) loves playing online games because, as he has said: 'They don't know I'm deaf so they treat me like anybody else.'"

CLASS AND RACE, BE GONE!

The fact that everyone is an *avatar* inside the game pretty much rules out issues of class and race, bringing some much-needed fairness to human relationships. Although people are bound by their skin color in the real world, in the game world, all skin colors are available (even purple and green)! You can be a member of any class or race you wish (unless there's a hierarchy that you have to climb). The key is that you are not limited by the class or race you were born into, as you are in the real world. In-game money is also independent from money in real life, leveling the playing field even more. This is a basic quality of games and one that will become even more significant as online gaming spreads to the rest of the planet. Gaming allows the warriors within to do battle and the medics and priests within to heal them in make-believe, "friendly" wars.

Mage	Priest	Warrior	Thief
Lich	Priest of Mitra	Guardian	Defiler
Necromancer	Scourge of Derketo	Halberdier	Lotus Master
Herald of Xoti	Scion of Set	Conqueror	Master Thief
Demonologist	Druid	Liberator	Barbarian
	Bear Shaman	Crusader	Reaver
	Stormcaller	Dark Templar	Ranger
			Walayer

Character classes associated with the Mage, Priest, Warrior, and Thief archetypes in *Age of Conan: Hyborian Adventures.* Funcom

WE'RE GONNA NEED A BIGGER PLAYGROUND

Playing games during our free time is already an intense activity. When we start playing with the whole world, the stakes get considerably higher. As competition and cooperation reach new levels, games take the player on a much more dynamic, unpredictable journey.

Since learning is so prevalent in games, we believe that a full chapter can do a much better job than a few tidbits here and there. In Chapter 5, "Playing to Learn," you'll see how games can be a very effective learning tool and how you can make better use of the teaching power of games.

5 Playing to Learn

In Chapter 4, "The Social Game," you saw how games promote social growth through healthy competition and cooperation. Games are tools for social learning, training grounds for human interaction. Many benefits can be reaped from balanced, supervised gameplay—and parents are starting to take notice.

It's still surprising to most that games have a powerful effect on learning. Although games are now expected to connect kids with their peers through social experiences, the notion that kids can learn from a game still hasn't been fully embraced. One of the reasons for this may be due to the association between video games and toys, an old-fashioned concept that remains alive within part of society. It is true that games were put in the same category as toys throughout the 1970s, 1980s, and most of the 1990s, but recent generations have put this concept to rest. There's just no way to look at a PlayStation 3 and see it as a toy!

If you think of games as very sophisticated software that runs on even more sophisticated hardware—dozens of times more powerful than the supercomputers of the 1990s—their true nature becomes obvious: Games are the building blocks of an alternate reality. What we have today is just a few notches below the virtual reality utopia envisioned 15 years ago, and if we had affordable VR goggles, we'd be there already. Jumping over platforms in *Super Mario Bros.* might have improved your kid's reflexes and fine motor skills, but being part of a community in *Second Life* can actually give him enough experience to run his own businesses. The technology we have available today is nothing short of a quantum leap in immersion and interaction—two features that all classic consoles sorely lacked.

It's actually quite difficult to *not* learn anything while playing a game. The experience is so intricate and deep that we invariably "pick up" concepts, procedures, story structure, character development, physics, culture, and more. Where some games opt for abstract universes, others' obsession with realism bridges the gap between "game" and "real life," producing real, tangible knowledge in the process.

A game always teaches you something. Otherwise, it wouldn't be enjoyable, and no one would care about mastering its rules. According to Professor Richard M. Ryan, Ph.D. (University of Rochester), kids and adults play games because they provide opportunities for achievement, freedom, and connection to other players. "It's our contention that the psychological 'pull' of games is largely due to their capacity to engender feelings of autonomy, competence, and relatedness," says Ryan.

LEARNING THE STEALTH WAY

While learning is always fun, we unfortunately cannot say the same about the traditional school system. Somehow, decades after the Information Age, schools remain largely the same. Many classrooms of today resemble time capsules of the Victorian era, outdated and inefficient learning systems. This is a hot topic among parents and scholars alike. Although we have our theories, we're not here to outline ways to fix the system. What we can do, as authors and gamers, is to show you how to supplement your kids' education with the best technology can offer.

Back in the early 1990s, the *multimedia revolution* (the popularization of CD-ROM drives and sound cards for computers) brought with it more than FMV (full motion video) titles. The CD-ROM was seen as the perfect medium for educational software. This trend was eventually known as *edutainment*,—the combination of education and entertainment. As we discussed in Chapter 1, "Where It All Began," edutainment failed to deliver the goods. Most edutainment "games" weren't fun and ultimately didn't provide the education they promised. In fact, many edutainment titles managed to attempt at home the same old learning system found in the classroom. "Edutainment" became stigmatized and was a missed opportunity for students and developers alike.

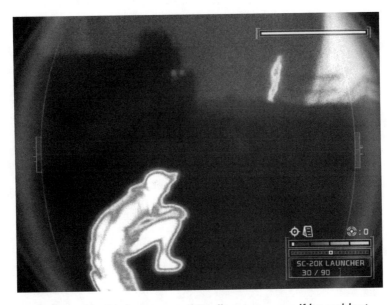

"Stealth learning" is incorporated in all games—even if by accident (*Tom Clancy's Splinter Cell Chaos Theory*). Tom Clancy's Splinter Cell Chaos Theory: © 2005 Ubisoft Entertainment. All rights reserved. Splinter Cell, Splinter Cell Chaos Theory, Sam Fisher, the Soldier Icon, Ubisoft, Ubi.com and the Ubisoft logo are trademarks of Ubisoft Entertainment in the U.S. and/or other countries.

Knowing that overt learning didn't do the trick, researchers have turned to what is now known as *covert* or *stealth learning*. Educator and scholar James Gee, Ph.D. (University of Wisconsin) defines stealth learning as "an activity where the learners are so caught up in their goals that they don't realize they are learning, or how much they are learning, or where they actively seek new learning." In short, stealth learning is to learn by default, with learning being a by-product of some other primary objective and not an end in itself.

On one hand, we have overt learning, which is what the "traditional" school system is all about. Kids are there to learn, teachers are clearly identified, and tests measure student performance from time to time. On the other hand, covert learning involves no school and most certainly no teachers; that is, not in the traditional sense. The main objectives in many covert learning scenarios are similar to those in the real world: solve a crime, survive, win the war, become a millionaire. The learning here runs *under* the main objectives, and players depend on it if they want to win the game. Contrary to school, players are tested constantly (hourly, maybe) and have enough room for mistakes—what is known as *learning by trying*.

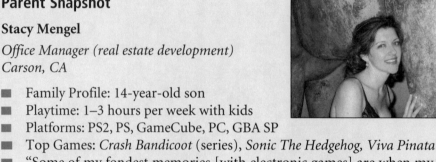

Parent Snapshot

Stacy Mengel

Office Manager (real estate development)
Carson, CA

- Family Profile: 14-year-old son
- Playtime: 1–3 hours per week with kids
- Platforms: PS2, PS, GameCube, PC, GBA SP
- Top Games: *Crash Bandicoot* (series), *Sonic The Hedgehog*, *Viva Pinata*
- "Some of my fondest memories [with electronic games] are when my son was very young and still overcoming a lot of hurdles with his autism. I have always been impressed at how quickly he picks up the concept of what to do and how to do it without knowing much about the game. I used computer games to teach my son how to use a computer and to reinforce basic lessons on colors, numbers, letters, and more when he was growing up. They helped considerably."

GAME GENRES AND LEARNING

Let's take a look at the genres listed in Chapter 2, "Games 101," and uncover the potential learning in them. We're focusing purposely on games that are not specifically created for educational purposes to show you how all games are educational, even if by accident!

ACTION

Action games are similar to big budget Hollywood action movies, focusing on large-scale set-pieces instead of a complicated storyline or deep characters. The difference between an action and an adventure game is the same as between a Universal Studios ride and a Broadway play. On the other hand, while action games are known to improve reflexes and visual acuity, we can't dismiss them for other purposes. Even the simplest *Mario* clone will have some learning potential, usually found far below the player's radar.

Platformer

Platformers are built on top of simple storylines, usually mere "support" for the many levels faced by the player. A game like *Donkey Kong Country* (*DKC*), the SNES launch for 1994, in which Donkey Kong must recover his bananas from the evil King K. Rool, has many interesting "tidbits" hidden in the gameplay.

Donkey Kong relies on his pal Diddy Kong throughout *Donkey Kong Country.* Courtesy of Nintendo

DKC is very team oriented with a tag system that employs both Donkey Kong and his friend Diddy Kong. If the player takes one hit, control defaults to the second character. On a second hit, the player loses a life; however, players can switch between the two in real time. This is necessary in certain levels, since Donkey Kong and Diddy Kong have different abilities. The theme of cooperation is repeated with the use of helper animals: rhino, ostrich, parrot, frog, and swordfish.

The first lesson in the game is that *cooperation is essential for survival*. Furthermore, it's also stated covertly that *each individual has a different strength* and also that *animals are on our side and can help us when we reach our physical limits*. All of this in a simple 16-bit platformer!

Shooter

First-person and third-person shooters represent one of the most popular game genres, and they're currently going through a Renaissance phase that began with

Goldeneye 007 and *Half-Life* in the late 1990s. Since shooters are still part of the action genre, story and character development are lightly used, and that's to be expected. Let's take a closer look at *Gears of War*.

Gears of War has the player issue orders to a small group of space marines. Epic Games

The game's story focuses on Emergence Day, when the underground Locust Horde start an invasion from below on peaceful planet Sera. The storyline follows Delta Squad on its strike against the Locust, with emphasis on the battles that take place on Sera's ruins. When we look at the game, we realize that the developers focused on giving players a visceral experience that is very close to Ridley Scott's film, *Aliens*. The game forces players to constantly take cover (an action nicknamed "stop-and-pop"), and the story is told after major battles. On one such battle, the captain loses his life at the hands of the Locust Leader, leaving the responsibility to the player's character, Marcus Phoenix. This is another game that stresses team play over "going solo." Assuming command of the squad is also dealt with in a very serious way, indicating to players that you don't always have a choice about being a leader, but you still need to do a good job once you become one. The AI characters in the game are highly responsive and will fight alongside the player, taking commands when Phoenix rises to captain. With the touch of a button, soldiers obey orders such as "regroup," "attack," and "defend," changing the way a situation plays out. Since players can be much more effective if they work with the rest of the team, it is learned quite quickly that leadership, respect, and organization make a team much more powerful than a single "super soldier."

Racing

Racing games teach players about different car models, including specs, features, performance, and handling. Realism is part of every successful racing game, even if the vehicle in question is a jet-powered hovering pod as in *F-Zero GX*. What the best racing games bring to the table is an understanding of the true meaning of speed.

Test Drive: Unlimited teaches about speed and safety by giving players close to absolute freedom. Test Drive ® Courtesy of Atari, Inc. © 2006 Atari, Inc.

Test Drive: Unlimited (*TDU*) is a pure racing game *and* an MMOG. What most ignore about the game, though, is that, due to its realism, a very important notion is taught: *Speed kills*. How can a game that glorifies expensive exotic cars and has no speed limits teach this? Precisely *because* it has no speed limits. During the game, the player must undergo delivery missions, where a very expensive car must be delivered somewhere on the island of Oahu. If the player delivers the car without a scratch, the player receives a bonus on top of the amount of money already made by doing the job. *Any damage*, even a small dent or scratch, will not result in a bonus, and if money runs out, the mission is over. A player can go through the trouble of delivering the car and get $10,000 U.S. or do such a bad job that the mission is cancelled altogether!

Another question arises: Does the fact that most cars in the game reach upward of 170 mph make it easier or harder for the player? The answer is *a lot harder.* When a delivery mission takes at least 20 minutes, the player faces a constant struggle between driving faster and getting there earlier (risking the cash reward) or driving slower but with less chance for mishap. Either way, the player will have to think about it. As you'd expect, it's when players get impatient that speeds rise and accidents happen, ruining the whole run. Players learn very soon that without patience and common sense, they'll never finish the mission or get the bonus associated with a perfect delivery.

The reason *TDU* shows the true nature of speed is that the game maintains a sense of realism. When driving very fast, keeping the car in control becomes a chore; the whole experience is actually quite scary. Horrific crashes ensue when players drive too fast, either because they lack the ability or because the speed is excessive for the road in question. In all our years playing racing games, we've never seen a racing game that shows this clearly the dangers of excessive speed!

Fighting

Fighting games were all the rage in the mid-1990s, when *Mortal Kombat* made the headlines due to its bloody "fatalities." In time, *Mortal Kombat* proved to be quite harmless, and other genres, such as first-person shooters (FPSs), took the spotlight. Currently, fighting games are either very "comic bookish" (*Marvel Vs. Capcom*) or photorealistic (*Virtual Fighter 4 Evolution*), and they usually contain a small amount of blood.

Now that the focus is not on the violence anymore, we can see fighting games as carriers of three important messages:

1. Keeping fit and training constantly are essential for victory.
2. Speed and intelligence far outweigh power and size (size will only make a difference if both players are equally skilled).
3. There's always time for a comeback.

All of the concepts stated above can be seen in fighting games—with the added bonus that they can be easily applied to real life. The concept of speed and intelligence is especially important since it might make a difference in your kid's life; growing up, we are constantly forced to deal with difficult situations at school and at home, and the frustration that ensues might lead to violence or self-destructive behaviors. Fighting games show us that intelligence can defeat the biggest adversary by choosing locations and actions wisely, and that comebacks are always possible, even in the very last second of the very last match. Fighting games also educate about current and classic martial arts styles and include snippets of the philosophy behind each style—seen in *Brutal: Paws of Fury.*

Soul Calibur III has a dazzling variety of characters and allows for different weapon choices. SOULCALIBUR ® III © 1995 1998 2002 2003 2005 NAMCO BANDAI Games Inc. Courtesy of NAMCO BANDAI Games America Inc.

ADVENTURE

By definition, adventure games allow the player to explore scenarios and environments in search of clues that will unlock the next step on a journey. If you're playing a good adventure game, the clues and steps will be logical but still challenging, while bad games do their best to present puzzles in the most illogical way possible, making players work overtime to put it all together. What adventures like *Myst* do best is to tell stories through exploration, in direct opposition to more action-oriented games like *Gears of War* and *Quake 4*.

Adventure games are less covert and more overt in their "teaching," but they still remain games, not educational software. By taking the time to tell a story and avoiding twitch mechanics, adventure games give players much more immersion and choice than action-based games.

Myst encourages players to explore worlds that hide clues to an intriguing storyline.
Cyan Worlds

Day of the Tentacle: Stimulating Logical Thinking While Teaching History

In *Day of the Tentacle* (*DOTT*), a seemingly good Purple Tentacle drinks from a polluted river and becomes evil as a result. Now with dreams of world domination, Purple needs to be stopped or the world will never be the same (literally; check out the game's ending)! The cast of heroes includes:

- **Bernard:** A well-intentioned nerd (first seen in another adventure game, *Maniac Mansion*)
- **Laverne:** An anatomy student
- **Hoagie:** A metal-head straight out of an Iron Maiden concert

With the aid of a time machine of sorts (the diamond-powered Chron-o-Johns), the three heroes attempt to go back in time and stop the river from getting polluted so that nothing bad happens when Purple takes a sip, changing the present for the better. Unfortunately, the diamond used in the machine turns out to be a fake, throwing Hoagie 200 years in the past and Laverne 200 years in the future, while keeping Bernard stuck in the present.

→

The well-developed storyline in *DOTT* allows for much more depth than usual, being light years more complex than the one found in *Doom* or even *Half-Life*. Also, the fact that quick reflexes and speed are not required makes *DOTT* very accessible to non-gamers; adventure games are notorious for captivating both genders *and* older adults.

DOTT was released in 1993, and two formats were available: floppy disk and CD-ROM. The floppy disk version had fewer sound effects and limited spoken dialogue, while the CD-ROM version employed professional voice actors, supporting voice throughout the game. The first version forced players to read and comprehend thousands of lines of dialogue (similar to the tasks given at school, but much more fun), and the second one played out much like an interactive movie, still requiring the player to choose between five possible lines of dialogue in every NPC interaction.

Immense value can be gained from playing through the whole game, since *DOTT* makes excellent use of the three available "time streams," a mechanism that allows the player to give items to characters that are in the past, present, or future. (Hoagie can bury items in the past, and Bernard can "find" them in the present; Bernard can send items in the present to Laverne in the future.) Many puzzles make use of this sort of time-dependent item exchange. Also, *DOTT* allows players to interact with renditions of U.S. founding fathers such as Thomas Jefferson and George Washington, among many others. When done right, these historical interactions can be very educational and may help players have a better grasp of what took place in the early years of the United States.

ACTION-ADVENTURE

Action-adventure games add puzzle-solving to seemingly simple action gameplay. A great example of an action-adventure game is *God of War,* Sony's very successful exclusive title for the PlayStation 2. *God of War* has many elements of action—and huge boss battles; however, it doesn't settle for reflex-based gameplay, but quite the opposite. To compensate for the furious action (and the word "furious" describes the game well), *God of War* (and its successor, *God of War 2*) has many puzzles spread throughout the game, mostly in the form of statues, levers, and switches that need to be moved, pulled, and operated. Having puzzles sprinkled over a foundation of action is a great way to enhance the game's pacing and at the same time motivate players to use their brains, resulting in added complexity and more satisfying gameplay.

God of War II is much more than a mindless brawler. Sony Computer Entertainment America

The best feature of action-adventure games is the pacing we've already described. First-person shooters (FPSs) and other fast-paced genres give players no reason to really think about their environments, instead focusing mostly on how to open locked doors and choose weapons. Action-adventure games, on the other hand, give players a fuller universe. Commands such as "open" or "walk quietly," might be available, and enemies need to be dealt with in specific ways; merely shooting them is usually ineffective.

Action-adventure games have also spawned a subgenre: stealth-based games. Starting with *Metal Gear* in the 1980s, copycats and sequels followed, among them *Metal Gear Solid* for the Sony PlayStation. Stealth-based games take most action-adventure traits to a higher level, giving players dozens of new moves. While firefights are almost arcade-ish in action-adventures, stealth-based games make weapons extremely lethal, and players can be killed if they vainly attempt to take on a room full of guards.

Both action-adventure and stealth games enforce thinking over acting, teaching players that patience and common sense are essential in crisis situations. When these games punish players for being merely reactive, they are in fact showing them the importance of thinking one's way out of situations, a skill we should *all* put to use more often!

PUZZLE

The one puzzle game everybody remembers is *Tetris*, designed by Alexey Pajitnov. *Tetris* was a pack-in for the original Game Boy; it successfully attracted a lot of casual players to gaming at the time, since it required fast thinking more that simply fast reflexes.

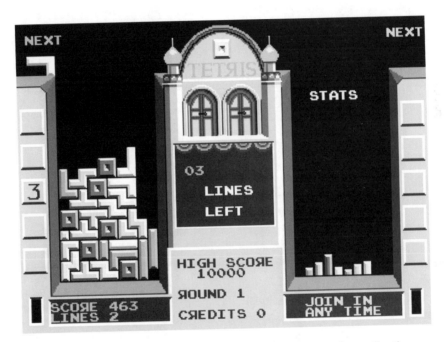

Tetris, the puzzle game that started it all—requiring eye-hand coordination and intense concentration. TETRIS® is a registered trademark of Tetris Holding, LLC; © 2007 by Tetris Holding, LLC

Modern puzzle games such as *Lumines* follow the same trend; they are intense, challenging, and maybe a little infuriating. These games require focused concentration and the ability to match colors and shapes into specific patterns. Sometimes puzzle games also require players to apply logic, critical thinking, and even mathematics in order to be solved.

Edutainment Reborn?

Throughout the book, we've been saying over and over again how edutainment died a horrible death in the mid 1990s. Although this is true, recent "puzzle games" have started to deviate from the genre and, surprisingly, may be inconspicuously realizing the promise of edutainment! Puzzle games can be thought of as workouts for the brain. Nintendo's *Brain Age* and *Big Brain Academy* take this concept to the next level: Each of these games is loaded with math, logic, and visual exercises that score players based on their brain age and brain weight, respectively, making it clear whether the player's brain skills are up to par. (If not, some "brain training" sessions can correct this!) Although each title focuses on different sets of skills, both are based on research conducted by Professor Ryūta Kawashim and have been a huge success for the Nintendo DS.

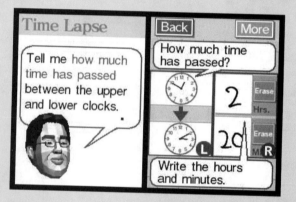

The time lapse game in *Brain Age* displays two clocks and requires the player to calculate the difference in time between these clocks.

Here's a list of skills measured and developed by *Brain Age* and *Big Brain Academy:*

- Pattern recognition
- Shape recognition
- Color recognition
- Logic
- Arithmetic
- Reading skills (*Brain Age* has the player read literary classics aloud!)
- Memorization
- Concentration

→

This is quality edutainment at work. However, since the genre is considered "dead," the *Brain Age* series usually falls into the puzzle or educational categories. Are games like these an indication that edutainment as a genre may have a future after all? (The series has already given rise to other franchises such as *Ultimate Brain Games* and *Brain Boost*.)

When they were smaller, my kids played many educational games. It helped a lot with their reading skills, as well as their problem-solving abilities.

—Travis Ogurek (parent/student)

My youngest son has learned quite a bit from games, including shapes, colors, and numbers. He is older now and less prone to the 'educational' games, but it was those types of games that formed his early addiction to gaming as a child.

—Guy P. Vance (customer service)

Early on in special day classes at a school for kids with learning disabilities, the visual aid of games was relied on with the use of *Reader Rabbit* and other math and puzzle games.

—John Francis Whelpley (writer-producer, Skibberrean Productions, Inc.)

The primary function of my kids' game playing is educational. My five-year-old daughter reinforces her counting, reading, and hand coordination through computer games.

—Bill Genereux (Assistant Professor, Kansas State University)

My youngest daughter (two years old) thoroughly enjoys her early childhood gaming console, which offers games that teach the alphabet and other toddler-oriented educational lessons. She watches and tries to emulate her brothers and sisters when they play games, and she loves it when there is a game that is just for her.

—Jacques Montemoino (Gideon Games, LLC)

My oldest son has a number of disabilities. Learning how to play *Sonic The Hedgehog* gave him a tool for enhancing hand/eye coordination. Once I realized this, I didn't mind the fact that the theme music was going through my head day and night! My other two sons, who are highly gifted and plan to get MBAs, enjoy strategy games. They get immersed in *Capitalist* and other business games. They also enjoy the challenges of *Sim City*.

—Catherine Clinch (Associate Publisher, *Creative Screenwriting Magazine*)

Parent Snapshot

Dennis J. Jirkovsky

Instructor (Metropolitan Community Colleges—Longview)
Lees Summit, MO

- Family Profile: Seven-year-old daughter
- Playtime: 4–6 hour per week with son
- Platforms: PS3, Genesis, PC, PSP
- Top Games: Disney, Cartoon Network, and Nickelodeon games
- "I believe my daughter learned her 'ABCs' from a computer game."

Parent Snapshot

Donna K. Kidwell

Commercialization consultant
(University of Texas at Austin)
Manor, TX

Donna K. Kidwell is a proud parent of three wonderful children and is also an international commercialization consultant and futurist. Donna specializes in commercialization strategies for potential of innovations in science and technology. She is a fierce advocate for using video games to teach leadership and management skills to children, and she blogs at *http://www.gamermom.com*.

- Family Profile: Three kids: ages 7, 10, and 13
- Playtime: 1–3 hours per week with kids (spouse plays 10 or more hours per week with kids)
- Platforms: Wii, PC, DS, GBA SP, GBA
- Top Games: *World of Warcraft, Wii Sports*
- "Reading skills are always reinforced, and with our youngest we use games to practice reading. When he was younger we used it to enhance alphabet recognition skills. My oldest now blogs about his experiences, which gives him a forum and format in which to practice his writing skills."

ROLE-PLAYING

With *Final Fantasy XII* and *The Elder Scrolls IV: Oblivion* topping the chart, role-playing games (RPGs) have been known to teach *responsibility*, along with *patience*, *determination*, and often even *respect* for social structure. Sprawling miles and miles of land, with memorable characters and a strong, plot-driven storyline, the best RPGs give players close to absolute freedom, allowing them to go anywhere and fight anyone. As we discussed in Chapter 2, the focus of RPGs is on character advancement (often set against a rich storyline), which means that every move made by the player character needs be carefully planned and executed. Without planning, it's very easy to wander aimlessly through the game, fail to advance one's status, or lose items and money in "freak" monster encounters!

Another feature of RPGs is the "side quest," an extra objective or mission (usually good for building character and collecting rare items) that functions as a "breather," providing the player with a break from the main quest. The balance between main and side quests is similar to life where main projects can be alternated with errands or smaller tasks.

The Elder Scrolls IV: Oblivion **requires time, patience, and attention to detail.** The Elder Scrolls IV: Oblivion ® © 2006 Bethesda Softworks, LLC, a ZeniMax Media company. The Elder Scrolls, Oblivion, Bethesda Softworks, and ZeniMax are trademarks or registered trademarks of ZeniMax Media Inc. All rights reserved.

Great RPG players are focused, resourceful, and diligent, and playing RPGs exercise this "muscle" in kids. By talking to as many characters as possible and assembling detailed notes, players are able to *sniff out* the next turning point in the plot, moving forward with the story, piece by piece.

Massively multiplayer online role-playing games (MMORPGs) add thousands of human players to the mix, turning it into a more social experience. While traditional RPGs only have players *level up* (gain experience points) and interact with non-player characters (NPCs), MMORPGs teach skills like managing people, leadership, and team-play, mimicking real life.

The extreme amount of effort required by an RPG is also beneficial for kids, since it is a testament to the importance of hard work!

SIMULATION

Simulation games have the distinction of being firmly grounded in reality. Other genres get away with a limited set of parameters—a general framework of reality—but simulation games are absolutely *required* to emulate reality faithfully.

In professional flying schools and air companies, flight simulators are commonly used to help wanna-be pilots log flight hours in order to avoid risking both crew and aircraft. More recently, flight simulators have also been used in disaster recovery and emergency procedures.

This is the origin of all flight simulators in game form. Despite the fact that simulations can be found nowadays as mere games, their original nature—training—remains alive inside the software. That's because simulations are all about learning a system of rules that corresponds faithfully to another system in real life. What's even more interesting, as we mentioned in Chapter 2, is that developers have also built simulations of fictional space ships such as *Star Trek*'s *Enterprise*, classic cars, vintage aircraft, and other vehicles that might not exist any more in real life (or haven't even been built yet)! In those cases, the simulator makes use of the rules of physics to project the behavior of products still on the drawing board, a feature heavily used by automakers.

If we think about it, it's clear that simulations comprise the most overt game genre, being absolutely unplayable without knowledge of the intricacies of both the real object and the game manual. The way *Flight Simulator 5* had the parking brakes set by default is still fresh in our minds, making a take-off impossible if the "pilot" didn't press the period (.) key beforehand. This little detail would prevent the plane from gaining any speed, frustrating those who didn't read the manual. Newer versions are even more sophisticated and now include lengthy tutorials that at least attempt to teach newcomers the basic real-world rules.

Simulations engage the player in the challenge of real life. Arcade racers are always easy to pick up and play, while racing simulations trick the player at every corner, rewarding the required attention to detail at the same time. Simulations instill in the player the desire to learn about what's being simulated, be it a 747, a large city like Chicago, or a Ford Escort Cosworth in the European Rally Championship.

While the tactics learned in *Super Mario World* might take some time to fully translate into useful skills, those associated with simulation games are instantly transformed into real-life skills. A humorous approach to this notion is seen in the film *Snakes on a Plane*, in which a passenger was able to perform an emergency landing solely because he was a hardcore flight simulation enthusiast!

In *Spore,* players learn to evolve a species from a microorganism to a space-faring race that explores the galaxy! Electronic Arts, Inc.

Process simulations such as *Railroad Tycoon, Sim City, Spore,* and *The Movies* have been also known as "construction and management" games, requiring players to build (construct) and maintain (manage) processes, whether it involves a railroad, city, galaxy, or movie studio. All simulations incorporate the educational theory of *constructivism* (learning by doing), which also involves customizing the experience for the player.

Simulations are part of what are now being called "serious games"—used by education, business, healthcare, and the government to either train, inform, recruit, or market to players. Examples include *America's Army,* a massively multiplayer online game (MMOG) that was created by the U.S. Army specifically to attract new recruits; *Dubai Police,* a game that trains traffic accident investigators; and *Real Lives*, a life simulation that shows how people live in various countries.

> I've always felt that we should pass a law forcing all of the candidates for political office to play in a competitive match of *Sim City*. It would show how they respond under pressure and how they make independent decisions about issues that impact citizens' lives. Of course, given that the people who would have to pass the law are those who would then have to play to win the *Sim City* game to keep their jobs. . . . Well, I'm not holding out much hope that this will ever happen. Still, it's a heck of an idea, don't you think?
>
> —Catherine Clinch (Associate Publisher, *Creative Screenwriting Magazine*)

Second Life as an Educational Tool

Jeannie Novak is producer and lead designer on a project that utilizes the *Second Life* (http://secondlife.com) multiuser virtual environment as a learning system. (Although *Second Life* might be described more appropriately as a social network, as discussed in Chapter 4, it has the capacity to exhibit features of a massively multiplayer online game [MMOG].) The course, developed for the Art Institute Online (a division of the Art Institute of Pittsburgh), is a Business Communications course that behaves like a game. It is planned that students taking the course will log onto the *Second Life* environment and "teleport" to Ai Pittsburgh Island, where they find themselves as new employees of a fictional corporation. During the 5-1/2 week course, students (player characters) will learn the inner workings of the corporation through real-world scenarios. They will also discover how to communicate with other employees (non-player characters) within the corporate environment. This is a big step forward in integrating games into education.

Eventually, we believe all courses will be taught as games. As we've emphasized in this chapter, all games involve "covert learning." The reverse can also be true: All courses could conceivably involve "covert gaming"! This is just the beginning of an educational revolution. See http://simteach.com for forums discussing using *Second Life* as an educational environment. Linden Lab, the developer behind Second Life, has also created *Teen Second Life*—open to teens 13–17. The only adults allowed in this environment are Linden employees—but educators have the opportunity to purchase private islands.

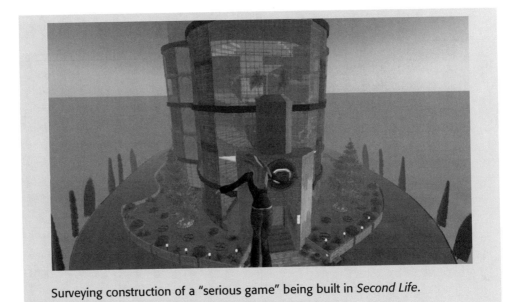

Surveying construction of a "serious game" being built in *Second Life*.

Strategy

Human beings don't really have a choice when it comes to talent, but they sure do have ample possibility to grow. If you look at our species as a whole, our vulnerability and savagery might seem incorrigible, but our intelligence has given us industriousness to turn our deficits into assets. Sometimes sheer effort may be just the thing to overcome the lack of sheer talent!

Resource management and strategic thinking are very important skills, so it's good news that both can be learned with the help of strategy games. There is nothing like winning a difficult battle despite being the underdog and having limited resources. Strategy games are especially useful because they force players to think on both big and small scales. For example, if you're playing *Rise of Nations*, it's not enough to solely research new technologies when battling for world supremacy; you have to build up troop numbers and vehicles as well. This leads to exhilarating and frantic gameplay typical of real-time strategy (RTS) games. Unfortunately, a certain degree of micromanagement is required in real life, and strategy games have the responsibility of portraying it somehow. *The Movies*, especially, utilizes micromanagement in a Hollywood studio simulation, making the game more of a strategy-simulation hybrid.

Resource management is a must in games such as *Rise of Nations.* Microsoft Corporation

The value of deep thought, leading to strategic thinking, is taught through challenges built on top of each other, imposing on players a need for multitasking and attention to detail that they might still not possess in real life. Players need to learn how to prioritize efficiently, assess risk, and organize their cities and armies, among many other tasks that would be at home in a *Fortune* 500 CEO's office.

> We have not used games specifically for educational purposes, but we play games such as *Star Wars: Empire at War*, *Age of Empires, Lego Star Wars*, and other "thinking" and strategy games that require one to organize, search, compile, build, etc. In this way, they are educational and entertaining.
>
> —Paul Orlando (professor, Art Institute)

SURVIVAL-HORROR

Survival-horror (SH) games such as *Resident Evil 4* have steadily increased in popularity during the 1990s and 2000s, beginning with *Alone in the Dark* in 1992.

Originally branched from action and adventure games (seen from the top and later with fixed "cinematic" cameras), survival-horror is now considered a major genre, having evolved from the wooden gameplay of *Alone in the Dark* into much more accessible (and terrifying!) experiences.

One of the traits that separates SH games from action games is the amount of ammunition. SH games never allow the player to feel truly safe; ammo is limited and difficult to find. The SH frame of mind is based on the notion of *scarcity*. Players should never feel like they have enough resources; in fact, they should perceive that there's a very slim chance they'll make it out alive! Of course, when you add horrific monsters to the mix, things get a lot more interesting, forcing players to face all their fears at once *and* manage their inventory at the same time.

Resilience is taught in SH games, as well as resourcefulness and courage. Those are important skills when times are tough or when we need to face our greatest fears. SH games tell us that we can only escape desperate scenarios with courage and ingenuity; they show us opposing forces: the fear that paralyzes us, and the courage that sets us free.

Alone in the Dark teaches players the horrors of scarcity and the importance of resilience. Alone in the Dark ® screenshot courtesy of Atari Interactive, Inc. © 2007 Atari Interactive, Inc. All rights reserved.

SH games are closely related to the adventure genre, and every SH game has a detailed storyline that "explains" the reasons for the horror. These are usually of very high quality, keeping players hooked even if they scream at their monitors from time to time.

> There are a few online Flash games that my daughters use for geography and math. I love to see them use those!

> —Chris Lenhart (network technician, NATO)

Parent Snapshot

Rosanne Welch

Freelance writer/college instructor
Van Nuys, CA

Rosanne Welch is a television writer/producer with credits including Fox's popular *Beverly Hills 90210*, CBS's Emmy-winning *Picket Fences*, and a five-year stint as a writer/producer on television's top-rated *Touched by an Angel*. In 1998, she researched, wrote, and co-produced a two-part special documentary for ABC News/Nightline *Bill Clinton and the Boys Nation Class of 1963*. Rosanne is also the author of two books: *Three Ring Circus: How Real Couples Balance Marriage, Work and Kids* (Seal Press, 2004) and *The Encyclopedia of Women in Aviation and Space* (ABC-CLIO, 1998). Prior to becoming a writer/producer, Rosanne was a high school English teacher and freelance writer with editorials for the *Los Angeles Times* and the *Cleveland Plain Dealer*.

- Family Profile: Nine-year old son
- Playtime: 1–3 hours per week with kids (spouse only)
- Platforms: GBA
- "I used to let my son play the PBS web site games. He liked *Cyberchase* as a TV show, and so he liked those games. Since they were math based, I let him play."

Parent Snapshot

Paul Orlando

Professor (Art Institute)
Atlanta, GA

- Kids: Two sons; Dante (7) and Ronan (5 months)
- Playtime: Paul and his wife Elise play 1–3 hours per week with their kids
- Platforms: GameCube, PC
- Top Games: *Lego Star Wars*, *The Incredibles: Rise of the Underminer*, *The Hobbit: The Prelude to the Lord of the Rings*, *Star Wars: Empire at War*, *Age of Empires*
- "I do feel that kids learn games faster than their parents and can understand how games work at a very early age. Since their minds are open to new things and don't have a history of such games, they see them in a different light or from a different point of view than their parents do. In short, they are capable of learning and adjusting to new technologies due to their developing minds. (They are not set in their ways like we are!)"

NEW FIRMWARE IN TOWN

Firmware is software that governs any hardware on a very low level; it can be thought of as a link between a system's hardware and its high-level software. (Operating systems such as Windows are "high-level" since they exist *above* the firmware.) In the case of humans, firmware could be the middle layer between mind and body, describing the way we process information on a basic level.

For example, early cinema audiences were ill prepared for the medium. This is because human beings at that time lacked the "firmware" to understand fast-moving pictures. In 1895, the Lumieres previewed a short film depicting a train arriving at a station; the film produced screams from the audience who were afraid that a real train was about to crash through the screen! Unaccustomed to this new medium, the audience had difficulty processing the information. As cinema

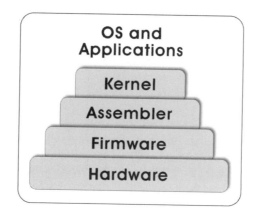

Firmware is the middle layer between a system's hardware and software. Diagram by Per Olin

continued to grow and mature, audience members eventually adapted. Due to the increased exposure, their systems overcame the earlier "shock" and enabled them to process that specific type of information. Today, the film industry is a major force in the entertainment industry.

Human firmware is first updated on a personal level with exposure to a new factor. It then proceeds to spread socially, inside families and companies, until it becomes part of humanity as whole. This works well with the original meaning of the word because real-life firmware is constantly upgraded, whether it's inside your router, DVD player, or computer. Not surprisingly, your childrens' firmware is newer than yours. Just by growing up during this time in history, they are already ahead of the curve, the same way newly built products carry newer firmware versions.

Our metaphor should clarify this point: As a general rule, the younger the person, the faster he will be able to interact with technology. Another facet of this rule is that newer generations have trouble with older media, the same way your Windows XP computer has trouble running DOS games. We're referring here not only to more arcane systems such as the telegraph, phonograph, and shortwave radio, but to traditional classroom lectures, books, and even television. Kids have more trouble with classic sources because they process information at a much higher rate (and in a less linear fashion) than their parents do. This becomes obvious in the case of television; teenagers currently spend only 27 minutes watching TV daily— less than their parents and grandparents, and much less than kids did in previous generations (since the advent of the medium).

The Firmware Divide

Children will always be the new and improved versions of their parents, personalities aside. This also means that they have different needs. As much as we'd like to have kids enjoy everything *we* enjoy, that's not usually the case. In a world that is being described as "wired" and simultaneously "wireless," kids are bound to find new ways to play games, send messages, listen to music, have relationships, and of course, learn. The problem is that few understand the divide between traditional learning and the kind of learning required by the newer generations.

	Boomers (60)	Generation X (40)	Millennials (20)
Work	Hierarchy	Self-reliance	Teamwork
Learning	Lectures	Workshops	Simulations
Researching	Books	Books/Internet	Internet
Playing	Sports / table games	Sports / video games	Video games*

* Millennials are also sports-minded but the generation is defined by their extensive use of technology.

The divide explains why the traits found in games are highly compatible with the firmware of newer generations. In order to overcome the divide, we need to do much more than merely "speak their language." We need to keep in mind at all times that kids today have a different relationship with technology. Older models—whether they involve learning, teaching, or socializing—simply don't work well due to the new "firmware."

A NEW WAY TO LEARN

In this section, we take a look at the new ways of teaching and learning—updated models that work well with our kids (and most Xers). They might seem obvious at first, but soon it becomes clear that human beings change much faster than the teaching standards currently in use at any time.

DYNAMIC LEARNING

One big problem with the kind of teaching practiced at schools is that it remains static for long periods of time. Everyone reading this book remembers how bringing computers to school was said to be a "major change." For example, Luis Levy went to Pueri Domus, a fairly progressive school in Brazil that was among the first to introduce computers. In fact, the school gave students access to labs containing Microsoft Office, multimedia software, and free broadband Internet. However, while Pueri Domus was on the cutting edge, the teaching was still the same style that Luis' older brothers had witnessed 20 years before when *they* were kids. For all purposes, computers were kept outside the classroom, leaving the teaching itself unchanged.

Traditional Instruction ("Factory")

- Every student receives the same amount of knowledge.
- Subjects remain the same for years.
- Students follow regular school hours.
- Tests are structured and are scheduled at certain times.

Game-Based Learning ("Sandbox")

- Players learn at their own pace.
- Challenges are dynamic.
- Hours are flexible.
- "Tests" may take place at any time and may follow a loose structure.

As you can see, game-based learning has all the primary elements of what we might call *dynamic learning*—a self-regulated engine that personalizes the difficulty to the user, maximizing learning potential. Real-life examples of that can be found in the relationship between master and disciple propagated by eastern religions. When a master takes on a disciple, he becomes responsible for the disciple's well-being and advancement. The master teaches as much as the disciple can digest and tests the disciple constantly, without warning. Challenges are tailor made for each individual, and there's room for "trial and error."

Games do the same thing, but the master here is software that adapts itself dynamically to each player's skills. While the events in the game might be the same for everyone, their difficulty will change, and the extra challenges available will also depend on who's playing. Not everyone unlocks every single secret in a game! In *Test Drive Unlimited*, you won't have the opportunity to drive some of the cars in the game until (or unless) you become more advanced. Ever. This is hard locked in the achievements system and requires that players win every time challenge, for example, so that the car becomes available for purchase.

Can you imagine a school that follows this model? The Montessori Method is a good approximation of the way games teach. Montessori schools are much more flexible than traditional schools. By avoiding the traditional "factory line" model, Montessori schools unlock creativity and self-reliance in students, similar to what games like *Sim City* achieve. Metaphorically, it's a battle between the sandbox and the production line!

ACTIVE LEARNING

Passive learning is easy to define: You make no effort—you don't even have to be fully "there"—and you end up learning something. This is how many kids learn in school even today, a constant rebellion of the senses against the physical obligation of being stuck inside a classroom. We all know by now that passive learning teaches the bare essentials and not much else.

We want our kids to learn *how* to learn and have pleasure while at it. We want them to learn laterally, by interacting with each other, rather than passively taking in a constant stream of information "pushed" at them from the front of a classroom. We want them to explore possibilities and take a shot at solving the universal problems. Sadly, endeavors like these rarely take place in school; at most, they're taken on by college students and researchers. There's little room for experimentation in school, and the memorization of dates and people hardly improves memory. We keep our students busy repeating other people's notion of knowledge, sadly keeping them away from their own vision.

It's Better to "Pull" than to "Push"!

In the early '90s, the Internet became a commercial medium with the help of the World Wide Web, which allowed text, graphics, audio, and video to be accessed through a user-friendly web browser. Before this, one of the primary methods of using the Internet involved sending email back and forth. Email is a form of "push" technology, where an individual pushes information to another or broadcasts it to many, as in some spam! (Speaking of "broadcast," all broadcast media such as radio and television are considered to be "push" technology.)

Web browsers, on the other hand, allowed individuals to browse and search through the Internet, accessing information by clicking on a series of hyperlinks. This "hunting and gathering" style of interaction is known as "pull" technology, where information is pulled by the user. Pull technology is *active* by definition, whereas push technology is *passive*.

→

This now-defunct Internet company characterized its own medium as a "push" rather than a "pull" technology by comparing it to television.

We have no doubt that the educational system could learn a great deal from electronic games. Games involve 97% active learning and only 3% passive learning. Players actively *play* games; they don't watch anything but the cinematics (which can sometimes be skipped anyway). Even a linear medium such as film can contain active components, especially when it leaves important plot points to the audience. Most of us don't want a movie that spells everything out for us. Good filmmakers always take the audience into consideration and *require* its participation in order to better tell the story. Games take this concept to the *nth* degree by having players make their own decisions along the way.

Isn't it refreshing to have the freedom to make mistakes and the autonomy to choose your own path? That's active learning—having power over the tools, sources, and end results in order to gain knowledge. While games use these strategies for entertainment purposes, the skills obtained throughout a lifetime of gaming easily translate to real life.

Passive Learning

- Observing
- Listening
- Following instructions
- Repeating

Active Learning

- Doing
- Speaking
- Improvising
- Creating

GOAL-ORIENTED LEARNING

Being a "go-getter" is a very desirable character trait in America. Go-getters get things done and never stop moving. All games are goal oriented. You have a list of objectives; how you achieve them is your responsibility. It's not a question of learning a button combination because the game explicitly asks the player what button combination is required to execute a Dragon Punch. The player needs to learn the Dragon Punch because it makes you more competitive in *Street Fighter 2*! Simple as that.

Process-Oriented Learning

- Focuses on step-by-step instructions
- Requires repetition
- Requires hierarchy (teacher/students)
- Disregards creativity

Goal-Oriented Learning

- Focuses on end result
- Requires trial and error
- Requires autonomy
- Encourages creativity

The best games in the market base their gameplay on the elements associated with goal-oriented learning. Multiple solutions to puzzles and scenarios are available so that players can be creative and never focus too much on "instructions" and recommendations. Once players know the rules and controls—taught in an interactive tutorial (learn by doing!)—games let players do their best against any obstacles that lie in their paths. There's always an end goal; beating the game means overcoming personal challenges as well as defeating the scripted challenges implemented by the designers.

Kids become go-getters when they trust themselves. They need to be loose in the world in a sense, but have their parents' support at the same time, a "backup" of sorts. Other combinations—having parents lead them by the hand or not having parents *at all*—are not as effective and usually create more damage than good.

WHERE GAMES AND SPORTS MEET

As you can see, games are much more than electronic toys. In a way, they are electronic hybrids of traditional board or card games and sports. How do you learn to play tennis or soccer? Do you read a book about the intricacies of swimming or watch an instructor use a blackboard to show quarterbacks how to score touchdowns? Probably not. In order to truly learn sports, you need to *play* them, and you always have an end goal in any practice session. The TV has taught you how the greatest players perform, so you have a role model. Now it's your turn to become that, and more.

Sports are games, but games are more than sports. Chess is a strategy game. Tug-of-war is a physical game. Hide-and-seek and cops-and-robbers are traditional games played all over the world.

The Music Connection

Although there have been DVDs released that teach voice, piano, guitar, and other music performance and composition methods, it's clear that there's nothing like actually *making* music during the learning process. In fact, many of these DVD-based learning methods encourage students to play back certain passages or even repeat patterns during the course of watching the DVD, which means that students must be near their instruments of choice at all times!

Games and sports are all dynamic, active, and goal oriented. They were the basis for electronic games. That's why video games differ so much from the methods seen in school; they have a different origin altogether.

Games and Sports Both Have/Require

- Victory conditions
- Winners and losers
- Rules (and manuals/playbooks)
- Teamwork (multiplayer modes/group sports)
- Flexible structures
- Mastery at certain levels/intervals
- Practice
- Contributions to personal growth

Considering the meeting points between sports and games, it's no wonder that sports simulation games have been one of the top-selling game genres. Players enjoy playing their favorite sports in the comfort of their own homes, where trying a limitless number of tactics and strategies is not only feasible but desirable. Players still love the "real" sport, but sports simulation games allow them to *expand* their knowledge and have fun at the same time. In this case, the sports simulation game has become a link between the individual and the sport.

GAMES AND CULTURE

If we want to use games as learning tools, we first need to grasp the real meaning of gaming from a cultural perspective. Gamers live life differently than people who don't play games. From the start, a gamer's life is based on knowledge. Hardcore gamers might depend on Google to find all the information they need, anywhere they go, with mobile devices like pocket PCs and smart phones. This is important because gamers have a need to know absolutely *everything* about their interests. Of course that doesn't mean that gamers don't read—they do, but they will go to books only if the topic deserves the extra level of detail.

INTERNET USE

Reading the latest news on the game industry is very important for gamers because their status among friends depends on how informed they are, and because they like to make conscious decisions. Gamers might read and contribute articles to Wikipedia (http://en.wikipedia.org), the free Internet encyclopedia. The Internet is, at its core, a communication medium, and it's essential for messaging and information exchange. Gamers are always in touch with friends and family, and they use email, social network web sites (e.g., MySpace [http://myspace.com]), and IM (instant messaging) for this purpose.

MEDIA CONSUMPTION

Gamers barely watch TV. Their version is YouTube (http://youtube.com); not even TiVo fully satisfies a gamer's idea of what television should be. YouTube is also popular because it is made up mostly of user-generated content—in stark contrast to the majority of what we see on TV. Moviegoing is also common for gamers, but attendance numbers have understandably gone down *due to* gaming. On the other hand, gamers watch a lot of DVDs and next-generation HD discs on Blu-ray or HD-DVD at home; they are the major force behind the new high-definition formats. Finally, gamers do read books, but only about topics that sit very high on their priority lists. "Readable" books need to be extremely updated, sharply written, and edgy enough in order to be in anyone's reading queue.

SOCIAL LIFE

Most gamers have very active social lives, and they use technology in order to:

- Keep in touch with friends and family
- Set up player matches and gaming sessions
- Make social appointments (clubs, restaurants, movies, shopping, dates)
- Discover the best entertainment in town
- Study for tests
- Hang out (taking over for the long phone calls of the past)

If gamers are not working or studying, they do their best to relax among friends.

LEARNING BRIDGES

Learning bridges are educational activities that, coordinated into a larger unit, enable learners to form their own body of knowledge. If we take moviegoing, playing an RTS, and using the Internet, for example, we can easily coordinate these three elements in order to teach the history of Rome. This is because the intersection between the three media "saturates" the minds of the learners with a large volume of information, allowing them to distill their own knowledge from those sources.

AIM FIRST

If you think about it, most of the elements of "gamer culture" that we've discussed in the previous section can be easily adapted for learning. Knowing how to find your way on the web, for example, ends up preparing kids to do deep research online, granting them access to a seemingly endless supply of human knowledge. Movies and books are also very positive since both habits are very effective learning bridges.

But first you need to figure out what you'd like your kids to learn. You need a clear set of objectives since they will point us in the right direction. Creating learning bridges is a three-step process:

1. Take a moment and think of possible topics of interest. We suggest that you write these topics down in a list.
2. List all relevant media formats available to you that might aid your kids in their quest for information on these topics.
3. Provide detailed information on items within each media format.

As an example, let's take a look at World War II as a topic.

Topic:	World War II
Media:	DVDs
	Games
	Internet research
	Books

Now we have our sources. The next step is to *detail* those sources.

DVDs (mixing documentaries and dramas in when possible):

The World at War 30th Anniversary Edition (BBC–1974)

Patton (20th Century Fox–1970)

A Bridge Too Far (MGM–1977)

Saving Private Ryan (Dreamworks–1998)

Games:

Brothers in Arms: Earned in Blood (PC)

Call of Duty 2 (PC / Xbox 360)

Call of Duty 3 (PS2, PS3, Xbox, Xbox 360)

Medal of Honor: Airborne (PS3, Xbox 360)

Internet research:

http://en.wikipedia.org/wiki/World_War_II

http://www.google.com/search?num=50&hl=en&lr=&safe=off&q=world+war
+2&btnG=Search

http://www.spartacus.schoolnet.co.uk/2WW.htm

Books:

Ghost Soldiers: The Forgotten Epic Story of World War II's Most Dramatic Mission (Hampton Sides)

Flags of Our Fathers (James Bradley)

THE FIGHTING FIRST: The Untold Story of the Big Red One on D-Day (Flint Whitlock)

Grandfather's Tale: The Tale of a German Sniper (Timothy Erenberger)

Anyone who experiences the entertainment on this list will learn a great deal about World War II. The best thing about this "method" isn't memorization; some of these sources might even contain inaccuracies and might contradict each other, so reaching a conclusion becomes an exercise in synthesis and common sense. No source is perfect, and assembling a coherent body of knowledge is a necessity. Going through this *once* is enough to teach anyone how to learn by themselves.

Active media (games, Internet) and passive media (TV, DVDs, cinema, books) should always be used in tandem in order to better educate your kids. It's not a good idea to leave them with a single source, whether it's a game, DVD, or web site. Kids must be able to access information from anywhere.

CHOOSE YOUR WEAPON(S)

As we've discussed, kids today make use of all sorts of media to entertain themselves *and* learn at the same time. You now know how to create "learning bridges" in order to help your kids grasp the maximum amount of content and then come up with their own conclusions. However, not every game suits every objective; sometimes, you'll have to be very precise if you want to reach a goal with your kids. Just letting them loose won't do it! Kids of all ages, teenagers or not, need incentive and guidance in order to learn this skill.

What if your children appear to lack certain skills that might help them become better learners? Let's take a look at three broad scenarios and how you can attack each of them.

1. Language Skills

What if your child lacks language skills? In this case, you need to fine-tune the media your child consumes to this objective. It is necessary to choose an adequate game genre, in other words. RPGs and adventure games are especially suited for language skill-building since they often contain a large amount of text and require reading and comprehension during the journey through the game's sometimes complex storyline. If your kid has a PS2, one option is *Tales of the Abyss*. The game is lengthy enough to keep your child interested for months!

Another important step is to reinforce the game with a book. The chosen book will depend on your child's tastes. However, if you take your child to the bookstore with you, we're sure you two can find something that really interests him. Some possibilities are books about technology (the history of Intel, Apple, Microsoft), games (game history, research, biographies), and politics (geopolitics, journalism). It's essential that the book act as a bridge with the game you chose.

Tales of the Abyss contains stunning special effects, accompanied by a lengthy storyline. TALES OF THE ABYSS® © Fujishima Kousuke Games Inc. © 2005 NAMCO BANDAI Games Inc. Courtesy of NAMCO BANDAI Games America Inc.

Finally, cover your bases with a healthy movie diet. Again, help your child choose a movie that has well-written dialogue *and* make sure to enable the subtitles corresponding to your child's native language; the latter is a known trick to improve language skills since the viewer can see, hear, and read the language at the same time. The triumvirate game-book-movie will attack the problem from all angles while also being fun and rewarding. In months, not years, you might find out that your kid's reading skills are getting substantially better.

Learning Is a Cycle

Everything we "prescribe" here needs to happen in a cycle. We mean that if you take these steps and then stop, the benefits will be minimal. It's much like love: We need to love our kids unconditionally and permanently, every second of every minute. Anything less than this is negative for their development. Learning needs the same care and attention; you need to constantly choose new goals and help your kids find the best possible material for their needs. It's your responsibility to be "on top of things," enabling your children to make the most of their natural talents.

2. Strategic Thinking Skills

What if your child lacks strategic thinking skills? These can also be taught, particularly through two types of games: real-time and turn-based strategy games. RTSs focus on speed, while turn-based games allow for deeper thinking. We'd start with a turn-based game so that your kid can take the time to reflect and make the best possible decisions; RTSs can be used later when your kid is more comfortable with the structure of strategy games.

The best bet would be to use both *Civilization IV* (turn-based) and *Rise of Nations* (RTS) and to supplement them with books about the civilizations portrayed in both games. If your child has any interest in history, your job gets that much easier: There are many books available that focus on the development and evolution of ancient civilizations.

Syd Meier's *Civilization IV* leads the pack in turn-based strategy games. Firaxis Games

Movies could be added to the mix also, depending on your kid's interests. Let's say he has a thing for Rome; *Gladiator* (2000) can be a great choice, especially when watched along with the director's commentary. Any good movie can supplement a study topic; Mel Gibson's *Braveheart* (1995), by the way, contains tons of strategy as well.

3. Management Skills

What if your child lacks management skills? These can be taught on all levels from interpersonal to large group. Games that deal with management from an interpersonal point of view are *The Sims 1* and *The Sims 2*, and games that focus on large groups include *Sim City 4* and *City Life*.

City Life adds some interesting twists to the genre. CDV Software Entertainment USA and Monte Cristo Games

The Sims is all about needs and goals. In a typical game, you'd have to organize your Sims' lives in such a way that allows each of them to attain whatever they need, whether it's recognition at home, work, or in their social lives. Players are required to carefully consider everything their Sims do to avoid wasting time and/or resources. *Sim City*, on the other hand, is more about larger, collective needs. You don't rule over individuals but large sectors of society—although the main objectives still involve how to best serve people in their quest for safety, money, and comfort. An alternative to the strictly simulation games would be massively multiplayer online games (MMOGs) such as *World of Warcraft (WoW)*. Becoming a Guildmaster in *WoW* can be great training in management, since the player leads a large group of *real* people. The complex dynamics involved are guaranteed to give your kid a nice challenge.

If you select overly "educational" books, the chances of your kid actually reading them are slim. Again, try to follow their interests (and everyone has interests) and pick a *relevant* book. Millennials have very clear ideas of what is useful to them, and they will surely rebel against a book that tries too hard! Hollywood has a good track record with movies that deal with management skills. Consider *Tucker: The Man and his Dream* (1988).

These three examples show you how to use games and other media as learning tools, emphasizing their positive characteristics. Although games are superior to film and most books in pure "learning potential," these other media can fill in the gaps left by some games since not all games are as deep as we would like them to be! It's always important to give kids access to opposing views on the same topic so that they develop critical thinking and problem-solving skills.

Education and learning are essential to the well-being of any type of civilization. As traditional school systems lose their edge, other systems arise—such as game-based education, in this case. In our hands is the power and responsibility to integrate gaming and learning, helping the birth of possibly the most effective learning system ever devised. As parents, you need to support games that teach valued lessons.

A BRIGHT FUTURE

Part II of this book has focused on the triumvirate of psychology, sociology, and education—three disciplines that have a vital role in games. Part III is all about how games may offer your kids a bright, unexpected future. We're most certainly not saying that working in the game industry is an easy job; it's not, and we won't let anyone think it is. What games have that no other career has is a perfect mix between being on the cutting edge and having fun at the same time, with a nice salary to boot. Despite long, crazy hours of production, the game industry is still one of the most dynamic, eventful, and visible segments of the economy, and the launch of three major platforms in 2005–2006 gives this already successful industry a major, major boost. In Chapter 6, "Game Makers," we will take a look at the inner workings of this fascinating industry and discover how games are made.

Part III

The Business

6 Game Makers

Game development is a career that increasingly attracts those who walk the fine line between technical ability and artistry; it requires the perfect balance between technique and talent. These talented individuals are known as "game developers." The "industry" (as insiders call it) is growing at a rapid pace, and consequently, professionals from Hollywood, advertising, and even major software companies such as Microsoft are steering their efforts toward the game industry.

Game development can be very lucrative, but it's also very risky. No less than 80% of all new games fail to recoup their investment in the first year, losing shelf space and value in the process. At the same time, a successful game such as *Gears of War* can spawn countless sequels and hundreds of millions of dollars in sales. Numbers like these—and the inherent "fun" associated with working in the game industry—are responsible for the attractiveness of game industry jobs. Everybody wants to jump into game development because it's more than a cool job; it's a chance to be forever on the cutting edge.

The focus of this chapter is to detail the roles of those who make games. We start with the basic structure of the business and advance to individual positions such as producer, designer, and tester. The roles played can sometimes be more interesting than the games themselves!

IN THE BEGINNING, THERE WAS A PROGRAMMER

Back in the late 1970s, making games was more a hobby than anything else. Despite the surge of jobs sparked by the success of the Atari 2600, literally *anyone* could make a game with the aid of a home computer. It seems almost unreal now, but at that time a whole game—graphics, audio, gameplay, and even packaging—could be done in weeks by a single person. This was only possible because games still had a very small footprint due to hardware and memory limitations. A game such as *Pitfall!*—one of the successes behind the early Activision—was solely designed by David Crane and was 4 Kbytes in size. Compare that with *Super Mario Bros,* which while still a small game, occupied 40 Kbytes in an NES (Nintendo Entertainment System) cartridge.

This trend lasted until the mid-1980s, when more sophisticated hardware (better graphics and sound) and larger cartridges made specialists necessary for the first time. This marked the shift from "the lone programmer" of the late 1970s and 1980s to a team of 5–10 developers. By the mid-1990s, with computer hardware running circles around consoles, teams grew even larger in number, reaching 20 developers on big titles such as *Descent* and *Quake.*

The market's shift to consoles in 2001 (attributed to the hugely successful PS2) brought to the industry the age of very large development teams with upwards of 80 developers on games such as *Gran Turismo 3.* Smaller games had more modest numbers, but the jump to 80 or 100 "devs" changed the industry's economics drastically.

Teams would get even larger with the next generation of consoles, such as the Xbox 360 and the PlayStation 3. For example, *Call of Duty 3* had a team of almost 300 developers and a budget of tens of millions of dollars. (Very few know the exact number!) This is a huge jump from the typical budgets of PS2 and Xbox games ($5–8 million in most cases). The reason for this is that gamers now expect much more from graphics and sound (especially graphics), forcing developers to have dozens of artists, specialized sound departments, orchestral soundtracks, and Hollywood-level scripts if they want to be able to compete with similar titles. This and marketing costs drove the budgets way up, making game development an even riskier proposition.

	1975–1985	1985–1995	1996–2001	2002–2006	2007–?
# of Team Members:	1	5–10	10–20	20–80	80–?
Media	Tapes Floppies Cartridges	Floppies CD-ROMs Cartridges	CD-ROMs Cartridges	CD-ROMs DVD-ROM	DVD-ROM BLU-RAY
Focus	1. Gameplay 2. Graphics 3. Sound	1. Gameplay 2. Sound 3. Graphics	1. Graphics 2. Gameplay 3. Sound	1. Graphics 2. Sound 3. Gameplay	1. Graphics 2. Sound 3. Gameplay

As you can see, there was a shift from gameplay to graphics starting around 1995 with the advent of 32-bit consoles (PlayStation, Saturn) and 3D accelerator cards for computers. Games in the late 1980s had a 3 to 1 ratio of programmers to artists. This was because gameplay was the major factor when making a game. With the shift to graphics, we saw an inversion of this as artists became more numerous than programmers.

THE BUSINESS MODEL

The game industry is divided into three major tiers: manufacturers, publishers, and developers. Each plays a different role in what is called the "industry cycle"—the ebb and flow that govern the creation and distribution of video games.

MANUFACTURERS

Manufacturers are companies that design and build hardware. For consoles, the "big three" are Microsoft, Sony, and Nintendo (PCs have multiple manufacturers). These companies are also known as first-party developers, since they also develop games for their own platforms. Manufacturers have absolute control over which games are sold for their respective systems because they have the games submitted to them before going to market. This is known as the "submission process." If a game fails submission, it goes back to the developer to be "fixed."

Manufacturers commonly buy studios and turn them into first-party developers. This was the case with Bungie, the developer behind the *Halo* franchise; before Microsoft got in the picture, Bungie had been developing *Halo: Combat Evolved* for Macintosh computers!

Manufacturer	First-Party Developer	Game
Microsoft	Bungie	*Halo 3*
Sony	Polyphony Digital	*Gran Turismo 4*
Nintendo	Intelligent Systems	*Metroid*

Manufacturer	Second-Party Developer	Game
Microsoft	Bizarre Creations	*Project Gotham Racing 3*
Sony	Insomniac Games	*Ratchet & Clank*
Nintendo	Sora	*Super Smash Bros. Brawl*

Mario makes a spectacular showing in *New Super Mario Bros.* for the Nintendo DS. Courtesy of Nintendo

PUBLISHERS

Publishers are similar to movie studios; they fund, market, and distribute games. In order to publish a game, the publisher first needs a license from the manufacturer. This license grants the publisher the right to sell games made for that platform. This is why the Sega Genesis used to display "Produced by or under license from Sega Enterprises Ltd." every time a cartridge was inserted; this was a "lock" implemented by Sega to defeat unlicensed games. However, it's important to mention that the reverse is true for the PC platform; virtually anyone can publish a PC game. This makes the PC platform the easiest to get into and, at the same time, the toughest to succeed at due to decreased standardization.

In the industry's early years, only first-party games reached the market. Atari games were only made by developers that worked *for* Atari. Activision, the world's second largest publisher in 2006, was the first third-party developer, making games for the Atari 2600.

In order to be profitable and efficient, publishers have an army of producers and executive producers (we'll explain their roles later) that keep tabs on both the developer and the rest of the publisher's staff. Even marketing, finance, and human resources must all work together to support the making of an AAA title!

Publisher	Developer	Game
Electronic Arts	EA Games	*Need for Speed: Carbon*
Activision	Treyarch	*Call of Duty 3*
THQ	Rainbow Studios	*Cars*

Need for Speed: Carbon is the latest installment in EA's lucrative franchise. Electronic Arts, Inc.

DEVELOPERS

Developers are also third-party. The big difference between publishers and developers is that the publisher normally has the money, while the developer has the talent. Developers live or die by milestones and sales numbers. Developers are either bought by publishers or hired by them. There's usually a lengthy contract that describes in detail the responsibilities of parties, milestones, and intellectual ownership. This contract will rule the relationship between the two companies for the duration of the project.

It's possible (and common) to have a game be created by two or three development studios at the same time, either by having them create the same game on a different platform (PS3 and Xbox 360) or collaborate on the same version. The former is necessary if a big game needs to be out for many platforms at the same time, while the latter covers enormous projects that simply can't be done by a single developer.

Third-Party Developer	Game
Epic Games	*Gears of War*
BioWare	*Mass Effect*
Stormfront Studios	*Eragon*

Second-Party Developers

Once an unofficial designation, "second-party developers" are now seen as part of the industry's landscape. Being a second-party developer means that you have very close ties to a certain manufacturer, either verbally or based on an exclusivity deal. Although not owned by the manufacturer—like a first-party developer—a second-party developer enjoys funding and close tech support from the manufacturers; this, in turn, allows it more freedom to ship ground-breaking titles. A good example of a second-party developer is Insomniac Games, responsible for the *Ratchet & Clank* franchise and the PS3 launch title, *Resistance: Fall of Man*. Insomniac has been working closely with Sony since 1996.

PRODUCTION

Illustration by Ian Robert Vasquez

Producing is "making things happen." Any job in production will be about making everything and everyone work towards a within-the-budget, high-quality game. Production is all about coordinating seemingly disparate elements into a cohesive whole.

There are many different kinds of producers, depending on location and hierarchy. Since the game industry is very nonstandard, however, some of the names and functions may vary, depending on the company.

- *External producers* work for the publisher. They might be executive producers in charge of the entire game.
- *Internal producers* work inside the development studio and usually are members of the development team. They supervise new builds, patches, and more earthly needs such as pizza orders and office space.
- *Assistant producers* are the green peas within a publisher. They may have risen from the QA department (more on that later) and are now responsible for certain areas of the game. Assistant producers are producers in training.
- *Associate producers* are sometimes one step above assistant producers. Producers of this level take care of daily tasks and non-mission–critical processes, allowing the producer to focus on more complex issues. Associate producers have a lot of responsibility but not much power.

■ *Producers* (or *executive producers*) call the shots in the making of a game. They represent either the development studio head or the publisher. Producers have a heavy influence on the game's design, although their main objectives are to keep the game on time, under budget, and on track for financial success.

Game producers hold the responsibility of keeping the lines of communication open between publisher and developer and also among the developers themselves. Producers solve conflicts, build and maintain schedules, secure equipment, *and* become champions for the game.

Microsoft Project is used by many game producers to track projects.

DESIGN

Design, contrary to the original meaning of the word (and the meaning often used in other creative industries), does not have much to do with the look of a game. Design is directly related to gameplay—*how* the game *plays*. Designers set the rules

Illustration by Ian Robert Vasquez

that define victory and defeat conditions and also plan and build the many levels in a game.

- The entry-level position in design is that of a *level designer,* who is primarily concerned about the levels themselves and is responsible for designing maps and environments. Level designers might also be involved in devising missions and/or writing dialogue.
- *Gameplay designers* are a step above level designers. In order to design gameplay, it's necessary to know the scripting languages used in the project. Scripting is very similar to programming, but it is easier since scripting languages are usually high level. So if the designer has a mission ready, on paper, he now needs to translate those rules and mechanics into terms that the game understands (so that it becomes part of the gameplay). Designers do it with scripting languages.
- The *lead designer* coordinates the design team. This includes supervising the work done on gameplay and often working along with the design director (or game designer) to create the master design. (Some lead designers don't actually code themselves.)
- *Design directors* might be known as *game designers*. This is a coveted position, since it's pretty much on the center stage of game development. It does involve management, including staff support, documentation, and the creation of prototypes.
- *Creative directors* interface with the design director while maintaining strong ties to the art director and other top development studio positions. They deal with the "big picture" of gameplay, making sure that the game is always fun and innovative.

The Interface Designer

Interface design is sometimes outsourced due to time constraints. The result is an interface that seems more like an appendage than anything else—because it wasn't done by the developers themselves. To counter this, some developers have added another position to the design department: interface design. Sometimes an entry-level position, interface design goes hand-in-hand with the art department; the interface designer supplies the mechanics and functionality, while the art department creates the 2D or 3D art assets. It's a great way to tackle the problem, since now the concept behind the interface is the same as the game's—helping usability and creativity go side by side.

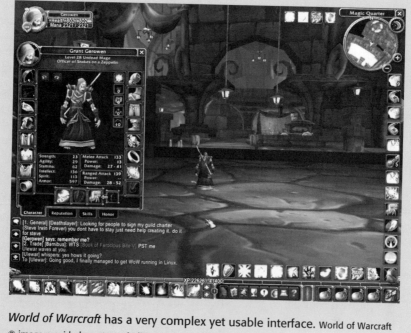

World of Warcraft has a very complex yet usable interface. World of Warcraft ® image provided courtesy of Blizzard Entertainment, Inc.

ART

The way a game looks depends in part on the technology used (such as platform or game engine), but despite the technology, it mostly depends on the art department. Game artists are responsible for concept drawings, textures, 3D models, and other assets required for a game.

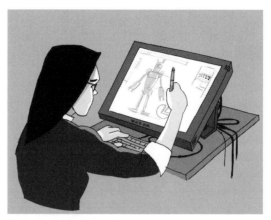

Illustration by Ian Robert Vasquez

- *Texture artists* are often entry-level positions. They take photos, and through image editing software such as Adobe Photoshop, turn 2D images into 3D, bump, and normal-mapped textures. Texture art is thought of as "easier" than other art positions, but coming up with detailed textures *while* preserving memory is no easy task. Texture artists must understand that their freedom depends on hardware limits (such as memory and bandwidth). Great texture artists work around limitations and deliver textures that look better than anything on the market.
- *Object modelers* are also primarily entry-level positions. These artists create the 3D models of objects such as furniture, foliage, weapons, and vehicles, usually using 3ds Max or Maya modeling software. Object modeling is regarded as an entry-level position because modeling objects is considered much simpler than modeling characters. Therefore, newbies are stuck modeling boxes and barrels at first!
- *Character modelers* work alongside the concept artist to model a game's characters in 3D. It helps to have a classic art foundation if you're a character modeler because it gives artists correct notions of proportion and other details of human and non-human physiology.
- *Lead artists* have seniority over other artists. A big production can have both lead modelers and lead texture artists; these are the "heads" of their respective departments. Of course, these positions are also skill based; the leads can help the rest of the team with undocumented functions or complex techniques that they wouldn't know otherwise.
- The *art director* oversees the art for the entire game, coordinating asset creation and orienting the art team to the look of the game. Art directors are in close contact with the creative director and sometimes the game designer, depending

on who's overseeing the project. Art directors are those responsible for the quality of the game's look, including how impressive it is. With graphics now on the forefront of game development, this position is more important than ever.

■ *Animators* are responsible for giving all characters and props personality, or "life," through movement. In the early days, programmers would do all the animation. Later in the game (mid-1990s), animation became a specialty, with animators migrating from film, television (where 3D animation had gained traction), and the traditional animation industry; they began working with the rest of the game art department. With realism being increasingly important in games today, animators also interface with motion capture (MoCap), a technology developed in Hollywood that allows actors' moves to be translated into in-game animation. Contrary to some opinion, MoCap is not a threat to animators; the imported "frames" still need to be fine-tuned and integrated into the game.

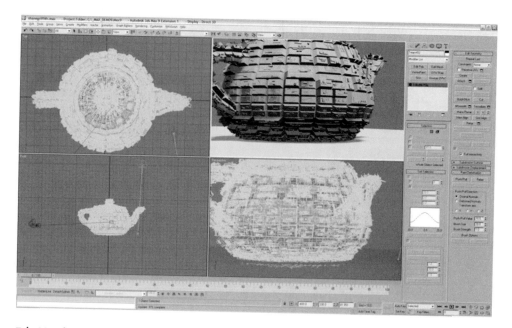

3ds Max is a standard game art tool. Autodesk, Inc.

The Concept Artist

Concept artists are not always part of the development team. Their role gets smaller and smaller as development continues. This is the reason why some concept artists work on a freelance basis, joining the project in the very beginning and then leaving when the look of the game is finalized. It is also common to have the art director do the concept design. In this case, the art director will have even more control of how the game looks, which can be a good thing and a bad thing, depending on who the art director is! Interestingly, a few major game companies such as Electronic Arts have recently hired some concept artists right out of college as entry-level art team members, evidence of the ever-changing game industry.

Set of concept drawings showing detail progression, created by art director Mark Soderwall. Art by Mark Soderwall

PROGRAMMING

Guess what element is always "behind-the-curtains" in games? The code. There are two types of code: low-level and high-level. *Low-level* code is known as machine or assembly language, and *high-level* code is based on languages such as C++ or

Illustration by Ian Robert Vasquez

Python. The code that governs a game runs in the background; if it weren't for programmers, there would be no gameplay, no artificial intelligence, no graphics, and no audio! Game programmers are those responsible for implementing the designer's design, the artist's art . . . pretty much everybody else's work.

There are many types of programmers. It's a very specialized position; programmers can have completely different sets of skills and still be part of the same department.

■   *Tools programmers* develop and give support to in-house tools that help the team make the game. Tools have myriad uses—file compression, formatting, listing, etc. Quality tools give developers an edge in productivity and help the team focus on more relevant tasks.

■   *Graphics programmers* are in charge of making the game run on the hardware of choice, whether that be consoles, handhelds, cell phones, or computers. They are specialists in application programming interfaces (APIs) such as Direct3D (Microsoft) and OpenGL, and they know hardware inside and out.

■   *Engine programmers* tinker and tune the game engine chosen to run the game. For example, if a developer has chosen the Unreal Engine 3.0 for a new first-person shooter (FPS), the engine programmers are responsible for adapting the engine to the game's needs by adding and/or editing features. The engine programmers are always in close contact with the engine licensor. (In the case of UE3, this would be Epic Games.)

■ *Networking programmers* are responsible for the net code that powers the multiplayer component of games. Since multiplayer capabilities are now a must for every game (otherwise, they're forgotten in a matter of days), networking programmers have quickly turned into valuable commodities inside game development studios. We can't stress enough how important is to have lag-free gameplay during multiplayer games, and this is the main objective of networking programmers.

■ *Artificial intelligence (AI) programmers* ensure that the game elements behave "intelligently." Players have become very sophisticated and now expect characters that display truly intelligent behavior, such as the marines in the very first *Half-Life*, working together as a team to set up "traps" for the players. AI programmers focus on intelligent behavior like this, whether for monsters in an FPS, highly sophisticated creatures in an MMOG, or a "simple" human in *The Sims*. Now that next-gen consoles allow for much more complex calculations, it's in the hand of AI programmers to provide game characters with truly engaging behavior.

■ *Audio programmers* ensure that music and sound effects play *how* and *when* they should. These programmers implement every audio element, including sound effects, musical soundtrack, and dialogue, to ensure that the sound code doesn't interfere with the rest of the game. (You'd be surprised the number of crashes caused by sound!) Audio programmers might also develop sound tools and compression codecs.

■ *Physics programmers* are becoming even more important (especially now that physics-based gameplay such as in *RoboBlitz* is going mainstream), not only on racing games but in every title. Technological breakthroughs are facilitating this; consoles now have hardware specialized in physics calculations, leaving the processor free for other tasks. Add-on cards (such as the Ageia PhysX) are now available for PCs. Physics lends a healthy dose of realism to any game.

■ *Interface programmers* help to implement the game's interface. These programmers ensure that every button and menu works and that the items in every character's inventory are *really* there!

■ *Quality assurance (QA) programmers* develop tools for testing. These tools are necessary because in certain cases it's better to have software test the game (e.g., trying all permutations allowed by the game's menus). *Forza Motorsport* had a system in which "automated testing" reported any bugs in the game's many menus to the developers with 100% precision and inhuman speed!

■ *Associate programmers* comprise perhaps the lone "entry-level" position. They tend to start small and work within well-defined boundaries. These junior programmers slowly learn about the game's script languages, tools, and hardware kinks—by taking on one small section at a time.

AUDIO

Game audio is now serious business. Game consoles rival the sound quality found on expensive home theater systems, and players have gotten used to multi-channel surround sound. George Lucas used to say that sound is 50% of the experience in a movie; this notion has been proven right in the last five years, especially since consoles such as the first Xbox introduced true in-game Dolby Digital 5.1 in 2001.

Illustration by Ian Robert Vasquez

Microsoft's DirectMusic Producer is used by game audio professionals because it allows them to create dynamic or adaptive sound. Microsoft Corporation

Audio used to be relegated to the background (or even as an afterthought) in game development; most of the development studio's resources were targeted toward graphics and gameplay instead. Now, games have well-staffed, well-funded audio departments that focus on extracting the most from the new hardware. Let's see who's who in game audio!

- *Sound designers* find sounds in the real world and transform them into effective in-game sound effects. It's a position that has been gaining prestige in recent years when players and the media have increasingly begun to take notice of extraordinary sound effects. Sound designers are also responsible for integrating new sound effects into the game engine, deciding when and how each of them should be used.
- *Voiceover artists* are actors who lend their voices to game characters. They record their lines at a studio, and sound designers integrate them in the game later in the process. Sometimes the same actor does more than one character in a game!
- *Composers* are also required to write the game's score. Lower-budget titles usually have soundtracks done with synthesizers, while AAA titles hire orchestras such as the Czech National Symphony and the London Philharmonic. With games, composers have the extra challenge of writing music for a non-linear medium and also have to implement multiple layers of tension within the same composition in order to portray various "moods" associated with a particular scene, which may change based on player choice.
- The *audio director* is the "big cheese" in game audio, the mind behind the game's soundscape. The audio director hires talent (including voiceover artists and composers), interfaces with audio programmers, and contacts licensors if the company needs the rights for pre-existing songs. The audio director has the responsibility of finding the game's "soul" through audio, which is no easy task in the game developer's rushed environment!

TESTING AND QUALITY ASSURANCE (QA)

As games get more complex, so does the possibility of having nasty bugs in the code. Testing and QA departments make sure that the game you just bought is playable, stable, and high quality.

However, testing is more than *bug hunting*; it also involves evaluating a game's fun factor. The only way to be sure a game is entertaining is to play it daily, nonstop, until the difference between "ok" and "great!" becomes obvious. This can be the difference between a failure and a market success, so it's very important that this kind of testing start early in the process.

Illustration by Ian Robert Vasquez

Devtrack helps developers track and fix bugs. TechExcel, Inc.

- *QA testers* usually work from the publisher's office or headquarters. These testers have checklists created especially for the game, and they need to go through them every day in order to find even the smallest issues. QA is the last line of defense in bug hunting.
- *Production testers* are in-house testers, working from within the development studio. Being close to the developers has many advantages over being isolated at QA, but the hours are even worse (12–18 hours a day, 7 days a week; QA tops out at 12 hours a day, 6 days a week). Production testers focus on high priority bugs, fun factor, and usability.
- The *testing manager* is the one responsible for supervising both in-house and QA test teams. The testing manager makes sure teams are working well together (personal conflicts chip away at efficiency), and he interfaces with the production staff to ensure that the testing department has adequate personnel and that the testers themselves are being well treated.
- The *lead tester* usually has risen from the ranks of production or QA tester. Being a lead tester requires good people skills, work ethics, and determination, especially since developers make leads work very long hours. Lead testers write the testing plan for a game and guide the team during normal testing processes, suggesting alternatives and organizing testers into subteams if necessary.

Three types of testing exist: compatibility testing, playability testing, and beta testing. *Compatibility* testing is more common in PC games; these testers make sure that a game works with the maximum number of accessories found on the market, such as sound cards, video cards, and controllers. *Playability* testers are very similar to production testers. *Beta* testing is a special type of testing that employs end users on a massive scale. Beta testers do their jobs from home, work for free, and get the chance to play the game before anyone else does. Beta testing usually tries to "stress" a game's servers (sometimes referred to as a "stress test") so that the system is prepared for the millions of users of the finished game.

THE LIFE CYCLE OF GAMES

Games have become so complex that they now must follow a strict development cycle in order to get to market. The times of merely having an idea and working days and nights for three weeks is over. Now games demand detailed planning and flawless execution, that is, if the producer wants to keep production on budget and on time.

There are many stages in game development, including:

- Concept
- Pre-production
- Prototype
- Production
- Alpha
- Beta
- Gold

Concept

Games start out as concepts, usually in the game designer's mind. There's usually at least one "visionary" behind every game. This is the person who had the original idea and somehow convinced others to join in making it a reality. The visionary begins with a basic concept of what the game is: who the main characters are, the chosen genre, gameplay type, and target market. With that in mind, the visionary then spends some time with the team leads and/or directors (programming, art, and design) in order to streamline the concept to prepare it for pre-production; often, the concept artist creates preliminary visuals during these meetings. It's very important that the concept goes through intense change and evaluation in this stage. Only a strong concept, one that resonates with both developers and market, has any chance of becoming a great game.

Pre-Production

Pre-production is all about getting the studio ready for the game. One of the main things that occurs during the pre-production process is the assembly of the remaining team members; every artist and programmer must be either contracted or taken from another project. This can take some time, but the game cannot truly begin until most of the team is ready for action. Once the staff is hired, the team starts the documentation process, producing an art style guide and a production plan. These are just the minimum elements necessary in order to organize the team and, at the same time, give them an idea of the game's style. The main driving force behind the project—the game design document (GDD)—is the culmination of the pre-production process. With a GDD, the team will know exactly what kind of game they have. The GDD gives the team guidelines for production, like the number of levels, type and tone of cinematics, and both basic and advanced gameplay. When the GDD is in everyone's hands and the production plan reaches a final version, it's time to create a prototype.

PROTOTYPE

Most publishers require a prototype (or demo) in order to continue. The prototype needs to prove to anyone involved that the game is viable, fun, and unique—necessary traits for any bestseller. Usually, the prototype is made in order to demonstrate the game's core gameplay. Graphics and sound don't really matter at this point; above all, the feasibility of the project must be beyond doubt, as well as the potential for success. And the only way to verify those two is to have something that anyone can play—a sample of the intended, finished game. Good prototypes will harbor the game's soul in spades, spreading the word around the developer's employees and from there to the publisher. Bad prototypes will immediately show the concept's basic design flaws, which can kill the project right there; nobody wants to work on a concept that doesn't have a strong foundation.

PRODUCTION

Once the prototype has been approved, the game moves into production, which might take at least six months on a rushed title to three years on an AAA, mega-budget game such as *Halo 3*. Some studios have the luxury of adopting an "it will be done when it's done" philosophy, while others might have to deal with the wishes of the publisher—period. Even worse, some games might go through over five years of "development hell" and never be released, such as *Duke Nukem Forever* (RIP).

Production might start as any other job—eight hour days, five days a week—but soon, overtime starts to creep in. With a year to go, producers might start what is called "light overtime," 12-hour days, six days a week. While this type of schedule is what anyone might consider "hard work," developers and publishers do their best to convince their employees that this is the very least for someone in the game industry. They make a case for "it's worth it because you love it" and that the game needs the extra effort in order to be truly great. Of course, the truth is much simpler than this: The fact is that game projects are sometimes mismanaged; in these cases, the only way to keep the game on schedule is to extend the working hours. This doesn't happen immediately, and it does follow certain stages, but it's all too common to drown game developers in inhuman working hours, especially during the last three months of a project. In any case, with or without overtime, production eventually goes into a higher gear, the very first milestone in game development: Alpha.

ALPHA

By the Alpha phase, a game is playable from start to finish. Some of the assets might not be final—placeholder sounds, menus, and textures are very common—but the game is now an entity of its own, with a clear concept and gameplay fully implemented. Most publishers hold onto any extra funding until a game reaches Alpha.

This is the stage where the in-house test team starts to hunt for bugs. Concurrently with bug hunting, Alpha is also the time to polish the game, making sure every feature fully delivers. If something still barely works by then, Alpha is the developer's chance to cut a feature without terrible consequences. Let's now see what Alpha means from a functional perspective:

- One gameplay path (full progression)
- Primary language text
- Basic interface with preliminary documentation
- Compatibility with most specified hardware and software configurations
- Minimum system requirements tested
- Most manual interfaces tested for compatibility
- Placeholder art and audio
- Multiplayer functionality tested (if applicable)
- Draft of game manual

The publisher evaluates Alpha candidates carefully. If a game doesn't deliver on any of these areas, it goes back to the developer until it is finally approved. Upon approval, production moves to Beta.

BETA

Beta is when a game is *feature complete* and needs only to be finished. The most important task of production now is to get rid of bugs and other issues, readying the game for launch. As all assets are integrated and placeholders are replaced by their final versions, a large number of testers (in-house and QA) struggle to make sure that everything works. Later in the process, the game will be in "code freeze," a state where changes are forbidden unless they're necessary to correct nasty bugs. Here's a checklist for Beta:

- Code
- Content
- Language version text
- Game path navigation
- User interface
- Hardware and software compatibility
- Manual interface compatibility
- Art and audio
- Game manual

When it is done—the publisher will say so. Once the publisher approves of the latest build, the game *goes gold*.

Patching a Buggy Game

Sometimes, even with all the hard work from QA, a game still ends up chock full of bugs. In the past, the only solution to this was to recall the defective copies, an impractical and expensive process. Thankfully, next-gen systems such as the Xbox 360 and PlayStation 3 have defeated the huge costs associated with recalls with easy, downloadable patches. However, although they deal with original problems more than adequately, patches have become infamous for making it easy for developers to launch a problematic game, since they know it can be fixed by a patch anyway. Some consumers even call themselves "guinea pigs" or "beta testers," since they already expect their shiny new game to be haunted by the most varied and annoying issues.

GOLD

The expression "gold" comes from *gold master*, the final version of the game that ends up in a gold-plated CD or DVD. Companies use this type of disc because it is the safest media available; gold versions are ready to market, so it's important that the content remain safe from scratches and fingerprints. For the next step of the process, a producer is usually responsible for taking the gold master to the mastering company. The golden disc is turned into a *glass master* and is then copied onto hundreds of thousands of blank discs along with the packaging. Once the copies are completed, the game is then shipped to stores worldwide.

FOR YOUR CONSIDERATION . . .

So this is how a game gets made. It's a huge artistic undertaking, rivaling most big-budget movies. The next time you see your kids playing a game, think of the hundreds of developers who spent 2–3 years making it—and of the many millions necessary to take the game to market. Soon enough, awards ceremonies such as the Oscars will share space with special *game* awards ceremonies—hopefully, without the long acceptance speeches!

7 Playing to Work

In This Chapter

- How About a Career in the Game Industry?
- Skills
- Education
- Starting Out
- Modding
- Beta Testing
- Networking
- Internships
- Player Communities
- Ports of Entry
- The Future Is Now

One of the greatest pleasures of playing games is being a valued consumer, catered to by those who create the entertainment. Without consumers, all companies would falter.

And being a consumer is more than just fun: It's *comfortable*. All these game developers, publishers, and manufacturers scramble for your hard-earned money day after day, nights and weekends, throughout the year. They create new hardware and games, and they pamper you with discounts, online communities, and free subscriptions to your favorite magazines. They will do just about anything to have (and keep) your business.

But being a consumer has one big problem: You are always *spending money*. And the royal treatment depends on your spending habits: You must spend constantly and reliably. As parents, you can get caught up in funding the playing habits of your kids, but there are other ways in which your kids can take part in this entertainment revolution.

Being a player does have its merits, but there are many opportunities for your kids to do something even more valuable with their knowledge of games: become *producers* rather than just *consumers.*

How About a Career in the Game Industry?

Your kid's skill behind a gamepad can easily be worth money in the game industry. Since game development degree programs are still in their infancy and there's a history of young people contributing to game projects while they're still in high school (or even younger), getting your foot in the door at a game company does not necessarily depend on having a college degree. There are other factors besides education, and most of them simply involve personal effort. Although we'd never advocate having your child refrain from getting a college-level education (especially since one of us teaches at the college level), there are some early opportunities available for your kids that could help them realistically decide whether they truly want to pursue a career in the game industry.

Once an off-the-beaten-path career, game development is now more than a possibility; it's a viable alternative to the traditional 9-to-5 desk job. Not every gamer is suitable as a developer, but developers are *always* gamers. (Try to keep this in mind the next time your kid stays up trying to get to the end of *Zelda!*)

Skills

Development skills are divided into four areas: design, art, tech, and management. *Design* focuses on storytelling, character development, gameplay mechanics, and level design. *Art* focuses on concept drawing, modeling, texturing, animation, and special effects. Tech involves more mathematical thinking and less aesthetics, consisting primarily of programming and scripting skills. Management is for producers and leads. It takes a very special individual to pull a team together and get the best performance from everyone. Management positions attract organized, determined candidates who like to lead (and who do it well).

In general, artistically minded individuals move to an art position, while tech people quickly learn programming and other useful skills. Those who move into design positions could lean toward art, writing, scripting, or programming. While it's possible for one individual to be talented in many ways, one way will often dominate, so it's crucial to help identify your kids' main talents long before they make a career choice. However, if your kids don't fit any of those categories, there's always hope that they are, in fact, "producer" types. You can spot this trait with school assignments; the more organized student or natural leader in a small group will almost always have management skills lurking somewhere.

Sorry, Previous Game Experience Needed

Sometimes, professionals from other industries, such as software development, music, and movies try to make the jump to games. Imagine their surprise when companies ask them to start as testers, despite their years of work experience. This is a unique trait in the game industry. Developers always require *game industry experience* for any position above tester because companies need to know that candidates understand the development cycle of a game, are familiar with all major platforms, and have *in-game* experience. (They absolutely need to be gamers themselves.) Somewhat of a "Catch-22," this limitation scares some candidates off: Once they used to be well-paid professionals, and now they're forced to take entry-level positions before doing anything else in the company! An exception to this rule is now sometimes made for producers; the game industry is beginning to realize that leadership skills from other industries might be transferable to games, especially when many developers who work their way up to producer positions never attained these same skills during the process!

Parent Snapshot

John Hight

Director of External Production (Sony)
La Canada, CA

In 1991, John Hight built his first game, *Battleship*, for the Philips CDi player. Since that time he has worked on over 25 games and 9 edutainment products on various consoles and PCs. He's been fortunate to experience game development from many different roles: programmer, artist, writer, designer, and producer. Prior to joining Sony, John held management and creative positions with Atari, Electronic Arts, Westwood Studios, and 3DO. In his role as Executive Producer and Director of Design for Electronic Arts, John contributed to the design and production of *Nox*, *Command & Conquer: Red Alert 2*, and *Yuri's Revenge*. He is currently working on games for the

→

> PlayStation 3 for both retail sales and direct-to-consumer digital distribution. John holds a BSE in Computer Science from the University of New Mexico and an MBA from the Marshall School of Business at the University of Southern California.
>
> - Family Profile: Two boys, ages 11 and 17
> - Playtime: 1–3 hours per week with kids
> - Platforms: Xbox, PS3, PS2, GameCube, PC, PSP, DS
> - Top Games: *Resistance, Motorstorm, Warcraft 3*
> - "My kids have contributed design ideas and critiques of games that I work on. They want to make games for a living."

EDUCATION

Once upon a time, getting a "game studies" education was far from possible. There weren't any college courses focusing on game development—period. So gamers had to rely on unofficial sources: Internet FAQs (Frequently Asked Questions), user-powered forums such as gamedev.net, and retail books. This produced many "do-it-yourself" types who learned everything by themselves but had no formal education. (With luck, some had college degrees!)

With the industry's growth, employers realized that, more than skilled workers, game companies needed educated and disciplined employees. This is how the partnership between game developers and educational institutions began. The demand soared, and the very first game degree programs in the country were launched.

One of the very first schools that focused on game education was the DigiPen Institute of Technology. In 1994, through a partnership with Nintendo, DigiPen kick-started its diploma in the Art and Science of 2D and 3D Video Game Programming, a pioneering two-year course on game programming that spawned many others throughout the decade.

Fast-forward to 2007. With the game industry in full stride, students now have many different schools to choose from. Well-known colleges and universities with game degree programs include The Art Institutes, DeVry University, Westwood College of Technology, ITT Technical Institute, Full Sail, Carnegie Mellon University, and the University of Southern California. (See the "Resources" section of this book for a complete list.)

If your kids are serious, finding an appropriate school is essential, but it is also often the final step in a candidate's preparation for a job in the industry. In this chapter, we'll show you how kids can start making games way before they utter the word "college."

Parent Snapshot

Destini Copp

Professor (South University)
Alpharetta, GA

Destini received an MBA with a concentration in marketing from Keller Graduate School of Management at Devry University and a BA in accounting from Clemson University. She is currently attending class to obtain a doctorate in business with a concentration in marketing. Destini previously worked with a *Fortune* 50 company in its marketing division. In her most recent position, she was responsible for the company's overall product strategy for a $700 million portfolio, including the prioritization and development of new products, enhancements, and the ongoing management of existing products. She spends a lot of her time at soccer and baseball fields, and she enjoys running and playing competitive tennis—both singles and doubles. From a volunteer standpoint, she serves as a coach/captain for the Tennis Association for Kids in Atlanta and the junior ALTA organization.

- Family Profile: Two boys, ages 7 and 10
- Playtime: Spouse plays games with boys 1–3 hours per week
- Platforms: Xbox, GBA
- "My 7-year-old son saw an advertisement on TV for DeVry University. They were soliciting students for their program to create video games. He thinks that is what he wants to do when he grows up!"

STARTING OUT

The very best way to help your kids take games seriously is to take them seriously yourself. If you do your research and keep up to date with the latest developments, there's a good chance you'll be talking to your kids about games when they're old enough. And every kid on the block likes fun, informative conversations with their parents.

Your attitude toward games will reflect on your kids. If you see games as silly and mere escapism, your kids will probably either mirror this view or rebel against it, with negative outcomes for both alternatives. It's important that parents understand that they are always role models, not just when they teach etiquette or good manners.

One way of introducing information in your kids' day-to-day gaming is to have them browse targeted web sites or magazines with you before buying a game. Show them how games can be evaluated by different people; how international news and events can affect games; and the role that advertising plays in "convincing" people that one game is better than all others. Make this a ritual before a new game is bought. Soon enough, your kids will read the reviews and tell *you* what to buy!

The second step is to give your kids their own computers. Nowadays, it makes more sense to provide them with a mid-range laptop on which they can play games, one that doesn't cost $3,000. The sweet spot for a good laptop is around $1,500–$1,700—plenty of power without breaking the bank.

Laptops are also good because they come with recovery discs. If your kid wreaks havoc with Windows, you can always put the disc in and return it to factory settings. However, since this erases about everything on the hard drive, get your kids an external hard drive as well and teach them about the importance of backing up their work. This way, if push comes to shove, they won't lose any important school assignments (or game saves).

Let's now recap your first two steps for a gaming-focused upbringing:

1. Read game magazines and targeted web sites (Gamespot, 1UP) with your kids prior to buying a game (ages 7 and up).
2. Buy them a mid-range laptop and add a large external HD as a backup. Keep your recovery discs safe (ages 10 and up).

Next: how to use the power of modding to introduce your kids to game development.

Last year around Halloween, I let my daughter use my drawing tablet to design some Flash characters. I also made some scenery and other characters. I then animated these characters and added code to make them interactive. Very basic stuff—but the kids enjoyed watching my daughter's drawings come to life, allowing them to move things around. Right now, one of the things my daughter and I do together with the computer is write stories. She comes up with a story, I type it up, and she supplies me with crayon artwork. I scan her work in, and we make a printed copy. As she gets older, I see us expanding this activity into interactive storytelling, Flash game development, etc.

—Bill Genereux (assistant professor, Kansas State University at Salina)

My son has expressed interest [in developing games of his own] but has not had time with the school year and sports schedules. My daughter has done quite a bit of game design, working out interaction designs and rulesets for games she creates.

—Donna K. Kidwell (commercialization consultant,
University of Texas at Austin)

Parent Snapshot

Kenneth C. Finney

Author/instructor (Thomson Learning/Art Institute)
Bowmanville, Ontario CANADA

Kenneth Finney was a commercial and industrial software engineer from the '80s until the mid-'90s. He is an associate developer for GarageGames (Torque Game Engine) and an author of three books on game development (including *3D Game Programming All in One*). Kenneth has also been an instructor in the Game Art & Design program at the Art Institute of Toronto since 2004.

- Family Profile: Two children, ages 9 and 11
- Playtime: 4–6 hours per week with kids (spouse plays 1–3 hours per week with kids)
- Platforms: PS2, PS, Wii, GameCube, N64, PC, PSP, DS, GBA SP, GBA
- Top Games: *World War 2 Online: Battleground Europe*, *Airheads* (in closed beta), *Legend of Zelda: Twilight Princess*
- "My kids are working on helping with the family game, Return to Tubetti-world!"

Parent Snapshot

Joseph Welsh

Student (Art Institute Online)
Age: 39
Location: Shirley, NY

- Family Profile: 11, 9, 4
- Playtime: 1–3 hours per week with kids
- Platforms: Xbox, GameCube, PC, DS, GBA SP
- Top Games: *Star Wars Lego II*, *Star Wars III: Revenge of the Sith*, *NHL Hockey 2007*
- "My son wants to develop games. We came up with an idea a while back, and it is still in the brainstorming stage."

MODDING

Modding is related to our skills section earlier in this chapter. The easiest way to learn game development skills, contrary to common sense, is not to wait until "game college," but to start earlier with modding.

When players take an existing game and modify it (usually through the use of editors or *world-building* software that is shipped with the game), this is known as *modding*. It may sound complicated, but modding is always a lot easier than developing a game from scratch. Let's use a metaphor to illustrate this.

Imagine that you just bought a Camaro from the late '60s. But instead of an SS with a big block V8, you got one with the inline 6. . . . (Let's just say you bought the crappy one.) No one likes six cylinders in a muscle car; it's like having the Mona Lisa in your living room, but with a Mario-style handdrawn moustache. You want a V8 in that car, and in order to do that, you're going to have to "mod" it. The first step is to go to a web site that sells Chevy V8s and buy one for your Camaro. However, right after giving them your credit card, you realize that just upgrading the engine might get you killed when you take the first corner; you go and buy better brakes and a stiffer suspension!

Two weeks later, the parts arrive at your home.

Modifying the car (modding) takes time and effort. Nonetheless, imagine the time it would take to build a whole new Camaro from scratch. You might not be able to do it at all! This is the same with modding games. Making a game from scratch takes a lot of time and millions of dollars (AAA titles, that is), while modding the same game might not cost anything. Like the Camaro, it's better to upgrade and modify a sturdy product than to try and reinvent the wheel.

Modding games teaches scripting, 3D modeling, art asset creation, and even interface design. It also allows your kids to use their own creativity to carve their very personal flavor of the games they love.

GoldenEye: Source—A Successful Mod

GoldenEye 007, covered extensively in this book, was made by Rare back in 1997 (almost two years after the similarly titled movie), and it was a smashing success for Nintendo, selling over 8 million copies. However, when a sequel came out, Rare's magic touch was nowhere to be seen. The rights to a 007 game had been sold to a new publisher, which, in turn used a different developer to make the game. Since then, gamers and fans alike have been waiting for a chance to play *GoldenEye 007* in a modern platform, but until now, this was impossible due to legal and financial issues.

$\rightarrow$

While there's hope the game will eventually show up in the Wii's Virtual Console (a paid emulation service provided by Nintendo), James Bond's game rights are now with Activision, and the original copyright holders are known to aggressively protect their property.

Based on the original *GoldenEye 007* game, *GoldenEye: Source* is a mod created by gamers for gamers; the mod uses the *Half-Life 2* engine as the basis for the extensive modifications seen in the game. The players who created the mod knew very well the risks they were taking. Modding protected IP (intellectual property) is questionable. However, their dedication and hard work have paid off, and the mod is getting a great deal of attention. *GoldenEye: Source* is free, and all it takes is the download of Valve's Steam software along with a $9.95 license to *Half-Life 2 Deathmatch*.

In this total conversion, maps and characters from the N64 game are re-created with current technology while allowing for full-featured online play, typical of games like *Quake 4* and the *Battlefield* franchise. This is really a dream come true for fans of the original because the N64 just wasn't capable of pulling this off, and an official sequel has 0% chance of being produced.

The main advantage of modding a game is the friendliness of the process. The game industry has learned its lesson, and it is now more accepting of modding. The user base stays interested and active through modding, and it also has the power to *expand* through added features and more compelling multiplayer modes. Smart game companies such as Valve (developer of *Half-Life)* and id Software (developer of *Doom* and *Quake*) bundle their games with level editors, assets, scripts, and map builders. With those in hand, teenagers can make their own maps for *Half-Life 2* or *Quake 4*!

> I have bought my son his own version of *Unreal* and told him I would help him build his own levels.
>
> —Tommy Smith (student, Art Institute Online)

> One of my kids has played around with GameMaker and the level editor for *Counterstrike.*
>
> —Jim McCampbell (department head, Computer Animation; Ringling School of Art & Design)

> My youngest son (age 11) has enjoyed games that allow you to develop your own player and/or game field (such as *Robot Arena* and *Ricochet*). He also is very talented with just about any development program he tries (even 3D programs), and he learns them on his own with little direction from me or his father.
>
> —JoAnna Almasude (Media Arts & Animation instructor, Art Institute Online)

Modding the Valve Way

Half-Life, released in 1999, made waves with one of the best game storylines in history. But *Half-Life* had another ace in its hand: the engine on which the game was built, a heavily modified version of the *Quake* engine. *Half-Life: Counter Strike*, a player mod, is still one of the most popular multiplayer FPSs around! With *Half-Life 2* and its famed source engine, history repeats itself: *GoldenEye: Source* is another great example of the flexibility of Valve's second-generation game engines.

Having a successful mod under his belt almost guarantees employment for your kid. When developers play through a finished mod and see map-building, scripting, and even art skills working together, they pretty much have everything they need to hire your kid. Once the mod has been completed, it's important to post it on the developer's official site so that it can be experienced by developers and other players in the modding community. This can lead to additional work with other modding groups and, eventually, a job interview.

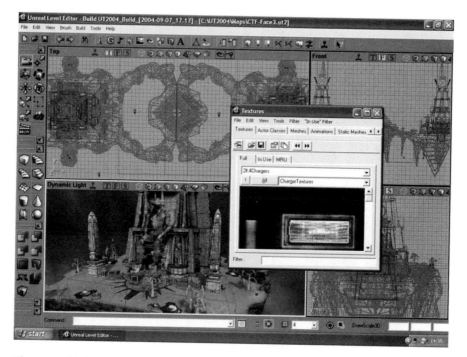

The Unreal Editor makes modding easier. Epic Games

Mod Checklist

1. Find out your kid's favorite genres.
2. Choose a quality, stand-out title.
3. Make sure the game in question is moddable.
4. Make sure it comes with the SDK (or that you can download it for free).
5. Check for support over the Internet. Look for forums and bulletin boards.
6. Help your kid develop an idea for a mod. Watch movies, and play similar games together.
7. Let your kid loose and see what happens!
8. Have your kid post the mod on the developer's official site.

Parent Snapshot

Jacques Montemoino

Gideon Games, LLC
Austell, GA

Jacques is a veteran dice- and paper-based role-playing game creator. Including an internship as an assistant to Mike Lackey, associate editor of *Spider-Man* at Marvel Comics, he has written numerous novels and has created over 30 paper-based games. Jacques is a father of four and also an avid video game player. As a Hispanic-American, he believes that the video game industry is still in its infant stages and needs cultural diversity that isn't based on stereotyped stigma.

- Family Profile: 13, 11, 5, 2 (2 boys, 2 girls)
- Playtime: 4–6 hours per week with kids
- Platforms: Xbox, PS2, PS, GameCube, Genesis, PC, PSP, DS, GBA SP, GB Color, GB, Super Joy (has hundreds of older games from Nintendo, Sega, and Atari)
- Top Games: *Final Fantasy XII, SOCOM 3, Axis and Allies*
- "My oldest son has expressed an interest in developing games. He frequently proposes new game ideas and offers critiques and suggestions for games that I have used when testing my own. Although not able to develop any games on his own, he has taken many of my paper-based games and altered them, producing variations of my own role-playing games."

Parent Snapshot

David Ladyman

Publications Manager (IMGS, Inc.)
Austin, TX

David got his start in gaming with Steve Jackson Games (paper games)—first as a tester, then as a developer and editor. He was *GURPS* and *Car Wars* system guru for awhile and then edited and developed for TSR (AD&D) and FASA (*Mech Warrior, Renegade Legion*) before turning to computer games. He spent six years as Origin Systems Publications Manager; his department then spun off into its own company, Incan Monkey God Studios (IMGS). Since 1997, IMGS has been a freelance content and design house specializing in strategy guides for MMOGs (*Ultima Online, EverQuest: Ruins of Kunark*).

- Family Profile: Three children: Evie (13), Will (10), and Jesse (8)
- Playtime: 1–3 hours per week with kids
- Platforms: PC, Nintendo DS, Genesis
- Top Games: *AdventureQuest*, *Nancy Drew* series
- "My two sons have developed elaborate add-on adventures for some of their games, especially *Super Mario*. These are only on paper so far. When they are with their friends, they sometimes pretend they are in a computer game and plot out strategies and their next actions in the game."

BETA TESTING

As we discussed in Chapter 6, "Game Makers," game testing is a profession. People need to first get hired by a publisher or developer, and then they get to test games for a living. However, this applies only to pre-Alpha and Alpha phases. Beta testing is often a completely different story. The good news is that your kids could have a foot in the door if they jump on it right away.

Not all games have open Beta testing. This is especially the case with some console games more on the old-fashioned side. However, if a game has a big online following (as all modern games do), they will need external Beta testing—period.

Open Beta testing has become the norm with big online games like *World of Warcraft* and now *Halo 3*. These games have a huge user base, and the mechanics behind them are also extremely complex, as far as online components go. If the developers didn't do a huge open Beta, all kinds of nasty and fatal bugs would still creep through QA (quality assurance) and hit the users at launch. That's why smart developers open their Beta to end users; it's better to have 2 million players testing your game and stressing the servers day and night than a noodle-fed team of 15 geeks and jocks working 14 hours a day, 7 days a week (Hint: Noodles and far too many hours of work per week don't go very well together!)

Your kids can easily enroll in open Beta programs. It's free (and doesn't pay), and it will give them real-life experience with testing and game development in general. Beta testing can also be done from home, and your kids will still have plenty of time to be kids and do their homework.

Beta testing is fun and cheap, and it provides kids with very valuable experience. There's really no negative side to it. Beta testing is a win-win scenario for both players and developers.

Halo 3 Beta Program

The Xbox Live multiplayer public Beta, which is a prerelease version of *Halo 3*, went live on May 16, 2007, exclusively on the Xbox 360. Through the resulting feedback, Bungie Studios was able to further refine and hone the final version of the game. There were three ways to participate in the *Halo 3* Beta:

1. Register at *www.halo3.com.*
2. Qualify and register as part of the "Rule of Three" program.
3. Purchase *Crackdown*, which links to the *Halo 3* Beta download.

NETWORKING

Networking, which has become almost an art form, is a way to connect and keep in touch with people in your industry so that you can pool those resources in case of need. Most of you are intimately familiar with this skill and have probably exercised it in your careers. It sounds like hard work (and it is), but networking is an undeniable part of life, and all successful career-minded individuals do it very well.

Remember the "six degrees of separation rule"? This is the basis of networking. The rule says: "Anyone on Earth is connected to any other person on the planet through a chain of acquaintances that has no more than five intermediaries." Many studies have attempted to prove this rule, and most have succeeded. We can willingly make use of these connections instead of relying only on chance. If your kids want to work with games, they have the power to make it happen through smart networking.

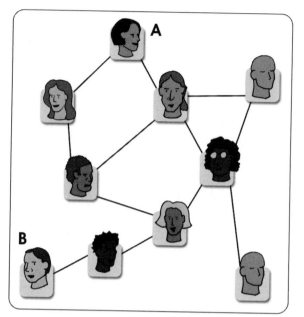

Diagram by Per Olin

Game Industry Networking in Five Easy Steps

1. Attend GDC (Game Developers Conference) yearly. Go to all parties, and attend every lecture. In short, become one of "them." And don't forget to hold tight to those valuable business cards!

2. Make sure you have *your own* business cards. (If your kids don't have them, they should.) Bring loads of them with you, wherever you go. Be generous as well.

3. Join IGDA (International Game Developers Association). Go to the regional meet-ups and make friends. You also get a free yearly subscription to *Game Developer Magazine* when you join, which is a cool thing in itself.

4. Participate in open Betas and in the forums, always sticking to the point and "respecting your elders" (the devs).

5. Go to *E for All*, the new E3. With some luck, you'll eventually meet some industry insiders. *E for All* should also give you plenty of ammunition in the form of industry topics, game previews, and the latest in the console wars.

The information gathered through networking is an invaluable asset when your kid looks for a job. In fact, it will give your kid a clear picture of the market, who's who among powerful players, and directions to the best companies and/or most rewarding jobs. Networking also teaches the value of being organized, since managing loads of business cards along with phone numbers and personal details is not an easy task.

Hopefully, your kids will end up being offered not one but many jobs if they network effectively.

INTERNSHIPS

Participating in internships is a surefire way to get the most interesting entry-level jobs in the industry. While testing is always paid, assistant producers and PR interns might only receive school credit, since "payment" for these positions is sometimes seen as raw experience plus the opportunity of working with such big name companies.

Production can especially put your child on the fast track to a lucrative, rewarding game industry job. On the other hand, although testing can sometimes be brutal—with low pay and long hours—production is truly at the heart of game development because it touches every sector (management, design, art, tech, and even testing/QA). Good producers work miracles with small teams, and bad producers might sink a large, well-established dev team!

The best part of internships is the networking possibilities that unfold when you "get inside" a company such as EA, Activision, or Vivendi. You end up meeting all kinds of interesting people, and you also get a chance to be part of AAA titles and their expensive marketing campaigns.

Internships are often announced on developer and publisher web sites or can be found at Gamasutra (http://gamasutra.com). Look at web sites associated with game companies that have been involved with games your kids love to play and see what opportunities might be available. High school or advance college credit might be offered in lieu of payment.

PLAYER COMMUNITIES

In the old days, if you had something to say, your best bets were pamphlets and newspaper ads (both with very limited reach), and television was for the very few who could pay the price. There was just no way to speak your mind, in public, to a wide audience.

But on the Internet, *everyone* has a voice.

It all changed with the World Wide Web, the graphical interface to the Internet launched in 1991. Web 2.0 took us even further, with blogs and YouTube empowering users in ways that previously were unheard of. The truth is that no one really knows where this is all going. The change is so drastic that it is currently affecting every single area of our lives.

Player communities are self-managed groups of people with similar interests who gravitate toward targeted web sites. In almost all cases, those sites have forums that serve as a meeting point for the users. Everyone creates an account and is then allowed to post messages in the forum, building the web site's database of knowledge through individual contributions.

Games, powerful media in themselves, also attract users, and game-related web sites such as Gamespot and 1Up have grown to become major media hubs. The forums on these web sites host thousands of users commenting on the games they love, hate, and ignore and exchanging secrets and "glitches" (bugs). Other forums, such as Gamefaqs, are more user focused and have almost no commercial and press components. Good threads may go beyond 40 pages, and flame wars between PS3 and Xbox 360 users are a constant attraction.

The last category of user-powered communities is official game forums. These sites are maintained by the game companies themselves and serve as meeting points for all the game's fans and users. This category is especially important for us because sometimes game companies recruit employees from these forums.

Official game forums such as *ForzaMotorsport.net* are crawling with developers.
Microsoft Corporation

You read this correctly. The official forums for a game, such as ForzaMotorsport.net for *Forza Motorsport*, are breeding grounds for possible hires. The reasons for this are simple:

1. Users who commonly post on forums have better writing skills than most.
2. Experienced users develop a "following" that knows and respects their opinions.
3. Those users might have been following the company for a while, so they're already deeply rooted in the company's philosophy.

When you couple this with technical abilities, it becomes obvious why game companies use these forums: They make it easier to spot the talented, charismatic individuals way before the competition grabs hold of them. It's an opportunity to catch them "fresh" and unspoiled by multiple jobs in less reputable companies.

The authors have seen this happen a few times with industry colleagues. One in particular was voicing his opinion about a certain RPG one day, and he was hired as a designer the next day. Just a few years later, this same person is now a lead designer on a major AAA title.

So what can we learn from this? Forums are excellent avenues for communicating with developers. Help your kids take advantage of this new type of media. It's your job to give them the tools to better use their raw and undeveloped talents.

Making Use of Player Forums

1. Remember that laptop? Your kids can use it to become members of whatever forums they choose.
2. Your kids can easily attract some attention by reviewing a game and posting it on YouTube. (Don't worry; game companies couldn't care less that a video of their games is being posted online.)
3. Follow through with your kids. A forum thread can often take on a life of its own; they will love to tell the latest on the 103-page "PS3 sucks" thread.
4. Make sure your kids are part of the official forum (that's the one where devs will be snooping around). We also happen to know that producers check Xbox.com to get feedback on Xbox Live-enabled games.

PORTS OF ENTRY

Now that you've read a few tips and tricks about breaking into the game industry, here's a quick guide to the entry points that will allow your kids to become part of creating the fun. To make things more interesting, we'll rate each position with stars for fun factor and financial reward, with five stars being best.

MODDER

Fun Factor *****
Money *

Modders get absolute creative freedom and a shot at their dream projects, reporting to no one. Modding is not a piece of cake, as some newspaper articles might suggest; it can take years to make a decent mod. No one hires you to create a mod; you have to be self-motivated and disciplined and take it upon yourself to start up a project or join one. Modders don't get money—that is, for creating the mod itself—but you could say that there's the possibility of deferred pay. The up side of modding is the visibility that modders get when their mod is featured in web sites and magazines. Small projects can easily snowball into main media events, like *Counter-Strike*, and then suddenly everyone in the project might find themselves hired by the developer. It has happened before, and it's bound to happen again.

INTERNSHIP

Fun Factor ****
Money**

Internships offer very little financial reward but can be an excellent avenue for networking. An internship allows you to work onsite, which gives you the possibility of meeting people from all areas of development and production. It can also be a straight shot to the company's headquarters, where you find the highest paying jobs in the company and where all decisions are made. One problem with internships is that sometimes you have to run errands or make coffee for the producers, but that's not *so* bad. Assistant producers (or APs) are producers in training, and their ascension is swift!

Beta Tester (External/Remote)

Fun factor ****
Money *

Beta testing is great in so many ways: You get to play the game for free, participate in an elite forum, submit bugs, and make suggestions that people actually listen to. However, Beta testers are *never* paid and might not even be credited in the game's manual. Still, Beta testing is a path to a game job because game companies have employees who monitor and moderate all Beta testers.

Game Tester (Internal/On-Site)

Fun factor ***
Money ***

Game testing can be rough, disheartening, and even tragic—because the hours are often long, and 15 geeks in the same tiny room can drive anyone insane. Testers work hard, get decent pay (for an entry level, no-college-required job), and are often very far from the spotlight. Here's the lowdown on the two tester varieties: QA testing is more standardized, but far from production (so suggestions get ignored); production testing is much more rewarding (it feels good to be a part of the team as a developer), but hours can easily go past 80 per week.

The Future Is Now

This chapter has provided some advice for your kids to start in the industry right away. These techniques all depend on your kids' talents and experience and the amount of time they can devote to their passion. A career in the game industry is not all fun and games. It's hard work, but it provides the pleasure of being part of a truly astounding industry, with room to grow and a firm grip on pop culture. Is it more fun to play games or make them? After years in the industry, most will have trouble answering this question!

The following bonus chapter deals with that often-overlooked dimension of games: the technology behind them. We try to tackle the impossible in this chapter and explain in simple terms the amazing world of displays, controllers, cables, and media formats. Having this knowledge is essential, especially if your kids are old enough to influence your purchasing decisions. You'll thank us later!

Bonus Chapter

8

Know Your Game

In This Chapter

- Lingo Recap
- Parts of a Whole
- Play the Game!

Video games might seem complicated, but they are really much simpler than appearances might suggest. Just like the dusty VCRs of the '80s, game systems have their own special cables, instruction manuals, and technological names and uses. Still, be not afraid: Understanding what a game console and display technologies are made of is not really all that difficult. All it takes is the same fearless curiosity you had when you were your kid's age!

SUIT UP AND GEEK OUT

If you find yourself having difficulty programming your VCR (or DVR), troubleshooting your computer hardware or software . . . or hooking up a game console for your kids, remember this:

1. There is no maximum age for learning.
2. VCRs are dead (RIP).
3. Video games and computer systems can be daunting at times, but they also are bound by logic, even if at first they don't *seem* to make any sense.

No parents will escape the day their kids start pressing for a new big screen HDTV—or ignore a 13-year-old begging for a new game console. Consider how this "game" used to be played; kids would invariably win the argument with either (a) knowledge, or (b) a "guilt trip":

(a)   It's tough to argue to the death with someone who knows much more than you do about the topic. It's uncomfortable, and it leaves no room for negotiation. Either the parents play the "I'm the parent, I do as I wish," card or they will eventually be humbled into accepting whatever their kids want.

(b)   Parents can feel guilty very easily, especially if they work long hours and make a lot of money! Their kids are always aware of this, and they will often find ways to make their parents feel guilty. It's a slow process and can easily take weeks and/or months, but we guarantee that most parents will crumble at the end. Parents simply have no stamina for this kind of thing.

Luis was 19 when Laserdiscs suddenly were a thing of the past. He needed a DVD player . . . badly . . . and thus decided to pressure his mother to no end, until she agreed to buy one. He would focus on technology, financing options, educational value, and so on. It worked, and Luis got his DVD player after only one week of nagging. His mother just couldn't go against such determination, knowledge—and sheer, relentless cunning (not to mention lack of modesty, Jeannie might add)!

Let this be a cautionary tale. This chapter will help you make informed decisions and engage equally in discussions with your kids on advanced topics related to game hardware and software, and this will bring you both knowledge *and* power. Whether or not to purchase a particular television or game console should be a *family* decision and not based solely on the needs of your children. The final decision should reflect a true team effort. You deserve to be able to talk to your kids as equals, not as a victim or executioner!

We are in a very important moment in history, right in the middle of the shift to HDTV. It's essential that you have in your hands proven, useful knowledge in order to keep the peace at home—and the money in your pocket. This could very well be a quantum shift in the way you relate to your kids.

LINGO RECAP

There are two words that are absolutely necessary for the next pages: current-gen and next-gen. We've seen them before, but it doesn't hurt to take a look at them again.

CURRENT-GEN

Current-gen applies to the Sony PlayStation 2, Nintendo GameCube, and Microsoft Xbox. They are put in this category because we are right at the turning point for next-gen, so game web sites, magazines, and developers refer to these "older" consoles in this way. In a year or two, those consoles will be a part of "retro-gaming," joining the ranks of Nintendo 64, Sega Genesis, and the Atari 2600!

NEXT-GEN

Next-gen applies to the Microsoft Xbox 360, Sony PlayStation 3, and Nintendo Wii. Throughout the years, many consoles have once been called "next-gen," such as the Sega Genesis, Sony PlayStation, and even the now current-gen PlayStation 2. Although Wii games lack HD graphics and normal mapping, the console is still categorized as a next-gen system because of its innovative manual interface (nicknamed *Wiimote*).

Manufacturer	Current-Gen	Next-Gen
Microsoft	Xbox	Xbox 360
Sony	PlayStation 2	PlayStation 3
Nintendo	GameCube	Wii

PARTS OF A WHOLE

Now, let's be proud, stand tall, and face the beast! This is your very first step into a sea of game tech; the risks are many, but the rewards far outweigh any possible danger.

Every console (and computer) has the following parts:

- Display
- Case
- Controller(s)
- Power supply
- Video and audio cables
- Network cables
- Physical storage (memory cards and hard drives)

MEDIA DISPLAY

The *display* is the screen on which the game is played. With console games, several types of television displays (SDTV, EDTV, or HDTV) are possible. In a computer, the display is the computer monitor itself (either CRT or LCD).

SDTV (Standard Definition TV) = 480i

SDTVs are the television sets most people are used to. Although they've been in production since the 1950s, they're still very common today. They are also called "480i" by some console makers because they can reach a maximum of 480 *interlaced* lines of resolution. This is now the lowest denominator in displays, so their cost is also very low.

EDTV (Extended Definition TV) = 480p

EDTV is a term that few really know. "Extended definition" only means that the television is at least capable of 480p—480 *progressive* lines of resolution. The technology's full name is "progressive scan," and it is most commonly referred to in this way. The big difference between 480i (SDTV) and 480p (EDTV) is that 480p gives you a much more stable picture, since it refreshes just like film: one full frame at a time. On the other hand, 480i *interlaces* two 240-line frames (half of 480) to get one 480-line frame; this introduces flickering and other picture artifacts. The possible resolution for DVDs, the Nintendo GameCube, and the Nintendo Wii is 480p. EDTVs are also rather inexpensive since stores are trying to get rid of them in favor of HDTVs.

HDTV (High Definition TV) = 720p/1080i/1080p

Everything above 480p is referred to as *HDTV*. The numbers 720 and 1080 mean "lines of resolution," just like 480i or 480p. And just like standard TVs, the maximum resolution of some HDTVs can be in interlaced or progressive video mode. (There are many types of HDTVs, such as DLP (digital light processing), plasma, LCD (liquid crystal display), and LCoS (liquid crystal on silicon), but trying to differentiate between them is beyond the scope of this book.)

HDTV has at least six times the resolution of SDTV. This makes a huge difference in gaming. For example, on an HDTV display, you can read small text written on an in-game billboard, while the same text on an SDTV would be barely readable. The resolution gain alone brings a lot of added value to newer console and computer games.

We bet many of you are wondering which one is the best for games, 720p, 1080i, or 1080p? As expected, the best resolution possible today is 1080p, and both the PlayStation 3 and Xbox 360 can display it. However, such a cutting edge display

HDTV is the technology games needed to become truly cinematic. Big Stock Photo

technology has a price; 1080p TVs are extremely expensive. They are luxury items, and the cost of consoles plus 1080p TV alone will prevent it from reaching the masses for several years.

CRT (Cathode Ray Tube) = Flexible Resolutions

Basic computer monitors are known as *CRTs*. These displays haven't changed a lot through the years; other than the transition to digital (in the mid-1990s) and quantitative gains in resolution, CRT monitors are the same clunky and impractical grayish boxes that most computer users trade in for flat-screen displays. CRT resolutions are flexible, which means they can display many different resolutions, from 640 × 480 (current-gen) to 1600 × 1200, much above any resolution an Xbox 360 or PlayStation 3 can achieve. CRT monitors are usually inexpensive but can be costly in larger sizes.

LCD (Liquid Crystal Display) = Fixed Native Resolution

LCD displays are very popular today due to their low weight and size. They usually have a native resolution, which really means "optimal" resolution, but it's possible for them to display other resolutions as well. Let's say your LCD screen for the computer has a native resolution of 1280 × 1024. This means that if you feed it anything *but* 1280 × 1024, it will distort the picture in order to match it to that resolution. This inflexibility makes LCD monitors a little "tricky" for gaming. As a general rule, CRT monitors are still the gamer's best friend.

Lag: The Gameplay Killer

Both LCD monitors and HDTV sets can suffer from *lag*: the time the display takes to draw the next image. Since most LCDs and HDTVs are slow, this can result in an image with trails similar to those that a mouse pointer leaves on some computer screens. Another name for this is "ghosting," and it's bad for games, especially first-person shooters and most other action games. Lag is measured in milliseconds (ms); a very good LCD monitor has a maximum lag of 6 ms.

"Input lag" is the difference between the moment a player presses a button on the controller and the moment a character in the game performs an action. In an ideal world, this would be an immediate process, but some HDTVs take time to "figure out" how to draw the screen, and this might introduce between 0.5 to 1.5 seconds of lag.

Here's an example: Let's say Mario needs to jump over a big hole in the ground. As a player, your eyes and brain can process exactly when to make the jump, but the actual jump is always a little late due to the slow display. The result? When you press the button to jump, it's already too late, and Mario ends up falling into the hole!

Both types of lag are very detrimental to gaming, and some gamers are wary of some HDTV technologies such as DLP and rear-projection LCDs. Hopefully, as newer models come to market, lag issues will become a thing of the past, from a time when TV manufacturers didn't take gaming into consideration when designing their $4,000.00 high-end TVs!

CASE

The *case* is the casing that holds the console or computer together, and it is what many refer to as "the box." Game consoles usually have plastic cases, while computers have metal and/or plastic cases. The case contains the disc drive, the audio-video and network ports, and everything else inside the console/computer.

CONTROLLERS

Controllers are sometimes called gamepads or joysticks (and academically, manual or physical interfaces), and they are used to control the games themselves. Computers may use add-on controllers, but computer games usually rely on a combination of keyboard and mouse.

The Wii Classic Controller resembles both NES and SNES controllers. Courtesy of Nintendo

The Nintendo 64 introduced the Rumble Pak in 1997, an accessory that allowed it to rumble in tandem with the action onscreen. It was such a success story that now every current-gen and next-gen console—excluding the PlayStation3, unfortunately—has built-in rumble functionality. It's a veritable hoot to play with most of the time, but if the vibration ever becomes uncomfortable or tiresome, it can also be turned off in most games.

Wired Controllers, No More!

In the early days of video games, every single console had a two- or three-foot cable connecting the controller to the console itself. Those wires were aggravating for a few reasons:

1. They limited the player's movement.
2. People would pull them by accident and drop the console to the floor.
3. People had to sit too close to the TV screen in order to use them.
4. They were easily tripped over and cluttered up many living room floors.

→

Today, next-gen consoles such as the Xbox 360 and PlayStation 3 come straight from the factory with wireless controllers. This is a much welcome change from the messy wires of the past. Playing games with a wireless controller is a lot of fun and may be an essential buy if you have a big screen TV. It's also safer for both your consoles *and* pets!

But nothing is perfect. Wireless controllers have a serious flaw: They rely on batteries. This means you will have to go out and buy some AA batteries or charge your controllers from time to time. Be careful of storing your controllers so that their activation buttons rest on other items; this will drain the batteries. When in doubt, take the batteries out when your controllers are not in use.

If you have a current-gen console, do not despair: Wireless controllers are available for these, and they are not that expensive. It's worth a try!

POWER SUPPLY

The *power supply* in a console is the component that transforms the 110-volt current originating from the power outlet into energy that matches the console's needs. External power supplies are often referred to as "power bricks," since most are as heavy as . . . bricks!

The Xbox 360's massive "power brick." Microsoft Corporation

A computer's power supplies are always inside the case, and they are crucial parts of the system. Heavy-duty power supplies allow for the latest, cutting-edge GPUs (graphical processing units, used to accelerate the display of games such as *Doom 3*), while weaker ones limit the owner's choices to low-end graphics cards. The power supply feeds the GPU; a weaker power supply might even cause the system to crash and freeze.

Consoles, in contrast, can have the power supply either inside or outside the case. The first PlayStation 2 model (the big one) had an internal power supply. This means there was a single power cable connecting the console to a power outlet. The PlayStation Two (the small one that some call a "mini") has an external power supply; the power cable goes to the power brick, and from there a second cable goes to the console.

It's very important to keep power supplies away from water. With consoles such as the Xbox 360, it's also essential to give your power supply a lot of breathing space because it can heat up considerably.

CABLES

Quality *cables* will become your new best friend. If you need proof, try playing the Wii with the original composite cables. You won't do it for long. Now plug in the optional component cables, and *Wii Sports* suddenly starts looking good! Bad cables lead to color issues, image fuzziness, sound distortion, contact problems, and myriad other issues, effectively ruining the whole experience.

Video

Video cables allow your console to display images on a TV screen. There are many types of cables. Since companies like to make money, the cables shipped with consoles are usually the worst possible: composite. We highly recommend that you: a) buy the most expensive version of the console, since it comes with component/ HDMI cables; or b) buy new cables, either s-video for current-gen systems or component for next-gen.

Composite

A *composite* cable is a single, yellow RCA cable that carries the picture to the TV. These cables mix color and light, so the picture quality will be poor. Composite is the lowest of the low in video cables.

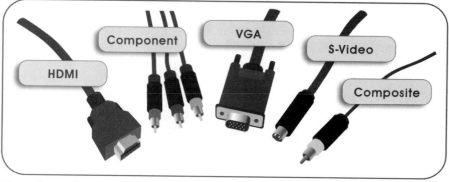

Diagram by Per Olin

S-video

The *s-video* cable is a major step above composite. With s-video cables, the light is separated from the color. Picture quality will be sharper, and color bleed (which usually happens with red) will be greatly reduced. This is our recommendation if you don't want to spend a fortune in cables.

VGA

VGA is the old standard PC cable, which is still in use and is of good quality. Some TVs allow you to connect your desktop or laptop through VGA inputs.

Component

Component cables divide color into three separate cables. This is great in many ways and allows for an HDTV picture. Go for this one if you want HD but don't want to spend HD money.

DVI

The *DVI* cable is PC-exclusive and a bit "dead" for other consumer electronics (such as TVs and DVDs) because it lacks built-in DRM (digital rights management). However, DVI cables carry HDTV signals and offer great picture quality.

HDMI

HDMI cables comprise the brand-new HD standard. This is the future—period. The only console that offers HDMI outputs is the PlayStation 3, but the 360 is rumored to have it as well in its newer top-of-the-line version. This is the very best cable available, and it will be good for at least 3–4 years.

Audio

Video game audio cables are a lot simpler to understand. They also come in only two varieties:

Stereo RCA (Analog)

Stereo RCA cables are the same ones used to connect old turntables. They are analog and can at most offer Dolby Prologic II sound (5.1 non-discreet channels). Most people cannot hear the difference between analog stereo and digital stereo, but they *will* hear the difference between Dolby Prologic II and Dolby Digital 5.1.

Fiber Optic/TOSlink (Digital)

Fiber optic/TOSlink cables provide a fully digital optical connection between your console and a home theater receiver. These cables skip the analog-to-digital-to-analog conversion that diminishes sound quality and allow for true Dolby Digital 5.1, the same surround sound standard used on DVDs. Fiber optic cables can be bought for Xbox, PlayStation 2, and all next-gen systems as add-ons. We highly recommend them over stereo RCA cables.

Network

In the past, computers and consoles used modems to connect to the Internet. While some users still rely on dial-up connections, the current standards are high-speed, broadband connections that make use of your computer's or console's network card in order to connect to the Internet and then to another player. RJ11s are traditional phone cables, while RJ45s are known as "network cables." Most modern games don't even support dial-up connections!

Modem Cable (RJ 11) = 56K Dial-Up

Modem cables are phone cables just like any other. The only recent consoles that still rely on a 56K modem connection for online gameplay are the Sega Dreamcast and PlayStation 2, but very few games make use of it. As we all know, this type of connection is very slow by today's standards.

Ethernet or Network Cable (RJ45) = Broadband

Ethernet or network cables connect consoles or computers to the Internet. In reality, they connect the console/computer to a router or cable/DSL modem. Their speed is only limited by your Internet provider. Both PlayStation 2 and Xbox have Ethernet connections, along with the next-gen consoles.

Storage

In the old days, the only way to save a game was to have memory built into the game cartridge itself. This is how SNES and Genesis saved games to memory: The manufacturers themselves had to pay extra in order to have memory chips built in. With the fifth generation of game consoles, manufacturers—Sega Saturn, Sony PlayStation, and Nintendo 64—introduced memory cards as *storage*. Later, with the sixth generation, hard drives became the norm.

Memory Cards

Memory cards are Flash memory–based and cost very little. They are still in use in the PlayStation 2 (8MB) and Xbox (8MB), but even the Xbox 360 has memory cards available (ranging from 64 to 512MB). The cost is great, but their capacity is definitely not enough for most users, forcing some to buy multiple memory cards.

Hard Drives

Hard drives in game consoles behave in exactly the same way as those inside your PC, holding the operating system, game saves, and media such as TV shows and movies. The original Xbox was the first console to offer a built-in hard drive with an 8GB model that made its name with hardcore gamers, while the PlayStation 2 followed suit with a 40GB disc that never really sold well. Next-gen systems (except for the Wii) have large-capacity hard drives built in; the PlayStation 3 comes with either a 20GB or a 60GB hard drive, while the Xbox 360 has 20GB capacity and a (rumored) 120GB version.

No Hard Drives for Nintendo

Nintendo decided not to include a hard drive on the Wii, contrary to the other next-gen systems. The Wii comes with a 512MB SD card that holds all the console's data, and Nintendo allows users to buy larger SD cards if they ever need more space. The big advantage of not including a hard drive with the Wii is that it allows Nintendo to keep costs down, as the sub-$250 price tag demonstrates.

Media

All consoles have some form of physical *media* that holds the game themselves. In the past, games were stored in cartridges and a few years later, on CD-ROMs. Modern game consoles, such as the Xbox 360 and, the Nintendo Wii, rely on DVD technology, while Sony uses its proprietary Blu-ray standard as the PS3's medium of choice.

DVD-ROM

*DVD*s hold 4.7GB (single-layer) or 8.5GB (dual-layer). They are used by PS2, Nintendo Wii, and the Xbox 360. All consoles except for the Wii are able to play movies on DVD as well.

Blu-Ray Disc

Blu-ray discs were developed by Sony. They hold 25GB (single-layer) or 50GB (dual-layer). Blu-ray discs are still very expensive to manufacture but hold many times more data than traditional DVD-ROMs.

Blu-ray Discs hold either 25GB or 50GB of data. Sony Computer Entertainment America

PLAY THE GAME!

We hope you found in this chapter all the information you need to "talk tech" with your kids, bridging the generation gap with some good, cutting-edge data. Navigating the new world of next-gen consoles and HDTV is not easy. Nonetheless, those technologies will become an even bigger part of life in the coming years, and it is our mission to deliver the facts on everything game-related, tech or not, to you—the parents. You can learn with your kids. You can show them why the NES was such a great system, and they will gladly show you a new world, a web of words like YouTube, HDMI, and Achievement Points. Let the games begin!

Resources

There's a wealth of information on game development and related topics discussed in this book. Here is just a sample list of books, news sites, organizations, and events you should definitely explore!

NEWS

Blues News—*www.bluesnews.com*
Computer Games Magazine—*www.cgonline.com*
Game Daily Newsletter—*www.gamedaily.com*
Game Developer Magazine—*www.gdmag.com*
Gamers Hell—*www.gamershell.com*
Game Music Revolution (GMR)—*www.gmronline.com*
Game Rankings—*www.gamerankings.com*
GamesIndustry.biz—*www.gamesindustry.biz*
GameSlice Weekly—*www.gameslice.com*
GameSpot—*www.gamespot.com*
GameSpy—*www.gamespy.com*
Game Industry News—*www.gameindustry.com*
GIGnews.com—*www.gignews.com*
Internet Gaming Network (IGN)—*www.ign.com*
Machinima.com—*www.machinima.com*
Music4Games.net—*www.music4games.net*
Next Generation—*www.next-gen.biz*
1UP—*www.1up.com*
PC Gamer—*www.pcgamer.com*
Star Tech Journal [technical side of the coin-op industry]—
    www.startechjournal.com
UGO Networks (Underground Online)—*www.ugo.com*
Video Game Music Archive—*www.vgmusic.com*
Wired Magazine—*www.wired.com*

DIRECTORIES & COMMUNITIES

Apple Developer Connection—*developer.apple.com*
Betawatcher.com—*www.betawatcher.com*
Fat Babies.com [game industry gossip]—*www.fatbabies.com*
Gamasutra—*www.gamasutra.com*
GameDev.net—*www.gamedev.net*
Game Development Search Engine—*www.gdse.com*
GameFAQs—*www.gamefaqs.com*
Game Music.com—*www.gamemusic.com*
Game Rankings—*www.gamerankings.com*
Games Tester—*www.gamestester.com*
GarageGames—*www.garagegames.com*
Moby Games—*www.mobygames.com*
Overclocked Remix—*www.overclocked.org*
PS3—*www.ps3.net*
Wii-Play—*www.wii-play.com*
Xbox.com—*www.xbox.com*
XBOX 360 Homebrew—*www.xbox360homebrew.com* [includes XNA developer community]

ORGANIZATIONS

Academy of Interactive Arts & Sciences (AIAS)—*www.interactive.org*
Academy of Machinima Arts & Sciences—*www.machinima.org*
Association of Computing Machinery (ACM)—*www.acm.org*
Business Software Alliance (BSA)—*www.bsa.org*
Digital Games Research Association (DiGRA)—*www.digra.org*
Entertainment Software Association (ESA)—*www.theesa.com*
Entertainment Software Ratings Board (ESRB)—*www.esrb.org*
Game Audio Network Guild (GANG)—*www.audiogang.org*
International Computer Games Association (ICGA)—*www.cs.unimaas.nl/icga*
International Game Developers Association (IGDA)—*www.igda.org*
SIGGRAPH—*www.siggraph.org*

EVENTS

Note: Most of the following events are restricted to attendees who are 18 or older. Please check the registration area on the event web sites for more information.

Consumer Electronics Show (CES)
January—Las Vegas, NV
www.cesweb.org

Game Developers Conference (GDC)
March—San Jose, CA/San Francisco, CA (cities alternate)
www.gdconf.com

Serious Games Summit (SGS)

March (San Jose/San Francisco, CA; at GDC) & October (Washington, DC)
www.seriousgamessummit.com

D.I.C.E. Summit (AIAS)
March—Las Vegas, NV
www.dicesummit.org

SIGGRAPH (ACM)
Summer—Los Angeles, CA; San Diego, CA; Boston, MA (location varies)
www.siggraph.org

Tokyo Game Show (TGS)
Fall—Japan
tgs.cesa.or.jp/english/

E3 Business & Media Summit
July—Santa Monica, CA
www.e3expo.com

Austin Game Developers Conference
September—Austin, TX
www.gameconference.com

E for All Expo
October—Los Angeles, CA
www.eforallexpo.com

COLLEGES & UNIVERSITIES

Here is a list of schools that have strong game degree or certificate programs:

Academy of Art University—*www.academyart.edu*
Arizona State University—*www.asu.edu*
Art Center College of Design—*www.artcenter.edu*
Art Institute Online—*www.aionline.edu*
The Art Institutes—*www.artinstitutes.edu*
Carnegie Mellon University—*www.cmu.edu*
DeVry University—*www.devry.edu*
DigiPen Institute of Technology—*www.digipen.edu*
Expression College for Digital Arts—*www.expression.edu*
Full Sail Real World Education—*www.fullsail.edu*
Guildhall at SMU—*guildhall.smu.edu*
Indiana University—MIME Program—*www.mime.indiana.edu*
Iowa State University—*www.iastate.edu*
ITT Technical Institute—*www.itt-tech.edu*
Massachusetts Institute of Technology (MIT)—*media.mit.edu*
Rensselaer Polytechnic Institute—*www.rpi.edu*
Ringling College of Art & Design—*www.ringling.edu*
Santa Monica College Academy of Entertainment & Technology—*academy.smc.edu*
Savannah College of Art & Design—*www.scad.edu*
Tomball College—*www.tomballcollege.com*

University of California, Los Angeles (UCLA)—Extension—*www.uclaextension.edu*
University of Central Florida—Florida Interactive Entertainment Academy—*fiea.ucf.edu*
University of Southern California (USC)—Information Technology Program—*itp.usc.edu*
University of Southern California (USC) School of Cinematic Arts—*interactive.usc.edu*
Vancouver Film School—*www.vfs.com*
Westwood College—*www.westwood.edu*

BOOKS & ARTICLES

Adams, E. (2003). *Break into the game industry.* McGraw-Hill Osborne Media.

Adams, E. & Rollings, A. (2006). *Fundamentals of game design.* Prentice Hall.

Ahearn, L. & Crooks II, C.E. (2002). *Awesome game creation: No programming required. (2nd ed).* Charles River Media.

Ahlquist, J.B. & Novak, J. (2007). *Game development essentials: Game artificial intelligence.* Thomson Delmar.

Aldrich, C. (2003). *Simulations and the future of learning.* Pfeiffer.

Aldrich, C. (2005). *Learning by doing.* Jossey-Bass.

Axelrod, R. (1985). *The evolution of cooperation.* Basic Books.

Bates, B. (2002). *Game design: The art & business of creating games.* Premier Press.

Beck, J.C. & Wade, M. (2004). *Got game: How the gamer generation is reshaping business forever.* Harvard Business School Press.

Bethke, E. (2003). *Game development and production.* Wordware.

Brandon, A. (2004). *Audio for games: Planning, process, and production.* New Riders.

Brin, D. (1998). *The transparent society.* Addison-Wesley.

Broderick, D. (2001). *The spike: How our lives are being transformed by rapidly advancing technologies.* Forge.

Brooks, D. (2001). *Bobos in paradise: The new upper class and how they got there.* Simon & Schuster.

Business Software Alliance. (May 2005). "Second annual BSA and IDC global software piracy study." www.bsa.org/globalstudy

Campbell, J. (1972). *The hero with a thousand faces.* Princeton University Press.

Campbell, J. & Moyers, B. (1991). *The power of myth.* Anchor.

Castells, M. (2001). *The Internet galaxy: Reflections on the Internet, business, and society.* Oxford University Press.

Castronova, E. (2005). *Synthetic worlds: The business and culture of online games.* University of Chicago Press.

Chase, R.B., Aquilano, N.J. & Jacobs, R. (2001). *Operations management for competitive advantage (9th ed).* McGraw-Hill/Irwin

Cheeseman, H.R. (2004). *Business law (5th ed).* Pearson Education, Inc.

Chiarella, T. (1998). *Writing dialogue.* Story Press.

Cooper, A., & Reimann, R. (2003). *About face 2.0: The essentials of interaction design.* Wiley.

Crawford, C. (2003). *Chris Crawford on game design.* New Riders.

Csikszentmihalyi, M. (1991). *Flow: The psychology of optimal experience.* Perennial.

DeMaria, R. & Wilson, J.L. (2003). *High score!: The illustrated history of electronic games.* McGraw-Hill.

Egri, L. (1946). *The art of dramatic writing: Its basis in the creative interpretation of human motives.* Simon and Schuster.

Erikson, E.H. (1994). *Identity and the life cycle.* W.W. Norton & Company.

Erikson, E.H. (1995). *Childhood and society.* Vintage.

Evans, A. (2001). *This virtual life: Escapism and simulation in our media world.* Fusion Press.

Friedl, M. (2002). *Online game interactivity theory.* Charles River Media.

Fruin, N. & Harringan, P. (Eds.) (2004). *First person: New media as story, performance and game.* MIT Press.

Fullerton, T., Swain, C. & Hoffman, S. (2004). *Game design workshop: Designing, prototyping & playtesting games.* CMP Books.

Galitz, W.O. (2002). *The essential guide to user interface design: An introduction to GUI design principles and techniques.* (2nd ed.). Wiley.

Gardner, J. (1991). *The art of fiction: Notes on craft for young writers.* Vintage Books.

Gee, J.P. (2003). *What video games have to teach us about learning and literacy.* Palgrave Macmillan.

Gershenfeld, A., Loparco, M. & Barajas, C. (2003). *Game plan: The insiders guide to breaking in and succeeding in the computer and video game business.* Griffin Trade Paperback.

Gibson, D., Aldrich, C. & Prensky, M. (Eds.) (2006). *Games and simulations in online learning.* IGI Global.

Gladwell, M. (2000). *The tipping point: How little things can make a big difference.* Little Brown & Company.

Gladwell, M. (2007). *Blink: The power of thinking without thinking.* Back Bay Books.

Gleick, J. (1987). *Chaos: Making a new science.* Viking.

Gleick, J. (1999). *Faster: The acceleration of just about everything.* Vintage Books.

Gleick, J. (2003). *What just happened: A chronicle from the information frontier.* Vintage.

Godin, S. (2003). *Purple cow: Transform your business by being remarkable.* Portfolio.

Godin, S. (2005). *The big moo: Stop trying to be perfect and start being remarkable.* Portfolio.

Goldratt, E.M. & Cox, J. (2004). *The goal: A process of ongoing improvement (3rd ed).* North River Press.

Gordon, T. (2000). *P.E.T.: Parent effectiveness training.* Three Rivers Press.

Hamilton, E. (1940). *Mythology: Timeless tales of gods and heroes.* Mentor.

Heim, M. (1993). *The metaphysics of virtual reality.* Oxford University Press.

Hight, J. & Novak, J. (2007). *Game development essentials: Game project management.* Thomson Delmar.

Jensen, E. (2006). *Enriching the brain: How to maximize every learner's potential.* John Wiley & Sons.

Johnson, S. (1997). *Interface culture: How new technology transforms the way we create & communicate.* Basic Books.

Johnson, S. (2006). *Everything bad is good for you.* Riverhead.

Jung, C.G. (1969). *Man and his symbols.* Dell Publishing.

Kent, S.L. (2001). *The ultimate history of video games.* Prima.

King, S. (2000). *On writing.* Scribner.

Knoke, W. (1997). *Bold new world: The essential road map to the twenty-first century.* Kodansha International.

Koster, R. (2005). *Theory of fun for game design.* Paraglyph Press.

Krawczyk, M. & Novak, J. (2006). *Game development essentials: Game story & character development.* Thomson Delmar.

Kurzweil, R. (2000). *The age of spiritual machines: When computers exceed human intelligence.* Penguin.

Laramee, F.D. (Ed.) (2002). *Game design perspectives.* Charles River Media.

Laramee, F.D. (Ed.) (2005). *Secrets of the game business. (3rd ed).* Charles River Media.

Levy, P. (2001). *Cyberculture.* University of Minnesota Press.

Lewis, M. (2001). *Next: The future just happened.* W.W.Norton & Company.

Mackay, C. (1841). *Extraordinary popular delusions & the madness of crowds.* Three Rivers Press.

McConnell, S. (1996). *Rapid development.* Microsoft Press.

Mencher, M. (2002). *Get in the game: Careers in the game industry.* New Riders.

Michael, D. (2003). *The indie game development survival guide.* Charles River Media.

Montfort, N. (2003). *Twisty little passages: An approach to interactive fiction.* MIT Press.

Moravec, H. (2000). *Robot.* Oxford University Press.

Morris, D. & Hartas, L. (2003). *Game art: The graphic art of computer games.* Watson-Guptill Publications.

Mulligan, J. & Patrovsky, B. (2003). *Developing online games: An insider's guide.* New Riders.

Murray, J. (2001). *Hamlet on the holodeck: The future of narrative in cyberspace.* MIT Press.

Negroponte, N. (1996). *Being digital.* Vintage Books.

Nielsen, J. (1999). *Designing web usability: The practice of simplicity.* New Riders.

Novak. J. (2007). *Game development essentials: An introduction. (2nd ed.).* Thomson Delmar.

Novak, J. (2003). "MMOGs as online distance learning applications." University of Southern California.

Oram, A. (Ed.) (2001). *Peer-to-peer.* O'Reilly & Associates.

Prensky, M. (2006). *Don't bother me, Mom—I'm learning.* Paragon House Publishers.

Prensky, M. (2007). *Digital game-based learning.* Paragon House Publishers.

Piaget, J. (2000). *The psychology of the child.* Basic Books.

Piaget, J. (2007). *The child's conception of the world.* Jason Aronson.

Rheingold, H. (1991). *Virtual reality.* Touchstone.

Rheingold, H. (2000). *Tools for thought: The history and future of mind-expanding technology.* MIT Press.

Robbins, S.P. (2001). *Organizational behavior (9th ed).* Prentice-Hall, Inc.

Rogers, E.M. (1995). *Diffusion of innovations.* Free Press.

Rollings, A. & Morris, D. (2003). *Game architecture & design: A new edition.* New Riders.

Rollings, A. & Adams, E. (2003). *Andrew Rollings & Ernest Adams on game design.* New Riders.

Rouse, R. (2001) *Game design: Theory & practice (2nd ed).* Wordware Publishing.

Salen, K. & Zimmerman, E. (2003). *Rules of play.* MIT Press.

Sanger, G.A. [a.k.a. "The Fat Man"]. (2003). *The Fat Man on game audio.* New Riders.

Saunders, K. & Novak, J. (2007). *Game development essentials: Game interface design.* Thomson Delmar.

Sellers, J. (2001). *Arcade fever.* Running Press.

Shaffer, D.W. (2006). *How computer games help children learn.* Palgrave Macmillan.

Standage, T. (1999). *The Victorian Internet.* New York: Berkley Publishing Group.

Strauss, W. & Howe, N. (1992). *Generations.* Perennial.

Strauss, W. & Howe, N. (1993). *13th gen: Abort, retry, ignore, fail?* Vintage Books.

Strauss, W. & Howe, N. (1998). *The fourth turning.* Broadway Books.

Strauss, W. & Howe, N. (2000). *Millennials rising: The next great generation.* Vintage Books.

Strauss, W., Howe, N. & Markiewicz, P. (2006). *Millennials & the pop culture.* LifeCourse Associates.

Tufte, E.R. (1983). *The visual display of quantitative information.* Graphics Press.

Tufte, E.R. (1990). *Envisioning information.* Graphics Press.

Tufte, E.R. (1997). *Visual explanations.* Graphics Press.

Tufte, E.R. (2006). *Beautiful evidence.* Graphics Press.

Turkle, S. (1997). *Life on the screen: Identity in the age of the Internet.* Touchstone.

Van Duyne, D.K. et al. (2003). *The design of sites.* Addison-Wesley.

Vogler, C. (1998). *The writer's journey: Mythic structure for writers. (2nd ed).* Michael Wiese Productions.

Williams, J.D. (1954). *The compleat strategyst: Being a primer on the theory of the games of strategy.* McGraw-Hill.

Welch, J. & Welch, S. (2005). *Winning.* HarperCollins Publishers.

Wolf, J.P. & Perron, B. (Eds.). (2003). *Video game theory reader.* Routledge.

Wysocki, R.K. (2006). *Effective project management (4th ed).* John Wiley & Sons.

Index